BICYCLE LOVE

BICYCLE LOVE

STORIES OF PASSION, JOY, AND SWEAT

Edited by Garth Battista

BREAKAWAY BOOKS
HALCOTTSVILLE, NEW YORK
2004

Bicycle Love: Stories of Passion, Joy, and Sweat
Edited by Garth Battista

Individual story copyrights in the name of each author, 2004
Compilation copyright by Garth Battista 2004

ISBN-13: 978-1-891369-45-2
ISBN-10: 1-891369-45-8
Library of Congress Control Number: 2003116289

Published by Breakaway Books
P.O. Box 24
Halcottsville, NY 12438
(800) 548-4348
www.breakawaybooks.com

FIRST EDITION: APRIL 2004
SECOND PRINTING: DECEMBER 2005
THIRD PRINTING: JANUARY 2008
FOURTH PRINTING: DECEMBER 2008
FIFTH PRINTING: OCTOBER 2009
SIXTH PRINTING: SEPTEMBER 2010

Contents

Introduction

These stories tell of all aspects of bicycle love: not just the mad love we have for our bikes as objects, but also the love of cycling, the rides we do out of sheer joy, and the love that grows in our lives because of bicycles. You'll find everything here, from the wondrous infatuation we have as children for our first two-wheeler, to adolescent cycle-mania, to more subtle, complex adult relationships—with bikes and people. Here are children who disobey all authority for the rush of freedom on a bike; so does a grandmother, and a visually impaired young mother. Here are mountain bikers exhilarated and enlightened as they fly along the single-track. Road riders brought to exhausted ecstasy by long rides. There are bicycle dreams, crashes, and even bicycle warfare. An interesting group of tandem stories appears, in which it is said, "Wherever you're going in your relationship, a tandem will take you there faster." One tandem relationship ends; two go on. They just all got there faster. The bicycle heightens everything in life.

These stories were all submitted to a writing contest Breakaway Books sponsored. We read over three hundred excellent entries and suffered miserably trying to select the best, which meant rejecting some beautiful writing (and beautiful bikes). We read them again and again, sorting and shuffling. The top three are: Jayne Relaford Brown, Dan Trabue, and Sally Palaian, whose stories are arranged in salutatorian-valedictorian style, with Dan and Sally opening the book, and Jayne giving us the final word before we return to the outside world. The other fifty-nine stories are the best of the rest, just inches from the podium. You'll have your own favorites, no doubt, as you read these through. And unless, for some tragic or pathetic reason, you have never had the pleasure of riding a bicycle, your own bicycle love will light up, and lead you out the door, handlebars in hand, wheels turning, your body and spirit more alive than ever.

—G. B.

Surprised into Flight

Dan Trabue

Having once tasted freedom—wind-howling, heart-blasting, soul-soaring freedom—how now shall I return to the cell?

For *twenty years* I had been caged like an animal. Cramped within four walls. Two tons. Heavy metal and plastic and wheels.

I entered my prison daily and worse, I did so of my own free will. My heart's desire was to be caged within my car. I longed to drive, even if it was only around the block.

Worse yet, I paid for the privilege to enter my prison. Month after month, I'd make payments to the insurance company, to the loan company, and to the parking lot. I paid for gas. I paid for oil. I paid to have the oil removed and replaced. I paid for antifreeze, for windshield wiper fluid, for air-conditioner coolant. Poisons, all.

I'd daily shill out my contributions to the oil industry and yearly to my government. I paid to build more and more roads on which my rolling concentration camp might lumber along. I paid to protect the oil on which I was dependent.

I paid.

Daily. Yearly. Dearly, and in ways I hardly realized.

You see, I didn't realize I had been caged. No one told me. According to all the advertisements, personal liberty and beautiful women could only be had by owning and driving a car. The cage was a necessity. Thus I was told and thus I believed.

Or perhaps I knew it was a lie all along. After all, it has never been a secret that cars vomit smoke and oil and all manner of noxious muck, that they cost personally and societally.

Whether I knew or was deceived, whether by my fault or society's, the fact remains: I had become a captive of my car. It determined my path and separated me from the great outdoors.

But now, now I am free. And it was a bicycle that led me to liberty. My cage door has opened and outside, amid the sunshine, trees, grass, and fresh air, a twenty dollar beat-up bicycle bade me come into the presence of this world and share in its pleasant grace.

Now, when I need to get from home to work, I open my house door, roll my bike out into my neighborhood, and greet the little girl next door waiting to go to school. I pedal along the streets of my city, enjoying the tree-lined urban setting, old brick houses on either side, history rolling past.

As I head north through downtown, I can make my way down to the river and bike along the riverfront. I can zoom along rapturously embracing the glory of the day, moving at just the right pace. I can get to work just as quickly as I could in a car, but the journey is entirely different.

When cycling, I move at a speed that gets me where I need to go promptly enough, and yet slowly enough that I can watch the mallards swimming in pairs on the Ohio River.

I can watch downstream as an elegant great blue heron slowly stretches and leaps to the air, filling the city with feathered grace unknown to all but me.

When I travel by bike, I know the earth in a way that was lost to me while driving blindly around in my car. I can truly know the delight and challenge of each season as the year spins like a grand wheel.

On my bicycle, I can embrace the coming spring, and revel in the newborn daffodil and crocuses as they colorfully bid winter good-bye. I can laugh at the tickle of a sweet honeysuckle-scented shower.

On my bicycle, I can know fully the heat of a humid August day and accept it as evidence that I am alive in this world. I can appreciate the cool escape of an early-morning ride through Louisville's summer, mocking the fever of the soon-rising sun.

On my bicycle, I can rattle through autumn leaves lying on the street, scattering crisp joy as I ride. I can race the sparrows, darting out of bushes as I surprise them into flight.

On my bicycle, I can breathe deep frigid winter breaths, exhaling my own clear clean exhaust into a bright December sky. It can be cold and I can dress warmly and it is okay.

As I've become a bike commuter, I've discovered that I do not need to isolate myself from this earth for comfort or safety. In the past, I tended to view The Environment as some separate thing, the good stuff of this planet that needed us to protect it. I have found, instead, that the environment is us all: the oaks, the river, the mallards, the squirrels, and me. By biking, I've found my place in this beautiful fragile wild world and been made whole.

I've entered into the community that I was never truly apart from except in prisons of my own creation. In traveling this path, I've had to move deliberately in a direction opposite from the norm and accepted wisdom, but I've not been alone. I ride upstream with all of nature and the goodwill of friends who wish to break away from the foolishness of man.

On my bicycle, I've found freedom and more. With my two-wheeled connection to the world, I've no reason ever to be caged again, and that's been my salvation.

Dan Trabue is a cartographer by trade and a writer by avocation. He is a father, husband, reader, Anabaptist, bicyclist, and gardener. If he had free time, he would likely spend it poorly.

Pedaling Fool

Sally Palaian

In April 1993, at the age of thirty-five, one month after completing my Ph.D., I took Effective Cycling, a class for learning to bicycle. I didn't buy spandex quite yet, but good student that I was, I did buy the book for the class. I didn't know it then, but bicycling would change my life. Maybe not as much as Harry Potter or a thousand years of psychotherapy, but it is definitely up there in the top three.

I thought it odd, but we brought our bikes to class. I guess riding in class was experiential learning. Our instructor never told us our distance—that was his trick. We were too young to know about computers and mileage obsessions. Our greed for speed or distance hadn't been awakened. In fact, the only thing that had been awakened was I now noticed the guys in spandex.

The rest is history. Now I watch the weather as landscapers do. I believe I can feel when rain is longer than an hour away. I now blow snot out of my nose without a Kleenex. One time I got cocky with my technique and the drip ended up on the right shoulder of my fluorescent yellow jersey. I now talk openly in mixed company, sometimes even with strangers, about my crotch.

At the end of the class, I used my graduation money to buy a Trek hybrid bike. The salesman convinced me to go an extra four hundred dollars by saying, "At our age this may be the last bike we ever buy." My last bike, huh! I was just getting started. I mean, really, we still have to put his kids through college.

I am the kind of person who has been on a serious inner search. I have studied with healers in the rain forest, I have meditated with the Buddhists, chanted with the Krishnas, danced with the Sufis. I've been around in some funky places in my day, I can't even tell you the half of it. But biking has taught me way more than all of that. There's beauty and green. There's summer and fall and winter and spring. There are dead smelly animals in every stage of decompose until there is only a hide. No red, no bones, no hair, no smell, only a crumbled disheveled hide in every shape imaginable. After the flesh is gone, you soon forget that an animal once lived there. The snakes are the most interesting because no matter how knotted up, there's no mistaking that a snake lived in that body.

There are animals running from each other and animals feeding on each other. The squirrels do their back-and-forth cha cha dance, and the crows eat them for morning breakfast. I am a vegetarian and even this sight seems charming when on my bike. There are leaves flying, flowers blooming, and life everywhere. Green buds emerge from trees and then the brown leaves scramble across the pavement when the leaves are done with their life. There's the sun, and the rain and the snow and the wind.

I am a psychologist, when people ask me if my job is depressing, I always respond, "I have the best seat in the house—it's a privilege to sit in my chair." But maybe I'm wrong about that, maybe being in the saddle is the best seat in the house? You get to travel through so much space, seeing so many different things. You see kids dragging big giant trees across their lawn, kids fighting, kids street hockey, kids looking up waving at you as though you are a UFO. You see every configuration of toys strewn around lawns. You see sidewalk art. You see fathers chasing their kids with play guns or hoses, you see mothers yelling at their children. You see family and friends arrive for parties, you see them depart. You see neighbors talking to each other.

There's landscaping to notice, houses to lust after, and flowers to identify. There are so many people who labor over their homes, and so many who hire folks to labor. There are streets that get fixed, sewer pipes installed, highways paved, and sidewalks torn up. You see how construction projects work. This is a pretty interesting seat to sit in, this moving vehicle, which permits me to be a pumping fool taking it all in.

I see land developments. Each day as I see the progression, I wonder where the animals and critters go when trucks come and park on their homes, and when cement comes and covers the land. Where do those fellows go?

I now know just how much trash trashy people throw out. I can't help it, I look down on the litterers of the world. I see cigarette packs, teenagers who dump entire cases of beer bottles, Evian bottles, Gatorade bottles. I now see Burger King bags, Styrofoam boxes, plastic bags, pop cans, smashed plastic cans everywhere. In suburban Detroit, we have folks who throw ten cents out their car windows. On leisurely days, I collect these cans and cash them in for Gatorade.

But you know this; it is nothing new to you if you spend hours in the saddle. You already know about the pumping pleasure and the sights along the way. You already love riding 25 mph and not pedaling. And maybe like me, you also know how satisfying it is to climb at 3.5 or 4.2 mph in the granny gear. It is a great way to impress yourself with yourself at the top. A few weeks ago, a friend in my club asked me why I didn't see the pothole, after I complained about the sudden jar. What could I say; I was admiring my computer reading 33.9 mph down that hill!

From biking, I have learned about thirst, about salty skin, about what pancakes taste like with salt on them, what cantaloupe is like with salt. There are sweaty days and snotty days, foot freezing days and oh-so-happy-for-Gore-Tex days. Tired days, sore days, and everything breaks down days. There are days when you go slow no matter how hard you try and days when you can't figure out why you are going so fast—the wind can't be blowing that hard. There are hills that look like hills and some that only feel like hills.

There are discussions with other bikers about all sorts of things: mortgage rates, failed relationships, routes to conquer, how to cope with others who don't bike, bike trips we hope to take, equipment to buy, whether we are on a hill or not, movies we saw. One time we passed at least forty miles by discussing a possible sequel to the movie *American Beauty*. I mean, really, how are all those characters going to cope the day after the movie ends?

I sing songs from my lonely childhood. Peter Paul and Mary, James Taylor, Carole King, Melanie. I love to dance also. I swing my arms, I reach for the sky, and I extend my arms out like I am an airplane. It is great grooving in that saddle with the sights sliding by. I became a very good no-hands rider as a child because we used to tie a rope from one handlebar to the other and steered from the rope—pretending these were the reins and we were on horses. These days, my friends recognize me from far away because they recognize my bipedal upright stance on the bike—turning corners without holding on.

But the best part of riding for me is what happens in my inner world. Ideas serenade me when the endorphins pump. Round and around and around the legs go, sometimes I do complicated math to assess what it would take to raise my average miles-per-hour rate up. Round and around my legs go, I remember the dream from the night before when the Dalai Lama solved all my psychological problems—well at least the ones left over after therapy. Round and around they go, green possibilities hit the sky. I talk to my deceased father, and somehow my future comes crystal clear. I see myself as lovable and loving.

One day I even saw God in the trees—out there in the wind, rustling in the sky and planted in the ground. I saw God in the air when a tree shook its leaves free and then light shone on everything.

I was in the flow, the every lasting glory of nowness, whatever that is. I saw that all was okay.

Another day I was contemplating how short life is while riding no hands on my favorite training route. It was a fun part of the ride, more downhill than uphill. The sun was shining and a quiet question emerged, *What if this is it?* What if the heavens come to take me now? What if I have a brain aneurysm or heart attack or I hit a pothole and I land on my head? What if a teenager who just fought with his parents drives crazy down the street or a vulture picking roadkill decides to carry me away. What if I vanish now?

I was pedaling fast in this lonely moment with summer green everywhere. Here I was, little old me in my preposterous life, my so uncommon and so common life. All my insecurities, all that rejection by men. Maybe I really did wear the wrong nail polish? And all that money in therapy and schooling. Chubby little me, pedaling fool, the wind blows, my endorphins are loosening in my bloodstream and I wonder if the sky will open for me at this moment. All that screaming and pleading with God all those years. I have not gone down easily. All the pain of all the years when life was unbearable. All the lostness, all the struggle. My ancestors, my karma, my life. All those paintings I painted and songs I sang and dances I danced. All those fun zany parties I gave, and journals I wrote. What if this was it?

All the fights with my mother and all the joyous laughter we have now. All the outrage and sweetness at the end of hard work. All the beginnings and promises that did come true. And here I am: wind, quiet, sounds, hope promise, circles go around and around. What if this is my time? This day was a crossroads of sorts, one of those moments of complete utter connection to the whole universe. Buoyant evolution was carrying me and I wished someone could predict that my worst heartaches were behind me, but the truth is that no one knows when the winds will shift direction again. So, on that day, I realized there's joy here already in my life and I'd better just ride the bull and hang on for

17

dear life, like any other ordinary pedaling fool would do.

Sometimes it is like this, one transcendent experience after another, they just keep coming right in a row. Being a woman, I know what it is like to have one orgasm after another. You just open to the sweetness.

A few years back, *Bicycling* magazine had a contest: "You knew you were a biker when . . ." My losing response read, "When I didn't cancel my subscription to *Bicycling* even though you publish no articles for chubby forty-year-old, 12-14 mph women." The winner probably isn't even biking anymore.

But, I don't care much about that. I know it's official. Alchemy has done its trick and turned a regular girl into a person who loves being outside and keeps in shape only to bike. It became really official the day I put a helmet on two hours after paying ninety-three for my hair dye, cut, and blow dry. My hairdresser was horrified when I told him I was going biking that evening. He scolded me and said I should go look pretty and sit in Starbucks sipping tea.

Sally Palaian is a clinical psychologist from Royal Oak, Michigan. In addition to biking and writing, she's passionate about personal growth, travel, friends, growing tomatoes, and dancing around the living room. She's currently working on a book about money management.

Scratching the Surface

Kelley Crisp

I know myself from my scars. I have scars in both feet from running barefoot down back alleys and a scar above my lip from choosing the wrong role in a game of William Tell. I touch these scars and know the tomboy that cocktail wear cannot conceal. My bike is no sleek, sophisticated roadie, nor is she the grunge cool of a mountain bike. She is a touring bike, not because of her geometry and rack lugs and triple chain rings, but because of her scars.

I love her scars. Once, I put her together in the Charles de Gaulle Airport, repositioning the handlebars, the seat, and the pedals after their long cramped stay in the bike box. She had managed the fourteen hours of intercontinental plane travel unscathed until I stripped the threads of one crank arm trying to force it on in the wrong direction. At a local bike shop, the technician and I communicated with shrugs and nods. She now sports the sultry curve of a crank arm from Paris; the other crank arm is broad and straight. The pedals sit at the end of each crank arm like twins reared apart. Despite their diverse backgrounds, both pedals are happy and well adjusted.

Geometry and components, lightweight frames, formfitting saddles, expensive paint jobs and aero bars—these are the attributes of bicycle beauty. This is the language of love for the gear head. This is poetry to the spokesperson. I find comfort in her imperfections.

She sometimes suffers from a too-relaxed outlook. Her seat has a notched tear from when she leaned casually against a New England tree while fully loaded. The panniers, tent, air mattress, and sleeping bag put enough weight on her to force a tear. Like my waistline, the deep, organic tear grows a little wider each year.

Her missing decals flash an unfinished name like an old sign from a country road diner. After a long look, the missing parts of letters that once formed BRIDGESTONE now seem to read APRIL GESTURE. A manufacturer's name has been transformed into a sign of spring, a nod to love.

My bicycle has left paint and parts in the southern states, the New England states,, the East and West Coast states, and in France and Spain. She has left her purple calling card on trees and fences and road signs and buildings. She has traveled by train, plane, automobile, subway, and ferry. She has slept in a small hotel in Tallahassee, Florida, and in a youth hostel in France with a view of Chartres. She has been shackled and chained to a rack and lovingly boxed for flight. Like the old hounds that seem to live and loiter in the back of a pickup truck, she and I travel.

I sometimes imagine her at the bike rack outside a Florida diner. Surrounded by sleek techno brothers and sisters, she modestly recounts the experiences of travel while her preppy audience listens raptly. She carries her miles well, my pied beauty.

They say you know the depth of love from sacrifice. My bicycle has put many miles on me. I have carried her up apartment stairs, hauled her running to catch a train, and given her my berth in a sleeping coach on an overnight run to Madrid. I have given up dinner money for repairs and taken into consideration my modest teacher's salary to transport her to exotic locales.

My bike shop boys know our story. I take her in for tune-ups and repairs. Occasionally, while I wait, I give a passing wink to something more sleek and slender, faster and lighter. Always, these sometimes salesmen encourage my constancy. They've seen the fat, bald line of travel that runs the center of her tires after a long trip. They've seen the postcards of our travels and the pictures of us together with fat redwoods or crumpled farmhouses as the backdrop. They smile indulgently at my flirtations.

Nighttimes she rests on an oak bike rack in my bedroom. We share the apartment with a tandem and a fat-tire beach bike. The beach bike gets me from home to work and the tandem is good for a weekend lark. Yet never does she give me a reproachful backward glance from a dimmed headlight. She knows that holidays are all hers. In spring and summer we honeymoon in the enchanted forests of a French château or the quaint towns along the Oregon coast. In the fall, we ride the MS 150 or the organized rides of cycling clubs. I cycle along singing her songs that are best left in the shower as herds of fleeter machines whiz past us. And at Christmas I deck her out in tinsel and lights with a boom box strapped to her rack. Blasting Wal-Mart Christmas carols, we go a-wassailing.

We search out like-minded couples to share our adventures. We have found few stalwart partnerships willing to forgo the lubed whiz of a short-term relationship, willing to see a smile in the gritty teeth of a chain ring. We have lost companions to the mechanical herd and others to the difficulties of a committed relationship.

Sometimes I think I have outgrown her. I get a taste for speed, a desire for what is current, and a yen for change. Then I look at her and think of loudly sung songs. I think of landscapes with views unbroken by power lines. I think of sunny days where a glimpse of the sea brings the bright smile of water. And I think of yawping in French down the hills of the Loire Valley and playing a kazoo up the hills of New England. The scars she carries are memories and reminders. Do you think she would like Italy?

Kelley Crisp has been a teacher for eighteen years. She is currently working as a volunteer for the World Teach Organization at Namu, a small coral atoll in the Marshall Islands.

Crash and Learn

Janusz Nagiecki

Lying prone near the bottom of Vail Pass, I did not love my bicycle. I cursed it for ejecting me and for the stabbing pain of my ripped, raw flesh. One moment I was crouched into an aerodynamic tuck, a chill wind fanning a tear from my eye, and the next I was in the air, flung into a forward rotation over the bars. As I flew over the pavement, thoughts vaporized in my mind and a blunt horror replaced them.

"This is a time for body thinking, a time when old-brain responses are fiercely appropriate," writes *T'ai chi* master and all-around sportswoman Denise McCluggage, describing how the body responds to danger. "Recognize these times and flick to automatic. It is more preservative of self."

But in the few moments that elapsed before I thumped to the ground, I did not recall thinking, *Well, seems like a job for the old brain. Better flick to automatic.* Instead, my mind simply locked up, caught between a feeling of utter vulnerability, helplessness, and doom and the belief that this couldn't possibly be happening to me.

Yet in spite of my seizure, my arms began to move. As I began my downward arc, they stretched wide like impromptu landing gear with palms opening toward the earth. No sooner had my arms extended than I slammed into the asphalt bike path on which I had been riding. I immediately went into a spontaneous tumble, completing a few rolls before landing cleanly on my back. It was a perfectly natural if not graceful maneuver that seemed to come from somewhere within my core. As I came to rest, a small cheer must have erupted from within the nerve center that guided me through the fall. Mission accomplished: The spread eagle had landed.

I lay there for a moment as the dust settled, fearing that movement might only increase the pain. Slowly, carefully, I lifted my body from the ground and checked for damage. My jersey and tights were in tatters from the slide on the pavement, and my legs, arms, and shoulders throbbed and were pulpy in spots. But my limbs did not seem disfigured in any way, and no bones jutted through my skin. My bike too suffered only minor damage: a slightly ragged saddle, torn handlebar tape, and a front rim that bumped against the brake pad when I gave it a spin.

I stood up and walked the pain off, cursing under my breath while looking around for some clue to what may have caused the crash. A few dozen yards from where I lay I spotted what had launched me skyward. A lump the size of a melon jutted from the center of the bike path. There was a hole in its middle where apparently a post had once been inserted—probably to prevent vehicles from driving onto the path. The way shadows were falling from the nearby aspens, the lump did not stand out on the flat black path. I never saw it and must have hit it squarely in the middle. Before I remounted my bike to limp slowly home, I carefully piled stones onto the mound, making a tidy cairn on the pavement in the hope that others would more easily spot the protuberance.

As the fog of pain that clouded my head cleared, so did my frustration and anger. I made peace with my bicycle, finding redemption in truing the wheel and in retaping the bars. But I stayed off the bike for at least a week after the accident, letting my wounds scab over and the swelling on my bruised legs and arms subside. When I finally did get back on the bike, I felt fragile and vulnerable, suspended in the air above what now seemed like two very thin tires. I clung to the brakes on long descents, inhibiting my speed to only a fraction of what I would have let it reach in the past. It took months, but I gradually overcame the handicap, regaining back my confidence to where I could again ride with familiar abandon.

Buddhism teaches that we should avoid being seduced into thinking that life is only to be lived for its temporary pleasures. We must accept suffering as a part of reality. The Buddha himself once said that "When we know about suffering, then there is no more to know."

As cyclists we may experience rapture in rolling along by the power of our legs and lungs, but there is also the burn from a steep climb, or the chill from a cold, rainy descent, or, yes, even the intense pain of an injury sustained in a bad fall. Bicycling thus brings together elements of pleasure and pain, teaching acceptance of one as a natural part of the other. In this way, riding not only tones the body and inspires the soul but conditions us to deal with life itself. What we so deeply understand from countless trials on the road or trail can carry us through the larger difficulties and challenges that we face in our lives.

I never rode Vail Pass again after the day of my crash nearly a decade ago. Nevertheless, I feel like I have revisited it many times over. It has served as my guiding metaphor when times get tough. It tells me that though the horror of a bad moment may seem to last forever, it is fleeting and will soon pass, that I should trust my instincts when tossed into a tight spot, and that when I am swamped in pain to take comfort in the knowledge that, with time, my wounds will heal.

Janusz Nagiecki is an American writer whose name is unpronounceable to most folks he meets. As with famed cycling coach Eddie B.—whose name is really not B but Borysewicz,—Janusz has had people take liberties with his name. Mostly, they started calling him John. He eventually conceded and began calling himself that too—though when pressed he will still recite his full Polish name with gusto and flourish. Janusz's bicycling career includes leading tours throughout the continental United States, Alaska, and Canada, competing as a USCF and NORBA racer, and being the first mountain biker to ride the full length of the

Colorado Trail. Bicycling invaded his writing career approximately a decade ago. Along with his other publications, he has penned bicycling features for the San Francisco Chronicle *and* Seattle Times. *He also coauthored the cycling guide* Road Biking Northern California *for Globe Pequot Press. Janusz currently resides and rides in Northern California. Drop him a line at* www.bikemuse.com.

The Perfect Bike

Ken Keberle

There is only one perfect bike for me. I have seen it a thousand times, yet I have never touched it. When I can't sleep, I see this bike. Last spring my daughter was sick in the hospital, when I needed to take my mind away from the hospital room for even a few minutes, I saw the bike.

Some people have religion or mantras to keep them focused, or bring them inner peace. I just see the bike.

I was a teenager when I first saw the bike. I was working as a two-dollar-an-hour mechanic and trying to survive a household I wouldn't have wished on my worst enemy.

The bike is fixed in time: the late seventies. Around the time Bernard Thevenet was winning the Tour de France, and before Carter canceled the dreams of hundreds of riders by boycotting the Moscow Olympics.

Bicycling has saved my life, brought me joy, and provided my livelihood. So when things start to overwhelm me, I see the bike. Even now, at night when I can't sleep, I force myself to see the bike. I find the calm when I see it. In my mind there in never room for both turmoil and the bike.

The bike has been the same for over twenty years. The color is dark blue, rich blue, a hint of metal flake. A blue you can lose yourself in.

The vision is always the same. I start looking at the top of the headset. The headset is the satin Dura Ace headset from the seventies. Not chromed, like a Campy headset, but that satin silver that looks like it was poured into place.

The flats of the headset are asking to have a wrench touch them, but I know what the headset feels like. It spins perfectly. Whatever Cosmic Wrench assembled the headset, he did so with such precision that the gentlest breath could move the forks. I've installed and adjusted thousands of headsets, but I know in my heart that I could never find that perfection.

The stem is the same satin, like a Cinelli or 3TTT from the same era. For some reason there are never any cables or housing on the bike. Just the tubing. Perfectly finished. The paint so smooth, it looks still wet.

My mind's eye follows the top tube back toward the seat cluster. Always slowly, not wanting to miss a drop of that paint.

The seat stays are somewhere between erotic and organic. They come together like the Raleigh fastback stays of the era. Cut so tight they look like they were grown together.

One chrome Campagnolo seatpost bolt holds it all together. The bolt is still carrying that perfect Italian chrome and the hex is still factory fresh, not messed up by some hack trying to fit a quarter-inch wrench into a five-millimeter bolt. If the bike was touched by the hand of a mechanic, it was a mechanic who cared.

So this is the bike that keeps me focused. I don't know where it came from. It will probably be with me the rest of my life. Like a messenger or an apparition, a mental safe place.

It comes fixed in time; a time of hope and possibilities, a time of fear and trepidation, and a time when the only thing that made sense to me was the bike.

Twenty-plus years later, my life is full of joy and gratitude. Yet even the most optimistic man has his demons. Some are exorcised by time, others by love. Yet demons sometimes return. And when they do, there is the bike.

Ken Keberle was raised in Arizona and is a graduate of Northern Arizona University. He has been married since 1988 and has twin daughters. He's a pretty good bike mechanic.

Morning Revolutions

Tara Austen Weaver

It's still dark as I pull myself from a warm bed, thinking briefly of those who slumber on. Shuffling around the house I fill water bottles and stuff work clothes into panniers while pulling on leggings and lacing up shoes. I clatter noisily down the stairs in the chilly predawn silence and wheel my bike out of the garage. There is no traffic on the roads, bar the clanking garbage truck, and I glide past houses still dark.

There are those who think I'm crazy, waking long before necessary in order to bike to work. There are questions they ask—about showering, transporting clothes, changing flat tires. There are answers I give—the environment, exercise, traffic—but they all fall short. It's hard to explain what can only be experienced.

Merging onto the bike path I speed past the salty marshes and wetlands of the bay. The tang of the air tickles inside my nose. Lights from the distant road reflect on calm waters rippling into infinity and I hear the tide swishing under wooden bridges as my wheels roll over them. The air is cold as it whips past, stripping away any vestiges of sleep. Soon there are houseboats and sailboats bobbing offshore, white beacons in the paling dark. There are joggers out now and we nod in greeting as we pass each other, sharing the bond of the early riser.

I was not always a bike commuter. There were days when I drove my car to the ferry terminal and sipped coffee as I read the paper, crossing the bay safely ensconced in a window seat. Other days I shuffled three steps up and onto the bus, feeding money into the machine and taking a thin paper transfer, fighting drowsiness as the low and steady sound of the motor threatened to send me back to sleep. I always seemed to arrive at work only half awake.

Cycling through the bayside town of Sausalito, the image of my bike flashes on storefront after storefront window creating a staccato pattern as I pedal smoothly onward. There is a break in the storefronts and suddenly the panorama of the city is before me: streets and houses and skyscrapers still outlined in twinkling lights, reflecting in the silent waters of the bay. The sky is blushing in the east, pink and gold fingers stretching upward.

Past Sausalito the road begins to steepen. I breathe deeply and the cold air knifes at my chest. Pushing harder my legs begin to warm and burn, first the right then the left, as I steadily climb the hill. Head down I push past stands of eucalyptus trees, fragrant in the morning moisture, and the delicate lacy green of fennel bushes lining the road.

My first ride into the city was serendipity. Deciding to bike from my house to the ferry I misjudged time and arrived just as the stout boat was pulling away from the pier. I had two options: leave my bike locked to a lamppost and take the bus, or ride all the way. Emboldened by the early-morning light I decided to go for it. I've never looked back.

Cresting the hill the Golden Gate Bridge is before me, glowing red in the radiance of dawn. The cars are thick now, bogged down among themselves, and I speed past them on the walkway. The bridge hums from the vibrations of many motors and I feel the movement through my handlebars. Leaning forward I wheel across the slight incline, stopping at the middle of the span.

Suddenly the flaming gold of the sun bursts over the eastern edge of my world, flooding the city, the bay, and the mountains with a generous light. The bridge is illuminated now, more golden than ever before. The moment is precious, worth waking up for, worth the work to get here, worth it just to hang suspended high over water—on a shimmering link of gold—to watch the day begin.

Eventually I move on, wheeling across the span in the warming light. Descents wait for me on the other side—coasting down hills to the sandy wetlands of Crissy Field, and the manicured green lawns and sailboats of the Marina. Cresting another grassy hill I glide down the curve of Aquatic Park where waves break rhythmically on a crescent of damp sand. The wharf is here, eerie without its daytime clamor. Restaurants are just beginning to stir as I speed past, busboys sweeping the sidewalk, a bakery churning out fresh bread. This early the air smells of yeasty dough, fresh fish, and the alluring scent of possibility.

There are days when I simply can't bike. Days when logistics require a car, or evening plans preclude bringing a bike along. These days are never as good. Try as I might, I am cranky; still sleepy at three; my brain set on some slower speed. I need the cycle spins in order to function properly. If this is addiction, I am not complaining.

Clearing the wharf I roll onto the smooth sidewalk of the Embarcadero. Piers flash by me on the left as I swoop around joggers, walkers, and graceful rollerbladers enjoying the early-morning sunshine. The world seems new, and waiting in patient readiness for something to happen. The water of the bay glistens to my left and I wheel past the soaring dome of the ferry terminal, its arched facade disgorging early commuters scurrying to offices, meetings, and industry.

The Embarcadero curves around the city, embracing its towers and buildings, and I follow the smooth pavement and wide sidewalk that borders the water. Here are the docks of yesteryear, haunted by the figures of longshoremen, the days when San Francisco was a real port. Rotting now, the sodden wood is slowly falling into salty waters; a century of history being forgotten.

To my right are the gleaming towers of the new San Francisco, an era of electronics and ideas replacing the might of ships and men. Here are the machines, the engineers, the high-tech speculation, the new concept that rules all. Never let it be said that San Francisco had only one gold rush.

The clear bright of the day is reflected in these sharp windows, the waters of the bay dancing with light. In a groove now I coast past coffee shops—the deep aroma coaxing me onward—and toward the end of the Embarcadero. Here are the last of the boats; pristine sails a brilliant white in the early-morning sunshine. Here too is the ballpark, its rusty brick solidity anchoring the shoreline. Memories of pitchers and peanuts cling poignant to the empty shell and as I sail past I glimpse a moment of velvety green through the open porthole door.

Leaving the Embarcadero I find myself on city sidewalks and dismount to cross the busy street. The train station bustles with commuters—coffee cups and briefcases in hand—eager to start their day. The flower vendor is stocked with deep purple irises, tender roses, and fragrant daylilies; the newspaper seller calls out headlines to a wakening world.

Crossing at the light, I stand before the low brick building that is my destination. Removing my helmet I shoulder my bike and clankity-clank my way up the stairs, maneuvering the landing, and up again to my floor. My bike clicks quietly as I wheel it down carpeted halls and into my office.

"How was your ride?" my co-workers ask each morning.

"Not bad," I say with a smile. Exhilarated. Invigorated. Alive. I am already eager for the ride home.

Tara Austen Weaver is a San Francisco-based writer specializing in travel, cultural issues, and adventure sports. She is co-editor of two collections of travel literature, Travelers' Tales Tuscany *and* Travelers' Tales Provence, *and is most happy when combining her passions by cycling or hiking through foreign countries.*

Streetpulse; or, How I Learned to Stop Taking the Bus and Love Bike Commuting

Andrea Kopp

As I fly through the gridlock I feel the street pulse around me. The beat of feet thumping around me, the revving of engines, the hum of voices, the moving shapes all around me. This is what makes me ride my bike. This is the street pulse. I push my pedals in circles, a constant flowing motion. Adrenaline rushes inside me. I feel the wind whip my face.

Ha ha! Look at those people . . . sitting in their cages . . . on their cellphones . . . somewhere else. I almost pity them . . . they have to spend hours ripped from the world in their metal enclosures to get to and from work. Hard work that goes to pay their cage's guzzling mouth. Good thing I'll have my sandwich once I get home . . . it's all I need.

A block ahead, a little light changes. Green. The mass of cars lurches forward.

Check six. I swing my head around. Never let situational awareness disappear. An SUV roars past me. I push harder. I want to make it past that light before it changes back. Still half a block to go. The little red man is already blinking at the pedestrians who look awkwardly at the kid on some old bike, speeding with the cars, the kid with a little tricycle on his helmet. Almost there . . . a couple dozen feet . . . the light turns orange. Not worth risking it. I switch gears down and slam the brakes and skid right to the white stripe marking the intersection. On one side, a bus, on the other, a Lincoln Navigator. It's gonna be important to really launch out of this one fast. I see the perpendicular traffic

33

rush through their now orange light. I stand on my pedals, stay in balance for a second . . .

Then I let all my force jettison me in front of the two massive vehicles encircling me. I grab my part of the lane and continue shooting on down Michigan Avenue. Eat this, gridlock!

I speed down three blocks, and get stopped by another light. I stand on my pedals, anticipating the release from traffic signals. Green. I slam the pedals. My chain skips. I stay put. I haul my vehicle to the sidewalk, push the derailleur forward, ease the chain back into its position. I check my bike quickly. Why are my brakes so loose? My trusty Allen tool, "Hexy," is immediately in my palm. I put it into action, tightening my brakes, making sure everything is all right. Within three minutes, I'm riding again. If other vehicles could be tuned up this fast, I might consider them. But my rusty old two-wheeled freedom is all I need to get to school, to get to the store, to get to my friend's house . . .

I stretch my arm out to my right and whip around another street corner, exhilarated by freedom.

Snow falls softly on Chicago tonight. I pat my good old knobby tires. Just the traction I need to get to school tomorrow. I'll be ready.

Bike Winter has commenced. I haul my bike onto the icy sidewalk, mount it, and pedal into the street. I shoot down the bike lane on Wells Street. "Are you crazy?" a motorist yells, driving by me.

"You don't know what you're missing," I respond. Snow continues to drift earthward, but that just adds to the beauty of it . . .

A couple of cars hiss by, but today I pedal slowly, enjoying the thousands of falling snowflakes around me. My balaclava, my two pairs of socks, my T-shirt, my rain pants, my sweater and coat are all there to keep me warm. Another cyclist rides down the bike lane on the opposite direction. I wave to him, and although we cannot see each other's mouths, we can feel each other's smiles.

I dodge a couple of cars parked in the bike lane . . . those people's disrespect irritates me, but as I drift down the street with the snow, feeling my legs pumping a bit faster, I smile. Road rage happens to everyone, but with your bike, it just makes you go faster. It never lasts long.

Of course, when I get to school, everyone thinks I'm crazy. Well, yes, I do still ride in winter. Why not? The bus is even more unreliable in winter, even more crowded and uncomfortable . . . my bike, on the other hand, makes me happy . . . unlike the bus, it releases me from negative energies instead of worsening them . . .

People often talk about the "dead of winter." Oh, but I feel incredibly alive.

My brother shoves a bike catalog under my face. Wow, that new "Specialized" sure looks fancy. And look at those new pedals! Those new tires! Those new derailleurs! Those new brakes! Those new . . . why do I need them anyway? My bike may not be "top-of-the-line," but I like my old reflective-tape-covered, sticker-plastered, winter-enduring bike better. After all, all I need to do is wash it down with soap every once in a while, adjust my brakes, and lube the chain . . . and since I've now learned how to do these things myself, why would I need to buy, buy, buy? All I need is a few good tools.

I am free. My bike is my freedom. I am not trapped, kept isolated from the life around me. I am not trapped where I don't want to be. I am not trapped by the need to always have the newest vehicle. I am not trapped by the thought of people disapproving of my transportation. I am one with my bike. When the adrenaline is pumping through me and I am shooting down the street . . . when I am slowly riding though the park, though the snow, through the world around me, appreciating it . . . when I take time to repair it . . . I am one with my bike.

A child walking down the street turned abruptly and pointed at the cyclist in the street: "Look at his helmet, Mommy! He's put a little bike on it! Look how fast he's going! He must be having too much fun!"

How right you are, kid. Hope you'll join me sometime, we'll commute together. You'll see, it's even more fun than it looks. Bring your friend along. We'll mass our ride together and take over the streets on our bikes. We'll all be free.

Andrea Kopp lives in Chicago.

To Africa and Back

Tokey Boswell

I learned everything I know about bikes and biking in the Peace Corps. I mean, I had bikes before, little cheap ones that got me across town, to campus, and the like. But it was when I left the country that I found out how wonderful a bike can be. I spent nearly two years in the Republic of Guinea, West Africa, with a 730 Trek Antelope.

There are roads in Guinea, and cars, but neither is in very good shape. There are thousands of miles of footpaths, though, just begging to be ridden. Some paths are through tall grass trodden down, some are across volcanic rock. Nearly all of them cross small rivers by means of fallen trees or rickety branch bridges. Many of the trails seem to start in the middle of nowhere, or end in the middle of nowhere, and none of them appears on any map, anywhere. I was a health education volunteer in Guinea, charged with the well-being of a county in the rain-forest-like coastal region. The county (or sous-prefecture, as they called it) of Tormelin is not overly large, maybe thirty miles wide and sixty miles long. There is one partly paved road that runs diagonally across it, and three or four other rocky roads that vehicles could traverse, depending on the weather and the courage of the operator. The sous-prefecture also has three major rivers, innumerable streams and marshes, and two significant cliff ranges. It was into this terrain my bike and I were thrust.

I rode that bike every day, visiting people and villages I wasn't sure existed. I rode through waist-deep puddles, across three-foot-wide trails of army ants, beside troops of monkeys. I rode through forests crawling with snakes, through streams filled with alligators and even more deadly bacteria. The trails and my Trek took me to seventy-foot waterfalls, to mile-long caves, to sheer cliff faces. They took me to the huts of people dying from malaria, dysentery, and AIDS. They took me and several hundred doses of polio vaccine to the farthest reaches of the county, tracking down children not yet inoculated.

Those trails and my bike took me to some of the most beautiful places on the planet—hidden oases where women washed clothes and laughed in the shade, groves of ancient trees—and to some of the saddest places. Guinea is not a modern country, and in many ways it is hard to live there, alone in a village of people with traditions so different. When I was sad, I rode home slowly and kept my head down. When I was angry I rode out hard and fast, eyes straight ahead. When the differences were too great, my bike took me away.

Some of my nearest Peace Corps neighbors were ten and twelve hours away, traveling by rickety car on crummy roads, or ten to twelve hours away on a bike, traveling those unrecorded footpaths. I often chose to take the latter, preferring the relative safety of two wheels. Those trips were true expeditions—I rode all day, weighed down by bottles of water, food, books, a flashlight, a few clothes, and whatever else I thought was needed. Once a friend made the daylong trek to my house across rain-swollen rivers just to present me with two cans of Budweiser that some benevolent visitor had left him. Those long trips were perhaps the most memorable part of my Peace Corps experience.

At every tiny village the whole town would come out, asking, "Little white man, where are you going?" I would tell them, and they would point me to a near-invisible route between two huts that carried me to the next village, and so on, until magically I appeared where I wanted to be. Well, almost magically. I remember the struggle of riding through wet soft sand, of carrying my bike and all those supplies up mountain trails too steep to ride. Of waiting, maybe hours, for a dugout canoe to carry me across the biggest rivers. I remember the pain of falling, the tears of relief when I saw my friends. I remember the successes, too—learning how to repair derailleurs and brakes, replacing the crappy complicated grip shifters with those old reliable thumb index shifters. Truing up spokes was most difficult, but eventually I did a passable job of it. After a while other people in Tormelin started bringing their bikes to me—old-school cruiser types that must have weighed thirty or forty pounds. No one else in town had the collection of Allen wrenches and screwdrivers that I did, so by default I was a mechanic. I would fix their bikes and we would talk. Slowly I would work into the conversation questions about their health, the health of their children. I asked what they were eating, where they got their water, where their latrine was dug. In the end I would make a suggestion or two, promise to visit, and hand them the repaired bike.

I think those moments improved my credibility in town far more than the many public speeches I gave. Spiked plants are everywhere in Guinea, and I must have punctured a tire at least fifty times during my service. For a while, I fixed them myself at home, but then I found an older man in town who could do it better, and faster, for the price of a few cigarettes. Every couple of weeks I would show up at his hut with a flat tire and a bloody leg or broken finger. He would smile and shake his head. "Crazy little white man, where did you go this time?" I would tell him, he would smoke and fix the tire, and then we would eat together. That was how things worked in Guinea. When it was time for me to leave the country, many people in Tormelin asked if they could have my bike. They had seen how fast I could travel and heard stories of my longest trips. I gave it to a new Peace Corps volunteer, though, with instructions to take good care of it: Oil the chain often. Let the tire guy in town fix flats. And every once in a while, take it on a nice long trip.

After returning from the Peace Corps, Tokey Boswell worked as a carpenter and a writer. He is currently enrolled in graduate school at the University of Iowa, in the field of urban and regional planning.

Callie's Gift

Sandra Schumann

This is a story about biking—about the love of a special canine companion—and how the two combined to teach me a lesson I will carry with me for life. I am one of those goal-oriented people. I tend to work hard, and play hard—sometimes to the point where it's impossible to tell one from the other. Thus, I took to biking like an ant takes to collecting seeds—with a focused intensity—completely shutting out the possibility that biking might actually be an enjoyable way to connect with the world. Well, that's not quite true. The first few times out, I actually did enjoy the ride. I could cover a lot more territory and see a lot more than I could when I was jogging—and with a lot less stress on my knees. In a short while, though, my normal way of biking was putting on a set of headphones, settling onto the seat of my Mongoose, and pedaling for miles—looking straight ahead—listening to a book on tape—and not stopping until I had finished my predetermined mileage for the day. Joyless, until a twenty-eight-pound bit of devotion on four paws changed my way of being on a bike.

Callie came to us as a yearling. A tricolor Border collie mix whom we adopted out of the local emergency hospital. She had been cruelly hurt by her former owners and, consequently, came to our home with a cast on her broken leg, a frightened gleam in her eyes, and an attitude. In spite of that all—or perhaps because of it all—she developed an intense devotion to me. The first night we had her, that little dog with the makeshift cast jumped up on the bed where I lay and began circling the perimeter—growling at my husband each time he tried to come near. Protecting me from a situation she, in her short life span, had come to see as dangerous. Putting my safety above her own pain. Of course, I let her know that all was well, and that people belong in bed, and dogs—usually—do not. She accepted the ruling with canine stoicism, and stuck to sleeping on the rug—just like she stuck to my side, and my heart, for the next fifteen years.

Now, I can't say life with Callie was always easy. Border collies tend to be extremely intelligent, endlessly enthusiastic, and always in search of work. If they aren't assigned a job, they will invent their own—quite often to the chagrin of the neighborhood children who find themselves being herded like sheep. Thus, it took all our combined inventiveness to find enough for her to do. She paroled the yard as I gardened, protecting me from snakes, and moles, and crickets, and all manner of frightening beasts; she carried the mail up our eight-hundred-foot driveway; and even helped with the laundry by retrieving any socks that escaped from the pile on the way to the washer. In her midyears, we found dog agility—a competitive sport that satisfied her need for employment, and further cemented our connection to one another. We also walked—daily—for miles—Callie enjoying the mingled sights, smells, and sounds nature had to offer a dog of her sensitivity; and I, in my own compulsive style, reading a book.

At age eleven, Callie developed problems with her neck and legs. She was no longer able to do most of the obstacles at dog agility and, eventually, was unable to walk more than short distances. Still, with her accumulated years of canine wisdom, she accepted her condition, and contented herself with those things she could still do. Instead of the jumps and A-frames of the agility courses, she stuck to the tunnels and chutes. Instead of long walks in the woods, she settled into a freshly dug hole and slept near me as I gardened. Instead of chasing the squirrels, she positioned herself beneath the trees—lying motionless for hours—furtively watching as the wildlings skittered through the over-hanging branches.

I, on the other hand, was not quite so content. I had stopped walk-ing because I missed my canine companion but I had not lost my need for more intense physical activity. I floundered for a while, and then I found biking. Or perhaps it would be better to say my husband gave it to me as a Christmas present that year of the no-walks. My Mongoose hybrid bicycle soon became my new exercise companion—a fact I dili-gently tried to hide from Callie—knowing it would cause hurt feelings. I should have realized that my creative attempts at deception were doomed to failure.

You see, from the time she came to us, Callie mourned even short separations. From the start, she took to sitting on the steps to the upstairs—peeking through the small windows in the front door as I drove off—adamant about remaining in sight of the driveway. We understood, and tried to lessen her burden by placing a chair at the front window so she could prolong our time "together." From then on, whenever I left the house, she took up her post—intent on saying good-bye; and, quite often, that is where she remained while I was gone. Her face was in the window when I left—and it was there when I returned. Still, she was content, and she understood the necessity of my leaving—as long as I traveled by car. The first time she happened to catch me sneaking out on my bike, though, was a different matter. Her howls followed me down the driveway, and the sadness of the call resounded in my ears throughout my ride. Feeling more than a bit guilty—and finally acknowledging the loss I was feeling without Callie at my side—I resolved to find a way to take her with me.

I searched the pet stores and the Internet—trying to find some-thing—anything—made for transporting little doggy beings on lengthy bike trips. I looked at bike seats, and dogcarts—contraptions of all shapes and sizes—and finally decided on a child carrier—a red-

and-yellow, canvas-covered two-seater that I pulled along behind the bike. It came complete with seat belts, a water bottle holder, and two pockets to carry the necessities of a small dog in tow.

I brought the cart home—assembled it—and plopped Callie in for a trial run. She balked—unsure that dogs were actually meant to ride in wobbly carts pulled behind even more wobbly bicycles. But, being game, she gave it a try. There was a bit of anxiety when she felt the rolling beneath her and, unused to her biking legs, she lost her footing and sat back hard in the seat. Then, just that quickly, she got it! She realized that was the way it was supposed to be done—not standing at the edge, straining against the seat belt, but sitting back against the seat—in the shade—out of the rain—at ease. Of course, there were some things she had to give up—the wonderful stretch-your-legs feeling; the short off-road jaunts to check out animal trails; the absorbing smell of fresh dog urine left as markers on the roadside vegetation. But she was happy. She was comfortable—she was outdoors—and, most importantly, she was with me.

For several years, we went out five or six times a week—her sitting in her carrier—me in front, hauling the load. At first, we were something of an anomaly. People expected to see a baby in the cart, and their expressions, upon seeing the cargo, were often priceless; but as the weeks and months went on, the folks along our routes came to know the little red-and-yellow wagon. They waved as they drove by in their cars—waved from their tractors—or looked up from their gardening to wave us on. We became a normal—and welcome—part of daily life. Even the ducks on the pond learned to recognize our approach, and they quacked their greeting as they paddled over for their daily portion of our Cheerios.

Now, I have to say, I'm not a really strong biker, so pulling a thirty-five-pound cart packed with a thirty-pound Border collie was quite a strain at times—especially over the hills of Maine; but it was worth it.

We were back together again, and that made me happy. Moreover, I felt proud of myself. I was giving Callie the extra time it took to lug that heavy cart around town, and I was even gratified to have some pretty sore leg muscles because of it. After all, that proved how much I loved her, didn't it? Yep! I was doing a really good thing; and in my narrow, human way of thinking, I felt really, really good about the gift I was giving her. It turned out that, as is often the case in life, I was only half right. In retrospect, I know I did give her a gift—and it was given with great love; but her gift to me was so much greater.

For, as I said, I was an intense rider; and when we rode, I noticed nothing of the world around us. Callie, on the other hand, noticed everything. Felt everything. Smelled everything. Soaked in every sensory aspect of the ride. She rode, head high, eyes wide open, muzzle lifted to the wind. Smiling. Zen-like in her appreciation of the moment.

Later, as she got older, and her kidneys started to fail, she couldn't get through a long ride without a pit stop; but even that became a learning experience. I realized I had been missing all the details—all the little things that made biking a work of the soul. The smell of the milkweed. The furtive movement of a weasel on the creek bank. The velvety feel of wild lamb's ears petals. The twittering of chickadees in the pines. I had overlooked all of it. She missed none of it. And I took joy in her joy.

We biked together for four years—from early spring until late fall—as long as the Maine roads remained ice-free. Then, at age sixteen, her kidneys began a rapid decline—and, along with them, she lost her joy in biking. In fact, she lost her joy in most of what life had to offer outside the comfort, warmth, and safety of her bed. She never once, though, lost her joy in being with me—and I never once, through the pain of those last weeks, lost my joy in being with her.

Callie died—smiling—in my arms—two weeks after our last bike ride together. We buried her in a coffin papered with pictures of our times together—including a picture of her sitting proudly in her cart behind the bike.

That was five months ago. I tried—once—to go biking without her; but that was a very short time after her death—and it was too soon—the memories too fresh. I tried to see things through her eyes; but the joy was missing, and I put my bike away. Yesterday, I took it out again—and I rode. I followed the path we normally took together—our path. I cried as I pedaled; but I kept going. I stopped to feed the ducks—and I cried—but I kept going. And, as I rode, I began to feel the joy coming back; but this time it was different.

Callie's wordless teachings had taken root—the lessons she had taught me were well learned. My biking had taken on a new dimension—and so had my connection with the world. I could see, and smell, and hear, and feel through my own senses now. And that . . . was Callie's gift.

Sandra Schumann is a psychotherapist who lives with her husband in the beautiful Maine woods. She draws inspiration from the woods and coasts of her home state, as well as from her experiences with the animal companions in her life. She enjoys gardening, dog agility, ballroom dancing, writing, and, of course, biking.

Full Cycle with Spin

Nenad Petkovic

The riding was easy. We were going down and across the rough dirt track and up across the ridge and along on the grass, unwillingly herding the sheep with our movement. It was fun and tears were streaming out of both temporal corners of my eyes and the tracks of the tears were horizontal due to the wind and the speed of the bike. This country was beautiful, lush and green with rolling hills and wildlife that added to the sky that made you ache to reach the end of it and not miss a single thing on the way. The riding was smooth and I felt so happy, light and free, and my bike was running like a gazelle and I didn't miss anyone and had no worries about the future or places I needed to return to or people I needed to see.

Most of the time, J. and I would ride alongside each other and all we'd talk about was how fantastic it was, nothing about people we knew and what they were doing or what they'd said, or who was doing what and with whom. It helped that we'd left both our mobiles at home, but I think it was the ride that made us forget everybody else. So we talked about the country, the sky, the light, and how well our bikes were running.

J. would ask me about the trees and I'd tell her about the oaks and maples, the birches, the yews, pines, and cypress trees and we'd stop while I showed her the difference in the leaves and how you tell a beech from a hawthorn when they're not flowering. This would make me all the happier, that I could talk to this country intimately and please J.

with my knowledge of it and watch her revel in her newfound ability to name the country and enjoy it even more. In the same manner she'd teach me about the bikes and the ride and give me the advice I needed to get the most of this ride. Happiness created happiness while the wheels of our bikes went silently and smoothly round.

Every now and again J. would pull off to ride on her own at her own pace. Reveling in pushing herself physically as hard as she could, she'd punch up the gears to a ten or twenty until her legs burned and she'd have to hit back down to a five or a three, which is where I would usually be found.

We'd been so lucky with the rain and with the bikes not having a single puncture and this part of the country being far enough away from any busy roads that sometimes all we could hear was the wind and the sound of our own movement. We'd seen hawks and kestrels chasing the rabbits and so we'd play at chasing the rabbits on our bikes, but the rabbits were just too unpredictable and agile and our bikes just couldn't turn anywhere near as fast. The chase was good and we laughed and when I could see J. smile and laugh again like that, part of me wanted to capture the moment in a piece of amber and wear it next to my heart.

The times we stopped for lunch we'd make it quick, grateful for the rest but anxious to get back on our bikes, so we'd make sure in the mornings before we set off that we packed easy things to eat and digest. Sometimes hard-boiled eggs, sausages, bacon or cheese, sometimes fish and mayonnaise wrapped up in lettuce leaves. Protein-rich fatty foods that made us feel so light as there were no starches or sugars in our diets. After all the sickness we'd had that wouldn't go away while we were eating breads and pasta and fruit, we felt so healthy on meat and fat alone. Full of energy, we'd ride all day, our bodies getting leaner and healthier adding to how good we felt about ourselves on this ride through such big and vibrant country.

Part of what I loved about this country, and the reason that J. had chosen it, was the numerous shallow streams and rivers that would cut up the land and provide balance to the rolling hills. Down and across and up and along and we'd hit a stream and we'd ride right over it splashing and enjoying the new sounds. At the wider streams and rivers we'd pick up our bikes and carry them across. I'd be laughing at J. using her little finger to lift up her bike and her laughing because she was showing off her bike and then me jealously laughing at her bike being so much lighter than mine. This all made us so happy and we'd wade across to the opposite bank, laughing so hard that sometimes we nearly fell in and we had such fun with it that she'd cross back to the bank we started from and do it all over again, holding her bike high above her head, watching me laugh.

The waters were so clean and pure and frequent that we didn't need to fill up our water bottles. We'd stop and drink when we needed to, but sometimes I would miss a cup of coffee, freshly made black coffee with no sugar, and if there was just one thing I missed on this ride it was that coffee, but the water was good and cold and thoroughly refreshing. We'd drink to our fill when we needed to and then ride on.

Earlier on J. had pulled ahead of me and I saw that she was moving fast downhill and I could see a river coming up, but she wasn't slowing down and I stopped to watch because she was going faster and faster toward the river and I knew she was going to try to take it at full speed and without getting her bike wet. I saw her negotiate toward a slight incline on the bank and she sailed off into the air whooping with delight as she arced over the river and landed with a 180-degree skid on the moist turf on the far bank. She saw me watching and smiling and she laughed as if to dare me to try the same, but she deserved that triumph on her own and I shook my head smiling and eased on down to the river.

In the evenings we'd clean the bikes down and make sure that all the nuts were tightened after all the jarring that the bikes took on our behalf. After an hour's attention the bikes were as good as new and frequently we'd want to ride them immediately under the light of the moon and the stars and accompanied by the owls. So we rode under the moon, at first fearful, but slowly gaining in confidence and reassurance and the bikes were so reliable and at night they seemed to have minds of their own and know how to avoid any danger. This made us incredibly happy, feeling somehow that all the Gods and Goddesses that made up the sparkling night sky were looking after us.

It was fantastic, the thrill of riding as fast as we could under the light of the moon, with the trees looking black and the ground looking black and no color anywhere to be seen other than the reflective strips of orange on our bikes. We'd even turn the bikes' in-built lights off when the moon was bright and we'd be the stars in our own black-and-white movie, with the deers and badgers making up the audience and we were so happy riding at night taking chances and risks and feeling so free. We never knew how long these night rides would last; sometimes they'd go on all night and sometimes just an hour or so.

I'd bought J. a new bike for her birthday since she rode everywhere, to work, to her friends, to the shops, for any activity and she couldn't afford to replace her rusting, forever failing, ten-year-old machine. She'd let me ride her new bike occasionally and I got to enjoy it and so bought myself a cheaper model, which I rode on Sundays. It was a movement toward doing some things her way. Doing things somebody else's way with no taste of bitterness from the compromise and sacrifice and all those years of argument and feeling under pressure. The biking holiday had been J.'s idea and while I hadn't thought I could enjoy such an intense period of biking I'd agreed to the plan and here I was enjoying every second of riding through this country with J. and feeling free and happy with no regret and not wishing that I was in a five-star hotel on a beach somewhere warm.

It didn't matter that our time here was limited, that soon we'd return to the city, because J. and the country and the excellent bikes made me realize that for the first time in my life I was having the one free ride of my life, with no payment at the end. I would have this ride for as long as it lasted and remember it for as long as I lived and I'd cherish the memory of it for as long as J. and I were together, which is an amount of time that no person can ever know.

Nenad Petkovic lives in London, England, with his son Joshua. He doesn't own a bike, drives everywhere, and spends a fortune on parking. He has tried alternate means of locomotion such as skateboarding, but has not yet made significant progress.

Another Way of Getting There; or, How My Bicycle Became My Lover After Many Years of Servitude and Neglect

Joshua Caine Anchors

The ochre glow of evening sun pouring through the tall white pines of western Maine helped confirm a thought I'd been having all day: There is no better way to perceive the world than from the seat of a bicycle. This was my first day on the road of a seven-hundred-mile journey and I was lighthearted, ebullient, and innocent to the rigors of bicycle trekking. I was aware that my euphoria was perhaps naive considering I didn't have any bike tools, I had never biked over thirty miles from my house in northern Maine, and it didn't look as if my ragtag tent would fare too well against the ominous clouds that were accumulating over the distant White Mountains of New Hampshire. However, euphoria is one of those rare emotional conditions of life that even logic or reason can rarely diminish, and after being in school for far too long, I was eager for the sensual, spontaneous side of existence.

Although I had recently finished a university course on the Pragmatists, those tedious American philosophers who believed strongly in the supremacy of scientific method over experience, less than a week after the course ended I embarked upon the least methodical, least pragmatic journey that I could imagine. With no map or directions I navigated viscerally, relying only upon what seemed right. Clearly, I felt an urge to rebel from structure, and my justification for rebellion had come to me in the form of a frantic Scotsman. His name was David

Sangster and he called me one muddy spring morning desperately in need of a director for the outdoor adventure program at his summer camp in northeastern Pennsylvania. With a thick accent, he informed me that I had eight days before camp started and that he'd reimburse me up to two hundred dollars for a bus or train. The job sounded intriguing and involved living in a platform tent on the top of a hill with a crew of rock climbers and mountain bikers. I was elated as I accepted the job: Nothing could get farther from a classroom of philosophy texts.

As I agreed to take the job, however, I knew that I only had twenty dollars in my wallet, hardly enough to buy a bus or train ticket from Maine to Pennsylvania. And since I had too much pride to tell David about my predicament or ask him for a cash advance, I began considering alternatives. Walking or running to Pennsylvania wasn't an option; my parents were in Canada on vacation so they couldn't help me out; and though I'd often read books about jumping trains, I didn't feel seasoned enough for that kind of adventure. But when I finally arrived at the idea of bicycling to Pennsylvania, I knew I had struck on something deep, something that I had subconsciously wanted to do for years but never had the reason, the time, or the mad desire to escape from pragmatic behavior. Now I had no excuses and, as I looked over at my Trek mountain bike hanging from a ceiling hook, it looked like a greasy saint, a twenty-one-geared savior come to carry me over the diamond-studded pavements of the world.

Before my decision to bike eight hundred miles in eight days, my relationship with bicycling had been simply functional. As a proud nonconsumer of motorized vehicles, I found myself bicycling everywhere around the small college town of Orono. Rarely did I embark on recreational bike trips, but I found myself biking fifteen to twenty miles a day just to get to classes, go grocery shopping, or visit friends. Therefore, my relationship with my bike was more like that of a dependent old mistress than a fiery, impassioned lover. And because my fondness for my bike was clouded by function, I often neglected buying it the most instrumental of tools. My bicycle tool kit consisted of a patch, an Allen wrench, and some contorted metal device that I didn't know how to use. Although I was terribly incompetent at fixing what I depended on for transportation, as I glanced over at my bike with its titanium frame and shining metallic gears, it looked invincible, as if it could ride the immensity of jagged Himalayan slopes without suffering a single flat tire.

Two hours later, after leaving an explanatory note for my parents that said, "Left for PA on bike—No $. See you in few months," I threw a few pairs of socks, shorts, and underwear in a Sierra Club backpack and took my first pedal toward Pennsylvania, towards that great clump of agrarian land that I knew was out there somewhere to the southwest, somewhere across the lazy Delaware River, somewhere millions of pedals away. The freedom of simply bicycling forward, to a place on the map I had never been and didn't really know how to get to, felt both exhilarating and slightly ridiculous. Did I really think the four cans of tuna fish, the bag of ginger snaps, and the six bananas in my backpack would nourish me during my trek? What would I do if my chain popped off or a tire went flat? Where was I going to spend the night? I didn't mind bivouacking, but in a place where blaze orange is the state color and enormous antlers decorate most fireplaces, I wondered if camping alongside the road was such a good idea. I began to think that Hemingway was wrong when he wrote that "nobody lives their lives all the way up except bull-fighters." As I finally reached Route 2, that interminable, windy, shoulderless artery of pavement that would be my path to New Hampshire, I felt like a bullfighter must feel when he enters a hot, dusty stadium in rural Mexico. There were no senoritas or rose petals in my case, to be sure, but I had committed to the long, bullish road, and I was eager to discover how I could live my life up, how I could bicycle my way into the very pith of existence.

Eighty painful miles later I cruised into a wet campsite in the White Mountains after I was sure that the owners were asleep, and came to the profound realization that I was alone with my bicycle. Rarely had I actually contemplated the meaning of my bicycle, but as I leaned its sleek red frame against a tall oak tree I felt a powerful impulse to make sure it was comfortable. Perhaps my affection was an indication of fatigue or of campsite loneliness, but I suddenly had the urge to show some sympathy for all those miles and countless hills that I'd ridden with rusty chain, squeaky brakes, and wobbly tires. I recalled Ralph Waldo Emerson's idea that the existence of every material object is an expression of the spiritual or real, and as I set my tent up on damp, humusy earth, it seemed that my bicycle represented something much more meaningful than a simple contraption of metal, rubber, and grease. After all the time we'd spent together, the sweat and grease we'd borne, and now as we reposed together under the silent canopy of our illegal campsite, a sensation of deep reverence and friendship swept over me, and though I didn't invite the bike into my tent for the night, I did swear to buy it some chain lubricant the next day with my remaining five bucks.

A unique blend of madness and tranquility consumed the next seven days. I ate warm deer roadkill with a man outside of Kerhonkson, New York, slept in a creepy, rat-infested barn near Calicoon, New York, was targeted for bottle-throwing practice by young drivers in New Hampshire, pedaled through deserted Hasidic Jewish communities in New York State, was refused hose water by a man watering his lawn in southern Vermont, found a five-dollar bill in a ditch near Mechanicville, New York, met a clan of rock-climbing hippies near New Paltz, New York, who helped me fix a flat tire, ran over and crushed a small turtle just as I crossed the Pennsylvania border, was given free bananas and Gatorade by a 7-Eleven clerk in New Hampshire, and had to flee from a campground ranger in Vermont when he discovered my site on an early-morning patrol.

I began to feel uniquely integrated into the fabric of humanity and earth. I was a biker, a pedaling nomad, wandering my way through the lives of roadkill-eating men, rebellious teens, benevolent clerks, friendly hippies, and innocent, struggling turtles. The characters along my path all seemed wonderful; they were now a part of my story, my bizarre journey across the Delaware, and for this, they all seemed beautiful. But what helped me transcend my hitherto functional relationship with my bike was not the characters or the stories, but those moments of simply being on the road, those elusive slices of rhythmic serenity when the thick pink honey of morning sun would blanket the roads and crisp mountain air would breeze through young groves of rattling birch. When there were no sounds of engines or commerce but only of my own breathing, my own lubricated chain winding its way around the endlessly revolving crank. Heat waves emanating from a long stretch of New Hampshire tar became a glorious thing. The pain I could ignore; the glorious sensations of being on the road I could not.

At six in the evening, eight days after leaving my house in Maine, I pedaled up the steep dirt road to the unreal realm of summer camp. Motorboats tore across a tiny lake with tubes in tow, a loudspeaker blared baseball scores, little girls emerged from the arts and crafts building with Popsicle stick Christmas ornaments, counselors flirted by the dock, and people on golf carts frantically raced around trying to organize the chaotic succession of events. After my calm afternoon meandering through the Pocono Mountains on bike, this almost seemed like an unnatural, unhealthy concentration of humanity, a consolidation of engines, radios, chatter, and screams. But despite my reluctance to enter this microcosm of summer sensation, I was now broke, hungry, smelly, and fatigued, so I leaned my bike on the smooth trunk of an eastern hemlock and went forward into the madness of children, golf carts, and fiberglass tepees to find the Scotsman.

Only when I stopped at the door of the camp lodge to look back at my bicycle, to make sure it was safe and content under the dense hemlock canopy, to make sure I had leaned it so that no pine pitch would drop on its seat and no twigs poked through the spokes, did I consider that I was now treating my bicycle as I would treat a lover. And how could I not adore my bicycle when all those miles of open road lay before us, when a whole country of vast peoples and sights and paths waited to be explored, when energy and youth still charged through my legs, when it was all just as simple as pushing down on the pedals and letting yourself go.

Joshua lives in Quebec City, where he spends a great deal of time trying not to sound foolish pronouncing words like feuille *and* seuil. *Since bicycling to Pennsylvania a few years ago, he has invested in a pump and tire levers, but is working to get his hands on some patches and glue. He is presently completing a book on Franco-American history in Maine.*

Wanted: Young Bike, for Adventure, Escape, and . . . Who Knows?

Susan O'Neill

I must confess: I use the bikes in my life passionately, selfishly, tirelessly (so to speak). I am not kind. I use them up, then I abandon them for newer, sexier and—dare I say it?—younger models.

It is a strange thing, not typical of my personality. I still wear sweaters from high school. I've been married to the same man for thirty-two years.

Ah, but my bikes . . .

I have had four. Four Grand Passions.

When I was young, I took the simple gifts my bike gave me, giggling like the girl I was, tossing my braids in the headwinds. But as I aged, I found myself demanding from each bike more and more. And more: I have urged them farther, higher, wilder, while insisting they handle me with a reverence I have not earned.

And they have complied.

My current bike, I blush to admit, is more than fifty years my junior. It has carried me around the world.

It has brought me fame.

Well, not quite. But the potential for fame.

Even my husband, bless his heart, hasn't done that for me.

And yet, I have been looking at others. Bikes, that is—not husbands.

My Grand Passion for these handsome machines began simply, as Grand Passions often do:

I grew up in the flatlands of northern Indiana. During the fifties and early sixties, I sailed down dead-level roads on a secondhand Columbia, blissfully ignorant of "English bikes" with gears and quarter-inch tires. "Blue Bud" was his name; I found him beneath our Christmas tree, blue paint peeling and rust patches nibbling his fenders. An experienced bike. He initiated me into the heady delights of escape—flying over tar and gravel, faster than the horseflies, too fast to glimpse the gargantuan field spiders lurking for me in webs slung between cornstalks. So fast, my mother couldn't catch me and nag me to clean my room. Bud carried me downtown—back before Wal-Mart, when there still was a downtown—and to my friends' suburban houses. Oh, yes, he hurt me, but he didn't mean it: I still boast a scar on my right knee where Bud launched me over a cement culvert into a ditch. I looked down at this little hard gray spot on my knee and picked at it in wonder, and a stone fell out. *Cool,* I thought. Then blood dribbled from the hole, thick and important, and I burst into tears.

Bud had been far too big when I got him—I swayed back and forth over the dropped "girl's" frame, vision thwarted by the wire basket hung from his handlebars—but only I grew, ratcheting up his hard rubber seat until I was a giant on two little wheels.

I never grew past five feet three, so being a giant was even cooler than having a stone embedded in my knee.

Blue Bud served me faithfully until I sold him and went off to nursing school.

The whole idea of biking got lost, then, in a swamp of books and a forest of IV lines. And for two years after graduation, as well: I'd joined the army, looking for Adventure, an even greater escape than Bud provided. And the army set me at Adventure's very epicenter. In Vietnam.

Once, in Hue, homesick and forlorn, I watched a flock of bright young butterfly-women on bikes—long black hair gathered into conical straw hats, split skirts of red, white, pink, blue, gold *ao dais* floating behind them—zip down the avenue between shell-pocked old French mansions.

I sighed. When I needed to fly, I had helicopters.

But . . . I would have preferred a bike. I saw myself whizzing down Route One, dodging convoys, chickens or flowers tied to my fender. A lie, because I was American; for me to bike there, then, would have been suicidal.

I survived the war, married a fellow survivor, and we escaped to stable ground in southern Maine and had a baby. We bought our first "real" bikes, with gears and butt-killer seats: identical Sears models, heavy steel with brittle white frames, and mystifying tangles of wires and levers. We lugged them from the Portland showroom in big, flat boxes atop our ancient Saab wagon and assembled them ourselves. It took forever, because we had no idea what we were doing. I never did get my gears right, but I was flexible, and adapted to using eight of the ten. I attached a rear child seat. It had no shoulder harnesses—just a narrow nylon waist belt—and neither I nor my daughter wore helmets. In the early seventies, no one did.

Searo, as I named him, was gawky but practical. I put hundreds of miles on him. While Kym slept against my back, I wound down every road in Wells, Moody, Kennebunk, Kennebunkport, York, Sanford, up into the traffic of Portland. Paul drove our Saab to work, and Searo was my liberation. I rode him at low tide on Ogunquit beach, over smooth-packed sand, through slack surf like layered glass. He had no fenders, so sand spockled my legs and tracked up the back of Kym's seat and into her wispy blond hair.

God, it was good.

Searo taught me how to clean a chain. And how to change a tire, patch a tube with goo and little rubber dots from a kit I kept in my pocket. I also kept Band-Aids in that pocket, until I learned to balance the overburdened bike during quick turns and sudden stops. My small daughter would shriek, "Not *again,* Mommy!" as Searo slewed and fell between my legs, hanging her by her nylon strap over yet another curb. I mastered the maneuvers in time, with no lasting physical damage to the child, but I fear that someday she will sue me for psychological torture.

Searo moved with us to Bar Harbor. And then to Hampden, near Bangor. I had been taking the odd college class as I worked and birthed and raised our kids; now all three were in school and I became a full-time student at the University of Maine in Orono, half an hour away by car.

I had been growing disenchanted with Searo. I saw him as a work-horse, big and plodding and not at all sexy. So, after I'd hinted and begged, Paul bought me a new bike. A Univega, sleek and gold and possessed of twelve speeds, skinny-tired and feather-light. A surprise gift; we had not met before, but by some miracle we fit together per-fectly as if made for each other. I fell in love. Vega carried me with no effort. He was quick and dependable. During clement weather, he schlepped me to school—a two-hour ride—my books bungee-corded to his back carrier. I drove him over gravel tracks in the woods, skew-ing his wheels. We made romantic escapes to Bar Harbor, starting at dawn and returning at sunset.

He followed me to eastern Massachusetts after I graduated.

He followed me to Washington, DC, when my youngest child hauled me off to play Stage Mother while he, at age eleven, acted in *Captains Courageous: The Musical* at Ford's Theatre. The play flopped, but Vega and I wandered every bike path within an eighty-mile radius of the city. It was Bike Heaven: strips of smooth blacktop, two-wheeled commuters calling "On your left," and gentle weather from late August to November, when the play closed down.

Nothing lasts forever; as we grew older, we grew apart. My Vega did not creak or complain when I hit fifty, but I—I creaked and complained like an arthritic auntie. He could do nothing right, I griped: his dropped handlebars numbed my hands; his wedge seat offended my tailbone. His low frame cricked my neck. I tried to settle our differences peacefully: I bought fatter gloves and shorts with extra chamois, talked him into a gel seat, and ate Advil like M&M's. But the thrill was gone. The postcard back roads called—farms, tiny New England towns, the Atlantic. And when I answered, my body chortled, *Sucker!*

It was in the fall of 1998 when I finally broke up with my little gold Univega. Paul and I had signed up for three weeks with a biking company called Discover Vietnam; after thirty years, we were returning to the land of bombs and butterfly bikers.

For the first time in my life, I did the equivalent of joining a dating service: I walked into a store and got measured for a bike. The young clerk—the *very* young clerk—matched me up with that dreaded Symbol of Aging: a hybrid. Fatter tires, upright handlebars. Lots of gears. I added bar-ends for my aching hands and a sweet Terry seat with a hole and the extra padding needed to accommodate my own generous seat design. My Trek 7500, Little Green, went to Vietnam with me. I dragged him from the box in Hanoi and reassembled him in minutes. Every gear worked.

Then we pedaled out into rush-hour traffic with our fellow bikes and bikers. It was madness, sheer brain overload. The medieval city was crammed with bikers. Hardcore, *working* bikers. Bikers on no-speed Chinese bikes, rock-sturdy cousins of Blue Bud, hauled three-foot-high baskets of cabbage, full cords of kindling and heaps and coils of industrial odds and ends. Bikers pushed and pulled five-foot-wide carts of produce. Bikers balanced birdcages and great piles of bottle-shaped bamboo tubes for catching catfish. And, of course, bikers toted chickens. Live chickens, and massive bundles of flowers.

Little Green and I bonded instantly in the chaos. We launched ourselves over concrete and red clay, on a quest for rediscovery: We limped up and raced down mountain passes, toiled through monsoon downpours and hundred-degree heat, dodged bike-eating potholes and

Russian dump trucks spewing black fumes, and narrowly evaded a small bull charging across the road in a market hamlet. We muscled through headwinds on headlands. We gloried in tailwinds on a sad stretch of chicken-pecked blacktop in ancient Cham tribal country, flying, flying, *flying*—until we crashed and I broke my elbow. It wasn't Little Green's fault; a Honda motor scooter turned in front of us, and wham!—we all flew, scooter, bike, me and the Honda's three riders. We struggled to our feet, all of us, and after much handshaking and hearty apologies none of us understood, I rode off, bleeding from knee and shoulder, my elbow a balloon. But the bike was just fine, a macho wonder: I reattached his chain and untwisted his handlebars and he was ready for action.

I returned from Vietnam and sent a story from my trip journal to *Boston Magazine.* They printed it. An agent read it. A few months later, he sold a collection of my short stories to Ballantine Books.

Little Green never brags about his role in my potential rise to fame. He loiters in my garage, as I tap at the computer in my messy little home office, spinning lies. Perhaps someday, if all goes right, you might find these new lies in your local bookstore, next to the old ones.

But this is no lie: When I am mired, when my plot lines won't untangle, when characters refuse to cooperate, I lumber out to the garage and pull out my bike. And as we fly over the blacktop, between fields of pumpkin vines and Christmas trees, everything gels. My bike, my go-to man. He is my mentor, my shrink, my incomparable friend.

But . . . I've met this spiffy little red Cannondale in Cambridge . . .

Susan O'Neill lives in eastern Massachusetts, and has biked all over the world, including Europe, Morocco, and a return to Vietnam, where she served as an Army nurse 1969-70.

The Mountain Bike Club We Started

Adam Hausman

I love our postride grub sessions the most. We attack the refrigerator and cupboards with a ferocious, desperate hunger. We eat with hands still dusty and bloody from the trail, as hygiene will do nothing to quench our ravenous appetites. We take great pleasure in creating scarfable rations from the mostly mismatched, donated ingredients available to us. Stale bagels topped with cheese and hot sauce is not only edible, but becomes our most satisfying meal of the week.

Afterward, we sit around with our hands resting on our swollen stomachs, moving little. We smirk at and feel superior to the others who've wasted away the afternoon playing video games. We condescendingly ask who got high score, as we exchange knowing glances among ourselves. It's not as good as beers and a hot tub, but hey, I work with teenagers.

We owe our beginning to a local bike shop that donated fifteen decent mountain bikes to the Boys & Girls Club where I work. I get to wear a lot of hats at my job, including homework tutor, therapist, game-show host, surrogate parent, and concert promoter. But nothing has had a more positive impact on my kids than the mountain bike club we started.

On a sweltering day in July, I took an inventory of my crew as we loaded the trailer for our first ride.

10 wary teenagers. Most of them didn't know exactly what they were getting into, only that they had been promised Slurpees at the end.

09 of them overweight. You've heard the statistics about today's youth. They're true.

08 bad attitudes. The Bailey brothers are up for anything, the rest loathed the very mention of the word *fitness*.

07 kids with felonies on their rap sheets. A ride in a van with other teenagers normally means work crew for them.

06 wallet chains. Long ones. Long enough to get caught in bike chains.

05 black T-shirts. "Marilyn Manson isn't wicking wear," I whined.

04 energy bars. Although it seems Twinkies will be tough to pack in.

03 helmets. Seven cracked heads will definitely get me fired.

02 pairs of combat boots. It would turn out to be a war of sorts.

01 pair of sunglasses. My own.

00 water bottles. I even forgot mine. They said, "Don't worry, we've got sodas." I started in on a lengthy lecture about dehydration before hearing my own voice trail off, as I realized I had much bigger concerns to deal with.

We set off anyway on the easiest ride I could think of. They complained about the heat, the rocks, the trail, me, their bikes, each other, the outdoors, me, the fact that they weren't currently playing X-Box, their thirst, their hunger, the hills, and me.

No one got seriously hurt, and for that I was thankful. On the ride home they sipped Slurpees and plotted to kill me, while I made a mental note to try to negotiate a group rate with the bowling alley to fill what I assumed would be my now empty Wednesday-afternoon program time slot.

Over the course of the next week I was shocked to receive inquiries about where this week's ride was going to be. Sometimes I feel I don't know teens any better now than before I started this job. I arranged for a shuttle so we could ride the largely downhill "Frizzle-Frazzle trail," which included a steep, windy BMX-like section complete with banked turns and tabletop jumps. They said it was "sick."

Next, I took them on the prettiest ride I know of. I led them past waterfalls, old growth Douglas firs, moonscape lava fields, and rushing whitewater that spilled into perfect blue pools. They good-naturedly complained about having to dismount their bikes to stop and "appreciate nature." But by scanning the peaceful looks on their faces in the rearview mirror of the van on the way home, I knew that I had reached them. They'd been touched by beauty.

I notice a remarkable improvement in their fitness levels from one week to the next. I see more confident, happy teenagers attacking hills they once cursed, and I attribute this boosted self-esteem to better health and newly toned bodies. They just know they feel better.

They confide in me that their problems seem to melt away for the duration of the ride and for some time after. I think their intense focus on the trail is allowing their minds to empty and shed worries. No one has ever used the word *positive* and *addiction* in the same sentence while speaking to them before. They don't realize it's their endorphins popping, but some of them are experiencing natural highs for the first time. They are learning to realize exercise as self-medication years before I ever did.

I'm jealous of the pure relationship they have with this sport. They're not interested in dial-type fluid-expansion compensators, magnesium lowers, or adjustable rebound. However, a few of the guys have expressed curiosity about alloy nipples. I still can't get them to wear Lycra, but they mostly remember to wear shorts and sneakers.

I introduced the kids to both "bonking" and environmental activism on one memorable ride, dubbed lovingly, in hindsight, the "death ride." We got detoured by a logging operation on one of our favorite rides, and my often lacking navigational skills failed us. We got lost, ran out of water, rode fifteen miles farther than intended, and barely made it out of the woods alive. There were some tears, but it made us even closer as a group. They were outraged about the destruction of their beautiful trail, and now we can all rant in harmony about the evils of development and urban sprawl.

The first couple of rides, many of the teenagers came along only in the quest for "catching air." After all, this is the X-Games Generation. Blame the media. But slowly over time, I've seen their riding begin to focus more on drawing that perfect line with their bikes, rather than on pulling tail whips or can-cans. When I wonder aloud about this shift in priorities, they can't explain why. They say, "I don't know, it's just fun to ride." I guess what they mean to say is that they're learning to not oversteer and overbrake. I'm noticing that they're coming out of corners with more momentum than they had going in. Charging up hills and smoothly riding technical descents is where it's at for them now. A couple of the standouts I can't seem to shake off my wheel anymore. I love it. They've become real mountain bikers.

Adam Hausman, thirty-two, lives and plays in Bend, Oregon. Besides mountain biking, he enjoys board sports, exploring Oregon, and working with teenagers.

Loving My Rockhopper

Jamie Kaminski

Of all my past relationships, the ones that still own a piece of my soul are the ones that most would consider to be in the love-hate category. There must be something masochistic about enjoying the journey of constant turmoil. I can sum it up to believe that the excitement arose from the relationship's constant ability to cause pain, the uncertainty of the connection, and the tremendous high when things were clicking. And, of all the activities in life, the ones that I am most passionate for are the ones that bring about the same sort of struggle with the incredible highs, as in some of my past encounters.

My passion began while running up Heavenly ski resort's beginner run, roundabout, in the summer months when the mountain was occupied only by a few hikers with sturdy dogs and mountain bikers. I ran past the guys who were biking up the hill, sweat pouring from their helmets, muscles bulging from their quads, with CamelBaks attached to their shoulders. Their bikes slowly swayed back and forth as they journeyed upward. Although I felt somewhat superior as I ran past the men in spandex shorts, it was then that I became intrigued. I wondered what the hill would feel like on bike, rather than foot.

After fifteen years of being an addicted distance runner, one who could not take a day off without guilt and anxiety, eventually my body began to rebel. Little aches and pains started to become chronic. It was then that I gave in to what coaches and friends have told me to do for years, to cross-train. Biking seemed to be what most of my running buddies had switched to, and a sport that could offer a freedom similar to running. I bought my first mountain bike, my specialized Rockhopper. Little did I know how much love and hate I would develop for the new sport and for my new bike.

My biking buddy, Bob, took me on my first mountain bike ride. We tested out my curiosity on Heavenly's roundabout climb. On the first climb through a somewhat sandy section, I felt as if I'd never been in shape. Maybe this was somewhat of a humbling experience? I was positive my heart rate was over the maximum, by the fact that I could no longer talk, which was much out of character for me. Not used to this type of anaerobic exertion, it was all I could do just to hang on. Even my biceps grew pumped and weary as I strained to grip the extensions on the end of my handlebars. I couldn't relax for a moment. I needed as much power as I could pull to pedal fast enough to gain momentum going through the sand, still on the steepest part of the climb. Bob reminded me to sit back on my bike, and to shift down a gear. As I gasped for air, while continuing to pedal up the hill, I was not sure if I was enjoying this type of discomfort. Something within allowed me to continue, despite my apprehension.

As the workload declined, along with the steepness of the grade, I began to appreciate the ambience of the ride. Soon I felt a oneness with my bike and the hill that words cannot clearly describe. Now able to relax, and my heart rate steadied, the scenery once again became vivid. I was able to take a moment to enjoy the breathtaking beauty of the blueness from the lake in the far distance. Able to talk once again, I filled Bob in on the many details of the drama of my life. I was not in my comfort zone for long before the feelings began to change.

The next switchback we came to was covered with gravel. My legs burned and beads of sweat dripped to my eyes underneath the colored shades, as I worked to pedal up the hill. Parts of the gravel were layered with sand. Instead of going around the messy clumps, I went right through the thickest part of the terrain. Although I was no longer having fun, I was determined to make it up the hill without pushing my bike. It was at that point when my muscles rebelled. They failed to supply enough power to continue. I ran out of steam and the bike fell over. I quickly picked up my bike as I voiced a few four-letter words. I tried to get back on, not wanting to admit defeat. Again, the bike went nowhere. The climb was too steep and my quad power too weak to get back on. As I pushed my bike up to a better takeoff section, I remembered the beefy mountain bikers I'd cruised by while running. Soon, I was pissed! It was then that I started a new love-hate relationship.

Unlike any of my past relationships, this one brought the reward of accomplishment when I reached the top of the hill. While the downhill section started the obvious reward and gave meaning to the term *a ride,* the sweetness came from the journey upward. Each sandy struggle and moment of discomfort left me challenging my own worst enemy, my mind's powerful ability to defeat my purpose. I believe that as we pull from an energy source, created in our own subconscious mind and are able to continue, even when utterly exhausted, we've won a personal battle. While there may not be a finish line, or crowds cheering our win, the simple pleasure comes from mastery of the mind over matter. The words of encouragement, "You're almost there. You can make it to the top," win over the devil's advocate stating, "Just turn around now. You don't have to go all the way up to the top today. You have nothing to prove."

Once I reached the top of the mountain I knew a victory had been won. Once I felt the breeze at top elevation and the chill from my own sweat evaporating, I put my windbreaker on, which signaled that a new sensation would follow. This incredible sensation was one that reminded me of being a child again, on an amusement ride, as I let gravity take my bike and me down the hill. This sensation allowed me to see a beautiful picture of the lake in the far distance, and the trees as I brushed by. It allowed me to feel at peace when finally, all clicked smoothly and effortlessly.

Soon the roundabout climb became a twice-a-week workout for Bob and myself. I enjoyed meeting him in the early afternoons, as we got ready to share stories with our sweat, and sometimes pain. By the second ride I was able to make it up the entire hill without getting off my bike. While parts of the ride left me gasping for air, spitting in an unladylike fashion, and complaining of the turmoil to get to the top, the feeling of thrill set in on the way down, as I watched for every rock that might throw me and each sandy section that would cause me to skid. I tried to go a little bit faster each time, enjoying the fact that once the speed was up, my security was less. The knowing, as I've known in some of my past relationships, that my comfort and feeling of serenity could be taken at any moment, created a special feeling of momentary peace—unlike any other. When I reached the paved section, closer to the end, I cruised at a faster, smoother speed. A chill that my rockhopper and I created left me feeling anxious for the finish. Yet once I pulled into the parking lot, reaching my car for the unloading, my mind jumped in anticipation. Now relaxed and warm, I craved the next ride.

Jamie Kaminski is thirty-four and lives in Stateline, Nevada. She teaches 7th-9th grade physical education in Gardnerville, Nevada, and coaches 7th- and 8th-grade cross country. She has been a distance runner since the age of thirteen, and now bikes as well—mountain and road. She also enjoys both downhill and cross-country skiing, camping, writing, and trail running.

Heaven is a Wide Berm and a Tailwind

Jan Allen

I called it a midlife crisis. Or maybe I was just in a rut. For whatever reason, ten years ago I decided it would be a great idea to quit my job and take off across the country in an RV. For three months I would explore the United States, have all sorts of adventures, and accrue memories to last a lifetime. I thought it was such a grand idea that certainly all my friends would want to join me and I would have a difficult decision picking the exact right person to accompany me on my journey.

Nobody wanted to go.

Then a friend told me about a group traveling from Virginia to Oregon. The time frame was right, the adventures could be endless— only the three months was by bicycle.

Well, I thought, how bad could it be—only fifty miles average a day? I did that on I-75 in less than an hour in my car. I would have to carry everything I needed on these things called panniers attached to the bike, but what the heck would I need anyway? Not dresses, not high heels, certainly not makeup. No big deal. I would suffer through the five hours or so of biking a day, then have plenty of time left to explore my country, make new friends.

It didn't turn out quite the way I expected.

The training I'd done was mostly inside a gym. Before setting out I stupidly pictured myself riding every day on a flat section of I-75, not climbing the Appalachian Mountains or the Ozarks or the Rockies. My five-hour-a-day ride turned into ten hours easily.

Also in my optimist's dreams I pictured perfect sunny weather. This was not to be the case. It rained constantly—hard—every day for the first three weeks. I always felt soaked to the bone because my clothes and towel and shoes never had time to dry out. It was the end of May in Virginia but unbelievably it was also freezing. Later in the intense heat of July and August I would have a hard time remembering the cold jacket-wearing weather.

I discovered too that when riding a bicycle there is something worse than heat or cold or drenching rain. Wind. As I pedaled it pushed against me like a trash compactor or a defensive football player in a play that never ended. It was even the strongest bicyclists' worst enemy, cutting their distance traveled sometimes to three miles an hour.

Because I suppose of the physical hardships our leader told us the first day that three or four of us probably wouldn't make it for the entire three months, maybe not even the first three weeks. When he said that I felt everyone in the room was thinking of me, as I was the only woman in our group of nine. It was grueling. Every night my body felt way beyond exhausted.

Yet in the midst of it all I realized I was falling in love. (I did meet my husband on that trip, but that's another story.) I was in love with this miraculous metal thing that was carrying me slowly but surely across the entire United States. When I pumped hard to reach the crest of a hill, the view at the top was so incredibly beautiful—my better-than-a-million-dollars reward for a hard workout. As I cycled alongside mountain streams for miles and miles, I felt I became a part of them somehow, experiencing their individual feel, smell, taste, and unique personality that is only possible on a bicycle.

The weather could make me miserable and discouraged, but I felt as if my bike and I were a team, and together our spirit could not be broken. I felt as if I'd mastered the elements and discovered a part of my inner being I never knew existed; I was strong, a conqueror of sorts.

I also discovered that on a bike the weather can become your conspirator in the making of a carefree happy day. Miracle of miracles, just as there is this dreadful thing called a headwind, there is also its heavenly counterpart called a tailwind—or as I can still hear my friend from Holland saying some mornings back in 1992, "Janet, the wind is our friend today." My bike would seem to come alive beneath me (or at least it felt like it had a motor) and the miles would click away so quickly on my speedometer it felt like I really was back in my car on I-75.

I did indeed accrue memories to last a lifetime that summer. Our country's diverse majestic views were intoxicating on a bicycle. There were many beautiful sights I knew I'd never forget, but the really special memories are the ones that are lost in some deep cavern of my brain, brought to the surface years later by another bike ride on another day. Also, many times I would have to wipe tears away as I laughed at the hilarious stories of the other riders' adventures. I realized later that when I am utterly and thoroughly exhausted from a long day's bike ride almost everything is hysterically funny, even tales of being nudged off the berm by aggressive truck drivers.

I returned to Cincinnati after three months with an enlightened attitude and physically stronger than I'd ever been. And I kept riding my bike. For a few years I never even let winter stop me. I biked to the store, I biked to work, I biked to friends' houses.

Now I tend to put my bike away for the winter. When spring returns biking becomes a brand-new joy again. I feel my muscles strengthen and my endurance improve. It's a good feeling as spring ripens into summer and I become strong enough to dart quickly off when the traffic light turns green and drivers in cars no longer rudely honk. By October or November I'm ready to give my buddy a rest and the cleanup—thanks to my husband—it deserves.

Ten years later I look back on my midlife crisis as a "youngish" person's indulgence. Now whenever I'm on my bike I feel like I'm thirty-six again. Worries fade and age is of no importance. I look at the trees and flowers as I pass slowly by, and the world is a beautiful place. It doesn't even matter if the rain moves in because when I'm on my bicycle I can weather any storm.

Jan Allen is forty-seven and lives in Cincinnati, Ohio, with her husband and her mother. She works as a medical transcriptionist. This is her first published story.

Haleakalā High

Shirley Moskow

At 4:15 A.M., when the sky above Hawaii is black velvet, hundreds of people are gathering atop the summit of Haleakalā, the world's largest dormant volcano. About a million people a year get up in the middle of the night to wait here for Maui's famed sunrise. World traveler Mark Twain described it as "the sublimest spectacle" he'd ever witnessed.

Most people drive up, view the sunrise, and drive back down. About eighty thousand a year, however, descend the 10,023-foot mountain by bicycle. I'm a novice biker, but I've joined a bicycle safari for the five-hour downhill trek. I'm seduced by the idea of not pedaling. Gravity does most of the work.

The safari brochure said I'd be fitted with a bicycle. Actually, it turns out that the bikes are all the same size and, much to my dismay, they're all men's bikes. Only the seats are adjustable. I'm barely five feet three. Because of the bar, my feet don't touch the ground when I brake. The first time I practice riding around the parking lot, I skin my ankle when I try to stop.

Now I'm standing among hordes of people milling around in the dark. Although the safari company has outfitted me with a neon yellow wind-breaker suit—pants and jacket as well as ski gloves and safety helmet—I shiver in the thirty-two-degree cold. Some onlookers are wearing only resort clothes or cotton sweaters. Some hug their children for warmth; others huddle under blankets.

A thin, almost imperceptible rose-colored slit appears in night's

77

black curtain. "Look," says someone behind me. "It's beginning." There's total silence; everyone stares at the sky. Like a blush, color deepens and seeps over the far rim of Haleakalā's crater, which measures nineteen miles around and three thousand feet deep, a spectacle in itself. A blanket of hot pink unfolds over the sides of the crater. Golden light crowns the summit with a scalloped halo. Clouds—large billowing waves like sculpted Styrofoam—fill the crevasse. A metallic orange arc glistens along the horizon. It heralds the arrival of the sun, a blinding ball of fire. The landscape is luminous.

Haleakalā—"House of the Sun" in Hawaiian—is appropriately named. And Mark Twain was right. This sunrise is worth getting up for in the middle of the night, even braving the cold. Haleakalā is known for extreme temperatures, summer every day, winter every night. The ride up the volcano is comparable to traveling from Mexico's subtropical beaches to Alaska's forests in less than two hours, then arriving on the moon. In fact, American astronauts trained here for the lunar landing.

Dawn is the cue for our guides to gather our group of ten for the thirty-nine-mile descent. Josh goes over the drill. He demonstrates hand signals for "stop" and "slow down." He shows us how to crouch and lean into the mountain on hairpin curves. We are to ride single file, leaving about twenty-five feet between riders to prevent a pileup in case of an accident. He leads. Ed follows in a van with our personal belongs and monitors traffic, alerting Josh via two-way radio.

If we run into trouble, Josh tells us to pull off the road. Ed will pick us up in the van or fix our bike. Josh tells of a biker who fell. He waited by the side of the road and waved when the van approached. Unfortunately, that driver was new. He waved back and continued on his way. Ed, we are assured, is experienced.

We line up according to weight, with the heaviest men at the rear, At first I feel comforted that I'm just behind Josh. But we're above the clouds, and much of the steep, lava rock road in front of me lacks guardrails. Suddenly, I'm terrified. What if I can't control my bicycle? I move as slowly as I dare. Forget the twenty-five feet I'm supposed to maintain between the next rider and myself. I'm about sixty feet behind. We've been warned not to look back so I have no idea how close the other riders are.

My bike glides downhill effortlessly. In spite of myself, I'm picking up speed. Even with the helmet limiting my peripheral vision, I see through the veil of clouds that Kipahula Valley is a long way down. When I'm about to negotiate the first of thirty-nine switchback turns, I lose sight of Josh. My heart is pumping. I swallow a deep gulp of thin air. I'm light-headed as I crouch, lean into the mountain, and gradually apply the hand brake.

I am euphoric to find Josh waiting in a rest area around the bend. When our group reassembles, he repeats, "Remember, keep your eyes on the road. Don't admire the view."

"What view?" squeaks a woman behind me. In the parking lot, she'd confided her fear of heights. Her husband, a Vietnam veteran, has urged her to accompany him. Later, she confesses that she never took her eyes off the road and prayed aloud the whole way down. "When I reached bottom safely, I was so grateful that my prayers had been answered, I said, 'Thank you, Lord.'"

Josh knows the mountain, every turn and twist. He makes the ride look easy. On straightaways and wide turns, he sits sidesaddle, cross-legged like a yogi, and watches us.

As I acquire more confidence, I focus on the experience. Muscles in my back and arms are taut. My senses are acutely alive. I hear the quick sucking sound of my tires on the road like peeling suction cups. I smell pine and hear birdsong. I am aware, too, that we are passing through different ecosystems, four in all.

Little rain falls at the top, the alpine/aeolian zone, so I see only a few hardy grasses and shrubs. The notable exception is the āhinahina or silversword plant, an endangered species. When Josh points to one, it appears smaller than a sword, more like a fan of kitchen knives. The long-lived plant produces a single six-foot purple bloom, then dies. There are more bushes and a greater variety of plants in the subalpine shrubland, food for the rare nene Hawaiian goose and state bird. Some travelers have seen it here. Not me.

On switchbacks, a ghostly gust of cold wind brushes my cheek. It signals our passage from the leeward to the windward side of the mountain. The windward slopes of the Kipahula Valley host one of the most intact rain forest ecosystems in Hawaii. I ride through a tunnel of elegant koa trees, a favorite wood of local furniture makers. By comparison, the leeward slopes are dry with only patches of trees.

About two-thirds of the way down the volcano, we stop at a restaurant for a prearranged breakfast. Many bike safaris stop here. The parking lot is packed with pickup trucks, vans, and bikers waiting for tables. When a biker steps from between two vans, I swerve to avoid hitting him and grab hard on my hand brakes. It's the wrong thing to do. I'm skidding and lose control. I land on the ground, my bike on top. Fortunately, only my pride is bruised. And I'm perversely comforted when another woman, also uneasy with the bar on a man's bike, topples, too.

Before breakfast, I peel off my yellow windbreaker suit and gloves. The sun is warm. A sweater suffices. When we continue, the road is not as steep. Turns are gentler. The way wends through open grazing land, where signs warn to watch out for meandering cattle. I ride past meadows where cows and horses graze, farms and nurseries selling tropical plants. By noontime, I'm biking in light traffic, under a fragrant canopy of eucalyptus. At a T-intersection, atop a small hill, there's a stop sign. I'm gaining momentum and decide to ride through. The sight of an oncoming car quickly changes my mind. Falling is safer.

I pick myself up, brush off my jeans, and walk the bike across the road. For the first time, the land is flat. I pedal along a road lined with pineapple plantations and fields of sugarcane gone to seed. Soon we arrive at Makawao, the biggest little town in upcountry, as this slope is called. Makawao resembles an old western movie set. Rustic one- and two-story clapboard buildings line the main thoroughfare. Some have open balconies on the second floor. Sidewalks are rough boards. Hitching posts stand by the curb for paniolo, as Hawaiian cowboys are called, who ride horses into town. Makawao's Fourth of July rodeo is the island's biggest event. The town is so picturesque I want to linger. Right now, however, I'm concentrating on keeping up with my companions and steering clear of pickup trucks angle-parked in front of cafés and art galleries.

The bike ride ends by the beach in Pa'ia, an old plantation town. While Josh and Ed load bikes onto the van, I climb the dunes to Ho'okipa Beach Park, which bills itself as the "wind surfing capital of the world." Watching the precariously balanced surfers as they test themselves and fall, I feel an instant kinship with them. I know the delirious exhilaration of being present in the moment. And, I recall a line in an essay by George Santayana, who wrote about those of us who need "to escape into open solitudes . . . into the moral holiday of running some pure hazard, in order to sharpen the edge of life." A bicycle makes a fine escape.

Shirley Moskow, a former newspaper editor, is a freelance writer with a special interest in culture and food. In addition to two books, she has written articles for metropolitan newspapers in the United States and abroad.

Break Up

Stephen Johnson

The affair with the magenta bicycle began in Chicago. I bought it for thirty-five dollars from an old man who ran a sports equipment store on the north side. He had a Polish name and his wife sat behind the counter fingering yellow receipts. I'd moved to Chicago to become an actor and writer. I didn't have a lot of money at the time I bought the bike, and in the five years I lived in the city, I never did.

The magenta bike was an old Schwinn Suburban, a cruiser with a huge frame and twenty-seven-inch wheels—perfect for my height. It had ten speeds but upright handlebars so you could sit comfortably. It was not built for speed. The shifters were cracked, the brake lines nearly cut through, flecks of red paint were chipping off the body, the name on the frame was barely legible, and the gears were rusted. The chances of the bike being stolen were slim. This would be a fine bike.

I discovered that Schwinn was a Chicago-based company from the nineteenth century, the Suburban a relic from the sixties and seventies, a collector's item if in good condition. I imagined the Suburban was designed for teenagers living just outside of the dangerous city. They could cruise through their green neighborhoods, going to each other's houses to play basketball until dusk, their bikes lying carelessly on newly paved driveways. Maybe mine was the last Suburban in Chicago.

I quickly reinvented my bike. With limited repair skills, I cleaned it, oiled the gears, stripped the rust, had the brakes fixed and new rims put on. I stripped the gears down from ten. It was now a one-geared freak, a fleet urban machine. The bike was heavy, and I carried it up many flights of stairs over the years, but I never complained because the bike had *heft*.

In gray, wintry Chicago, with an untrustworthy transportation system, the Suburban took me everywhere in every weather condition. I relied on it to get me to various jobs. I strapped a milk crate behind the seat so I could move groceries. I furnished my small apartment with old architectural pieces and furniture from salvage yards, and the bike carried it all. One day, you might have seen me riding two miles home balancing a six-foot-high bookcase. How else would I have gotten it home? The bike and I were young then and could do foolish things like that.

The Suburban did not attract classically beautiful women, athletic "bikers," or women who used bicycles for exercise. With its crate, taped-on lock holder, and upright handlebars, the bike tended to attract women with Betty Page haircuts who bought thrift-store clothes and listened to old country albums. Which was just the kind of girl I was trying to attract.

I got a job at an upscale restaurant and started dating a woman who had dyed red hair with short bangs. She liked Hank Williams and wine in juice glasses. She said she liked my magenta bike.

One bright summer Saturday afternoon, she and I dressed in our finest vintage clothes and rode over to a friend's place for his house-warming party. We'd bought the happy couple a sixty-cent wine rack and it dangled in my right hand as I weaved down Chicago's back alleys, the old immigrant routes. Riding behind me in the sun, she laughed and said it felt like we were in Italy. That was one more reason to fall in love with her that afternoon.

Time moved on and the woman with the bangs was gone, but the magenta bike was still with me. I was now working at a bistro and I rode to work in the freezing wind and snow because I couldn't afford car insurance. Drivers gawked as I pedaled along in three layers of clothing and a menacing ski mask. I took only bitter pleasure in staring at them from behind the mask and blowing billows of steam. They would stop glaring. After one last day of this billowing and grayness, I decided to move to New York to get something more out of my life.

I packed only a few essentials for the move. I put my antiques and old records in a friend's barn outside of Chicago, and I wanted to leave the magenta bike behind. Why would I need it in busy, dangerous New York? My friend crammed it into the tiny moving van at the last minute. I was glad he did.

I discovered that the streets of Manhattan were pure adrenaline, and the Suburban, with its hugeness and gangliness, seemed to fit right in with the other cobbled-together city bikes—of the messengers with their custom frames, and of the Mexican pizza delivery guys with their oversized, front-metal crates.

I rode all over the city, in and out of its precarious lanes. Buses, cabs, cars (and to a lesser degree pedestrians) became enemies. Your job was to keep moving and to survive. A fellow city bicyclist warned me that thirty-four riders a year die in New York City, but moving to the city had made me less afraid and more aggressive. The Suburban was big and I knew we could make it.

We just had to ride faster.

As you race down Fifth Avenue at rush hour for the hell of it, the city constantly smells of exhaust and gasoline and you feel the blue poison in your nose as you race downtown and you will not stop . . . you flit past a city bus and curl inside a stream of cars . . . there's the Public Library on the right, gorgeous . . . watch the cab on the left . . . fine he wants to cut me off, screw him . . . now you're squeezed to the curb now you're up on the curb and the lines of suckers waiting for the bus look pissed, as they always do . . . okay five more feet on the sidewalk and I don't want to do this people, I have to, and you do a quick take then hop the curb right back into traffic into the flow . . . another cab on the left now slow down, okay look at this asshole twitch and you know he's going to make a quick right without signaling so you slow down and yes! he cuts you off . . . ever so slowly now between the tour bus and city bus, slooooowly, okay just enough room to slice through, my god the exhaust . . . if the tour bus had moved forward you'd be crushed . . . don't think about that . . . weave between the miles of jay-walkers at Herald Square, yes, no, I'm not going to hit you . . . just make the light because if you make it . . . grip the foam handlebars on this magenta Cadillac that was never meant for this and pull god-damnit, and you urge your bike, you can do it baby, roll, get up on top of it and pull! . . . there's the light . . . you've got it, the green light at 34th, the promised land beyond, move it move it move it move move move move, there's the Empire State Building ahead (you beauty you) and there's nothing but four lanes of pavement to yourself if you can make this yellow light and cabs are stopping, and just a little more, time it, time it, and now . . . move move move move move move and . . . *yes* . . . you sit up on your saddle and you put your hands on your hips and feel the wind and exhaust and you veer to the middle of the empty four lanes and cruise along and watch the afternoon sun wash the buildings in golden light and for the next full city block—New York is yours.

Of course, an accident was bound to happen.

One afternoon, I was flying up Broadway near 96th, moving between roaring traffic on the left and parked cars on the right. I was trying to take the entire world into my vision, the only way to survive, but something didn't fit. Something flashed, a door opened out toward traffic ten feet in front of me. The options lasted a second. If I swerved around the door, I would move into traffic, get crunched, hit the pavement like a rag doll, and be trampled. Or I could keep my course, brace, and ram the driver and his door. Which I did. We were both fine after the impact, and he yelled and I yelled. Open your eyes, we said.

Something felt wrong in the frame and rear wheel of the Suburban after the accident. I was worried. Getting doored had done something to the bicycle that neither I nor the bike shop could figure out. The Suburban and I had been together for seven years. Now there was a squeal in the rear brake, a wobble going up the hill, a constant twitch in the crank—a death rattle.

Autumn in New York arrived. I was riding through Central Park at dawn one morning. A light dew reflected the red and yellow leaves everywhere. The sun blasting above morning joggers was so intense I had to cover my eyes.

I spun my way toward the park's exit to leave the calm and join the hubbub of midtown traffic. If you miss the thin exit path at 59th Street, you must take a wrong-way, one-way street and meet a head-on fate of pitiless cabs. I missed the path by a few seconds and slammed on the brakes. This time the Suburban's usually reliable tires locked up and screamed. We skidded to a stop just short of the cab onslaught. I was stunned that the bike hadn't responded. The rear tire was nearly deflated from the sudden stop. People were looking at us—mothers with strollers, buff young men in rollerblades, homeless guys on benches. I tossed the bike angrily to the grass, stared into the sky, and wondered almost aloud: What is *wrong* with you?

Reluctantly, I decided it was time for a new love, a new bicycle.

I went to a bike shop on the Lower East Side where a hundred years ago, Jewish immigrants probably used their old bikes to bring home challah and knishes in baskets and crates to waiting wives.

I locked up the Suburban—tattered and dying—to a parking meter. The bike shop was bright and mountain bikes and touring cycles and pastel bicycle pants hung from every rack. A salesman with a nose ring came on strong but was friendly enough. I looked at a brand-new "hybrid," a combination mountain bike/touring cycle meant for the new urban cyclist who wants his biking a little bit country and a little bit city.

I gave it a spin and the brakes were so tight I almost went over the handlebars. The bike was a white piece of metal as light as a baguette. As I floated around New York's old streets, I realized that newer bicycles are weightless and they are soundless. Gears whir, they do not click. The bike was a white puff of machinery. It had no heft.

I flew around the city without gravity or air resistance. It was not an unpleasant sensation, but I felt unmoored, not riding an object at all—but a cloud.

There was not even room for a crate.

I couldn't imagine anyplace to take this bike—not to a thrift store, not to a grocery store, not to a friend's house to play basketball in a languid suburb. You would just keep riding and riding with no point or end in sight, which might be the purpose of modern bicycles.

As the new bike and I drifted around a corner, unsuccessfully continuing our seduction, a young woman checked us out from a street corner. She was short and perky.

"Nice bike," she chirped.

But she wasn't my type.

Stephen Johnson is finishing his MBA at Columbia University. His work has appeared in Columbia: A Journal of Literature and Art, Mr. Beller's Neighborhood, *and* Gadfly. *Two of his nonfiction stories will appear in anthologies in 2004. He is also writing a book about life in 1992 Berlin.*

Riding to Freedom

Jean Brown

There is nothing like the exciting pleasure of receiving a gift that you have long hoped for. After two years of begging and pleading, I thought I would never get a bicycle, but my father surprised me, as he had only a few times before. He came from work one evening and told me to come outside. I thought I was in trouble for something like forgetting a chore. I knew he was going to make the same speech he had made a thousand times before: "You never listen, you're too thickheaded, and you always make up excuses for your behavior." This was all true. He had taught me well.

I hesitantly walked outside with my head hanging down.

"How ya like this bike?" he asked, with the smell of whiskey on his breath.

"Is it for me?" I replied.

I was more excited than I could remember ever being before. I thanked him as I held the handlebars in my hands and asked if I could ride it now. He walked over to the bike and removed a sticker from the seat that read "$2." He said that he would have liked to buy me a new one, but that was the best he could do for now. I told him that the bike was great, and it was the one I wanted. He looked at me with black, sad eyes and nodded his head, then reminded me to be careful. Then he set the ground rules.

"You had better not ride that bike in the road! If I catch you in the road with it, you'll never ride it again. A nine-year-old kid has no business in the road," the six-foot-three god advised.

The twenty-six-inch chunk of rusted metal had traces of red and blue paint visible only in spots. It had no gears and only pedal brakes which needed work. The chain seemed to be too large for the sprocket, and the spokes were bent, but it was workable. The seat was too high, so I had to push the bicycle up to a bank to get on and off it. To me, it was perfect.

The neighborhood kids called it the junkmobile, but I called it freedom. It was freedom to me because I knew when my chores were completed, I could ride as much as I wanted to. It was mine, and I didn't have to ask my brother if I could ride his. Better yet, I didn't have to do his chores in order to have a few minutes of riding his bike.

I followed Father's rules for about two months, but I was bored riding in the yard and fields. It was difficult to ride on the grass and I knew that it would be easier and faster on the pavement. I had to try it.

When I reached the pavement it was as if there were no ground underneath the wheels. I wasn't laboring to pump the pedals and turn the wheels. My feet seemed to just float in a paddling motion. I was soaring like a bird. Gradually, I turned loose the handlebars and lifted my hands high in the air. As I traveled down the road, I could feel the sun warm my skin and the shady parts of the road cooled the skin, creating perfect balance. How could something so wonderful be dangerous?

I made it back home without incident and without getting caught. My older sister was in charge of the younger children. She had been busy reading the March edition of *McCall's* magazine, and didn't realize that I had been gone for half an hour. I was already planning my journey for the next evening.

I managed to keep my secret for a few weeks until my brother came home early from ball practice and caught me in the road on my bike. I begged him not to tell, but there was a condition for him to keep quiet:

I had to do his chores. This agreement only lasted until our first dis-agreement.

My father was furious with me when he found out I was riding the bike in the road. He locked the bicycle in his storage building and dared me to go near it. He threatened to give the bicycle to my brother because I wasn't responsible enough. The idea of the bike locked away from me in the spider-infested building kept me awake at night.

When I would manage to fall asleep, I dreamed of riding the bicycle down a hill in the pasture while a bull that grazed the land chased me. In the dream, I knew if I could make it to the gate, the bull would stop chasing me. When I reached the gate that entered the road from the pasture, it was like crossing the finish line of a race. I rode through the gate, and it snapped like a ribbon. As soon as the tires hit the pave-ment of the road, the neighborhood kids would be cheering me on instead of laughing at me, only I didn't stop to accept the praise. I just kept riding without looking back. Night after night, I had this dream.

In a few weeks, I found the keys to the building, of course, and was back on the road. This time, I was more careful not to get caught, but I had decided if someone saw me in the road on the bicycle, I would just keep pedaling. My bicycle would be like a one-way airline ticket. It would take me away and not return.

After two days of rain, it was a beautiful afternoon. I was on the road cruising, heading for a sharp curve, when I realized the road had just been repaired. The next thing I knew, I was starting to skid on loose gravel. Out of panic, I pushed the right pedal back too hard and too fast. I went straight over the handle bars, hit the pavement, then slid on my left side enough to bury gravel in my skin. I felt a burning sen-sation on the left side of my body, and my left arm was throbbing as cruelly as a stubbed toe. I heard the sound of a huge engine chugging up the hillside. That sound motivated me to move, so I grabbed my bike and pulled it to the side of the road, forgetting about my injury.

As the huge truck passed by, I became scared, and for the first time, I realized the danger of riding a bicycle in the road. When I looked at my left leg and arm, I could see blood oozing from the torn skin.

All the way home, I imagined how angry my parents would be when they discovered what I had done. Dad would probably blame my mother for being at work and not at home, and she would blame him for having to work and him getting me the bicycle. Sometime during this argument, it would come down to the issue of money. "How will we pay for the doctor? What if she has to be hospitalized? We can't afford to miss work to take her to the doctor!"

As this scenario played through my mind, the pain was becoming intense, but the pain of facing my parents seemed more unbearable. Finally, optimism kicked in, and I began to think that there was a chance my parents wouldn't find out about this if I could just bear the pain and pretend that nothing was wrong. Maybe, if I was lucky, I wouldn't have to see a doctor at all. I was able to walk, so I must not have a broken leg. I was able to push the bike, so my arm couldn't be broken.

When I got home, I went to the bathroom to clean myself up. There was a pathetic sight in the mirror staring back at me. I was covered in blood, wearing torn clothing and looking like some creature out of a horror movie. I barely recognized myself. I took out an old washcloth, being careful not to use one of Mom's newer ones, and began to clean up. This is when I saw and felt tiny pieces of gravel half buried in my skin. The smell of asphalt and blood made me throw up. I knew I needed help, so I went to my sister, Laura. I pleaded with her not to tell my parents and help me clean up.

"There is no way you can hide this. It looks like you need to go to the hospital. Besides, if I don't call Mom, I'll be in as much trouble as you're going to be in," Laura screamed.

"You know, they'll blame you anyway, for not watching me closer," I bargained.

"Why can't you act like a girl sometimes and play with a Barbie or something? And for once, stay out of trouble, or at least not involve me in your harebrained ideas. Your lies have got you into this, and you still haven't learned. How can you hide something like this?" she lectured.

Well, I suppose I should have learned that lies had gotten me into this mess, but I also knew that lies would have to get me out of it. It would take lies and tolerating the pain of what might have been a fractured elbow to cover this up. With Laura's help, I was able to cover up the accident. My parents never found out. To relieve the guilt I felt from lying, I convinced myself that I had done my parents a favor by not telling them about the accident. If I had told them, they would have insisted on taking me to the doctor, and that was an expense they could not afford. They would have done a lot of unnecessary worrying also. It was best that no one knew about this.

I couldn't risk losing my bike and my freedom permanently, and I knew one day I would be allowed to ride on the road. After all, I had learned a lesson. The lesson wasn't about telling the truth but about the danger of a child being in the road on a bicycle. It was later in life when I learned the importance of truth.

Jean Brown lives in Graham, North Carolina, with her husband and two children, Jordan and Asia. She enjoys writing short stories and is currently working on a novel.

The Unbearable Lightness of Biking

Mackenzie Rivers

It was a Schwinn Varsity. Orange, with white handlebar tape, and *speeds,* five of them. I don't remember the exact size, only that even after owning it for ten years I still could not clear the top tube without leaning the bike sideways.

Size did not matter. I was eleven when I sold an entire and complete set of Nancy Drews for it. I sold Barbie and Skipper, their teeny plastic shoes, Barbie's bell-bottoms, Skipper's zippy pink convertible. Away went the troll dolls with wild eyes and ratty hair, the topsy-turvy doll that was Little Red Riding Hood, her grandmother, and the big bad wolf in one frayed calico bundle. I sold all of my worldly possessions in order to own the bike of my dreams. All for the grand sum of fifty dollars.

My parents were away the Saturday of my sale. The sitter apparently did not find it odd to see me lining the driveway with toys, or the cardboard YARD SALE sign posted by the street. After my parents returned and I had the Varsity and my newly sparse bedroom the big question was why. "Why not just ask us to buy the bike for you?" my mother asked, fretting about the forgone handmade dollhouse, the once adored teddy, the heirloom bone china tea set. Across the room the slouched hump on the sofa that was my older sister shrilled "she's not getting the money back!" whenever Mom began to reminisce over some forsaken toy. The Varsity had belonged to my sister, but since my parents had given her a car all she wanted was cash. Cold, hard cash.

"What about your bike?" Dad was referring to my Western Flyer.

What he meant was *Why, why wasn't your old bike good enough anymore?*
I didn't have an answer. The Flyer had certainly taken me places: I was
a Crazy Cat, a member of the all-girls biking club I started with my
three best friends. We pedaled to the mini mart for Pixy Stix, raced to
the neighborhood pool. It carried me to school every day, twelve blocks
past the teasing throngs of junior highers at their bus stops, past the
kindergartners clinging like kudzu vine to their moms. I rode it
through the humid glaze of summer nights, chasing the dim green
glow of the mosquito truck as it sprayed our neighborhood, filling it
with the pungent haze that signaled bedtime. I rode it every day, flee-
ing that peculiar and heavy Sunday-afternoon letdown feeling that
scratched the back of my throat so hard some days I thought I would
choke; I rode it to get away from simply staring into the blankness of
my room at the slow, tepid simmer of my eleven-year-old existence.

It was blue, with tassels dangling from the handles like they had
when it arrived under the Christmas tree, back in the first grade. It was
the bike I was a riding on my first attempt with no hands, the time I
knocked out two teeth when the front wheel hit the curb and I cata-
pulted over the handlebars. I lay unconscious in a congealing sunset of
red until Mrs. Hamby, washing her dinner dishes, spotted me and ran
down her driveway screaming. I had to have emergency surgery for the
split in my gum and eat baby food the rest of the school year. But I was
back on it two weeks later; pedaled all the way to Woolworth's, even
toted home a hamster in his little cardboard carton that I purchased
with the money the tooth fairy left under my pillow for losing my two
front, permanent teeth, now wired back in place. There it was, kickstand and tassels, propped in the garage against Dad's lawn mower: a
first grader's bike.

My friends all rode new banana bikes with swooped-up handlebars
and long plastic glittery seats. Those bikes held no allure for me; might
as well have training wheels again, or a three-wheeler like the ones

parked by the shuffleboard courts. No, what I wanted was a *real* bike, with real handlebars. Drop bars wrapped in white tape, curved downward like a ram's horns were sleek, grown-up, with cables and brake levers. Big kids cruising the street sat upright on bikes just like it, hands crossed in front of their chest or spread-eagled to the side like Walenda balancing on his tightrope. Those handlebars said one thing to me: freedom. Freedom from handlebars that clearly said *little kid's bike*. Or worse, *girl's bike*.

"You'll never bear children," my father cautioned, convinced of the notion that girls shouldn't ride bikes with a top tube, any more than swim on certain "days of the month." I rode anyway, out of my neighborhood cocoon, all the way downtown to the public library; I parked under the eaves where the winos hung out in the shade, made sure not to pass my uncle's service station, lest he mention to my parents I had wayfared beyond the allowed boundaries of transit. "Too many cars and who knows what," Mother would say, chiding my wanderings. Still I went, pedaling my way across the line, freeing myself from the tethering umbilical of parental control.

Growing up seems to be a continual process of pulling away and pulling *toward*. We stretch and strain to find our path, even as we retreat to what is comfortable and safe, the known and familiar. The trick is to balance the one against the other, on one hand lessening the impact of the return, on the other not blasting off too quickly in the first place. It is exactly like learning to pedal hands-free: If all the attention is placed on pedaling too fast there is too much force and the bike won't hold a straight course, but if there is not enough oomph at the pedals over you go. Eventually, though, there are those times when the cords of security stretch thin, pulled by the desire to pedal in a new direction, our own way, and we snap through, breaking away.

I can't remember what happened to the Varsity, only that one day the bike of my dreams became a Basso: glitzy but prone-to-chipping

Italian paint job, Campy Super Record, and heaven-of-all-heaven, Columbus SLX tubing. It was like switching to a glider plane after piloting a 747. Instead of a wedding ring I convinced my fiancé; it was 1985 and the Basso cost twelve hundred dollars, a thousand more than the Valiant I drove. It was my ticket; a ticket to freedom, toward a life I couldn't quite see, but knew was out there, somewhere. At any rate, the Basso might get me there faster.

It was during that first long winter of gray Appalachian rain when I realized my ability to be carried toward the hinterlands of the known and constant periphery that was the idea of myself. On my bike I was not me, I was someone faster, smarter, more talented. Better. I could shed the present and move forward, if only for the duration of miles and hours pedaling, levitated above my existence, beyond the drag of limitations, out of reach of my own hand at my entanglements.

On my Basso I could escape, the way I had on the Varsity when I rode away from the cement-block ranch-style existence of my parents fighting, away from the night we came home and I knew at once in the darkness that the shattering vial I knocked into the sink meant my sister had tried to kill herself. The day of my father's heart attack when I rode in the midday humidity to escape a far worse, angry heat. Then the marriage with its words and threats; I would ride into the creeping shadows cast by rhododendron and laurel, ride into the damp smoke smell of mountain coves, lift myself upward toward the glowing edges of my dreams. *You never do anything.* His words were rain slapping onto a pavement colored in bright chalk rainbows, and somehow, they stuck with me long after the clear memory of his face, that dull look in his eyes just before the thud against my face, the falling tree in my forest of emotions: If I wasn't there would I feel it? On my bike I surfaced for air: the familiar pedaling toward freedom, toward what I could not quite see but could always imagine, around the next bend.

Fifteen years later and when mechanics make that *tic-tic* sound before they shake their heads and call the Basso a "classic," I say that the Basso fits me. What I mean is I can't let it go. They don't know where it has taken me. They can't know how once you find that perfect fit you hold on to it.

But then that one ride; eventually there is that one ride, the one that forever stands in sharp relief, like a single bare blackened branch against the white of snow. It began near the top of a Sierra pass where the cleft of the road spliced the granite in a vague scar, a climb that began first with a soaring descent from the summit with its outcropping of rocks hunched and broken like little old men. It was too fast; the lake that was our destination winking in the distance like some small bright eye.

These days, I tell myself *not bad for a forty-year-old,* remind myself how the climb is obvious proof of my ability to endure, be tough. Biking is a talisman of how much my heart can endure, not that I ever used a heart rate monitor or cared about a target range. My mantra was never *spin,* but *climb.* As long as it is steep, my dream, the one playing in my head in that surround-sound big-screen kind of way, the 360-degree view of my life as I dreamed it might be where I break away, where I win, keeps playing.

I am standing, one crank at a time, when two younger, much younger, riders cruise up next to me. One observes that a bigger rear cluster might make it easier for me. *Easier?* I can't think of a time when cycling has been about easy. I look at their tricked-out titanium frames, two hundred dollar shoes, flashy jerseys, methodical pace fueled by PowerBars and Gu. They are lean and trim and I am old enough to be their mother and then the dream is gone, as if the reel severed mid-viewing, and I try hard through several choking switchbacks to get it back but it is gone. I am just a wannabe on a bike on a steep-ass climb who probably should get another rear cluster, better yet trade the Basso for a touring bike.

Then for some reason I think of my mother, a time when her hand rested against the seat of the Flyer, guiding me carefully as I pedaled in painfully slow, teetering pushes. My first day without training wheels. I begged to quit, in the same breath begging her to not let go, her hand the one variable I was sure kept my quivering body aloft. Then, after one long wobbling excursion down the driveway and back, I felt a lightness, and that was it: I could ride a bike. Freedom on a bike isn't about where you go or how fast you get there or what line you cross; it is as much about letting go as it is about holding on. The trick is in the balance, it is about not only knowing *when* to let go, but what to let go of.

I reached the summit and just let the old dream go. I let it go and pedaled away; I pedaled away, the way I had always done, feeling the freedom, the same wonderful, unbearable lightness of biking the way it had always felt.

Mackenzie Rivers had her first river adventure at age six, when her sister pushed her from a boulder into a small North Carolina stream. She has been entranced by moving water ever since, and after graduating Wake Forest University with degrees in English and art history became a professional white-water river guide. She migrated west, working between river seasons as a ski instructor, pastry chef, landscaper, barista, and assistant to a Hollywood film producer. In 1991 she guided the first official river trip of the Hopi Tribe down the Colorado River in Grand Canyon National Park, sparking an interest in water law and Indian law that led her to law school. To date she has completed ninety-nine Grand Canyon river trips, rowing enough miles to have circumnavigated the globe and be on her way back around again. Mackenzie lives with her husband and their three-year-old son in Idaho.

Riding for Nefertiti

Jeffrey Hammond

I learned to ride a bike in the late 1950s, when I was seven years old. The fact that I was the last kid in our neighborhood to do so reflected a blend of stubbornness and timidity that marked my entire childhood. A fear of water kept me from learning to swim; I refused to get on a Ferris wheel until high school; I was reluctant to try new foods or new variations on the old foods, as witnessed by the hamburgers with catsup and pickle—and only catsup and pickle—that I ate until well into college. When the first McDonald's arrived, ordering a hamburger with catsup and pickle became a problem, as the confused voice in the drive-through intercom proved. On this, at least, I held my ground: A born anti-adventurer, I figured that if I liked something, why change it?

So it was with bicycles. When I was small I liked my tricycle fine, and rode it until my knees nearly bumped my chin as I pedaled. The next logical step—the transition from three wheels to two—seemed an alarming leap from physics to faith. My older brother would hop on his bike and just *go*, supported by nothing, it seemed, but mysterious forces and dumb luck. This gave me the impression that when you got on a bike, all sorts of random things could happen. How could a person move so fast—and so high off the ground—and not be terrified?

Not that I wasn't curious, especially as the benefits of being able to ride became increasingly clear. Sometimes I studied my brother's bike, slowly lowering it on its side for a closer look. It had an intimidating complexity when viewed up close by a rabbity nonrider—its myriad bars and spokes, not to mention a sprocket and chain that seemed tailor-made to pinch a finger, as it once pinched mine while I was cranking the pedals by hand.

Anxious to save face as my neighborhood pals began to master these scary machines, I devised rationalizations for lagging behind. I bragged that by cutting through yards and climbing fences I could run to destinations as quickly as they could arrive on their bikes. Such defenses quickly grew stale, however, and full-blown shame emerged around the time my friends began riding their bikes to the city park. They quickly grew to resent my deadweight on their back fenders whenever they gave me lifts. I also learned that a bikeless kid had to leave for school twenty minutes before anyone else. Trudging along and only halfway there, I would wave halfheartedly as my friends sped by.

Noticing my sullenness, my parents rightly guessed that my inability to ride a bike had become a problem. In our house, problems were always addressed with "talks," and this one was no exception. My mother gently reminded me of my earlier reluctance to learn to tie my shoes: hadn't my life improved greatly—didn't I feel more grown up—once I mastered that? And didn't hamburgers taste better once I finally tried pickles and started adding them to the catsup?

I knew she was right. I tried to ride my brother's bike, but he was nine years older and it was way too big. I stood on a lawn chair, climbed onto the seat, and pushed off, but I balked at pedaling up to the speed necessary for balance. I wanted to ease into this—to go as slowly as my tricycle had gone—but Dave's bike refused to cooperate. I'd end up wobbling the handlebars to stay upright for a moment or two before pitching sideways and jumping free to avoid getting trapped under that finger-pinching sprocket.

It was my brother who finally took action. For some time Dave had been hauling me, perched on his crossbar, on occasional errands like dental appointments. His patience broke after the last lift he gave me, when one of my sneakers got caught in his spokes and we slammed facedown on a patch of gravel. Determined that I would learn to ride so he could live his teenage life in peace, he spent several days walking alongside and steadying his bike as I wobbled up and down Fishlock Avenue. But since my feet hardly reached the pedals and I was scared of the height, I just couldn't get the hang of it.

My father got me a smaller bike for Christmas, a used one of undetermined make. Dad proclaimed his confidence that I'd be riding it like a pro someday, just as soon as the weather permitted. By now I wanted to learn to ride as much as my family wanted me to. Aping Dad's optimism, I painted my bike red and placed reflecting decals on the fenders in anticipation of my future skill. But I couldn't dispel a suspicion that this skill might never come. With the rust spots scraped off and a fresh coat of paint, at least my bike *looked* good. Several more sessions with Dave allowed me to go several yards before teetering over. This was progress, but I was still afraid to ride without somebody walking alongside.

One day, when Dave caught me leafing through his high school world history textbook for the third or fourth time, he decided that this last hurdle could be overcome only with a bribe. A rabbity boy who cannot ride a bike to the park with friends might be expected to seek solace in reading, and Dave's textbook had sparked an interest in ancient history, especially ancient Egypt. The book's wonders included a half-page picture of the entrancing Queen Nefertiti. She looked like Audrey Hepburn, and I couldn't take my eyes off her.

My brother, who was indifferent to history but loved math and electronics, set the bait like a junior scientist. If I managed to ride my bike unaided between Point A and Point B—both points to be determined by him—he would get me my own copy of his textbook. Briefly lifting my gaze from Nefertiti's placid face, I made him shake on it. Dave scheduled the big test for the following Saturday, as soon as he got home from his ice cream delivery route.

It was early spring. I know this because I have a dated photograph that was taken soon afterward to commemorate the event. Late Saturday afternoon we went to the county fairgrounds nearby, my brother walking and steadying the bike with me perched on the seat and steering. Trying not to jackknife the handlebars, I barely noticed where we were going until Dave suddenly announced that we had arrived at Point A.

Point A lay in the middle of the road, on top of a hill near the crafts building. When I asked where Point B was, he pointed down the hill to a creek that lay about an eighth of a mile away. Crossing the creek was a flat concrete bridge, which was now covered by a foot of rushing water from the spring thaw. I would be given one chance, he said, to ride my bike down the hill like a regular person and bring it to a stop within five feet of the flooded bridge. If I fell over, jumped off, stopped too far from the water, or ended up wet, I would not get the book. The deal was also off if he had to touch the bike in any way. I begged for another Point B—couldn't I ride in the opposite direction from the creek?—but Dave was adamant. "No creek, no Nefertutu." I was almost crying from frustration when I corrected him: "It's Nefer*titi*!"

It was too late to back out now. Dave promised to start me off with a push and run alongside for the duration of the trip. True to his word, he gave me the push. Untrue to his word, however, he did not run alongside—a fact I noticed just before yelling "No fair!" and riveting my attention on the rushing water that was rapidly approaching. Not trusting myself to steer to the left or the right without falling, I decided that the only way to survive was to go in a straight line. I coasted downhill, wobbling the handlebars in what seemed like an endless effort to stay upright, until I got about fifteen feet from the water. Then I applied the brakes with clenched teeth and staggered a few steps, stiff-legged but upright, as the bike slid to a stop. When it was over I was straddling the bike like a regular person, about a yard from the water's edge.

As I rode home with a few steadyings and only one major fall, Dave explained that I couldn't have *his* book because he had to turn it in at the end of the school year. So the following Monday my mother picked me up after school and drove me to the administrative offices of the Findlay City Schools, where we exchanged three dollars of Dave's ice cream earnings for a worn copy that a secretary retrieved from a storeroom in the rear of the building.

That book contained all the ancient history that a kid could possibly want, from Mesopotamia up to the discovery of America, and it was mine to keep. The ability to ride a bike was mine to keep, too—a fact commemorated in that photo, which shows me pedaling down Fishlock Avenue with the fairgrounds behind me, steady on my wheels but too nervous to do anything but glance up quickly at Dave's camera.

Small things can have huge consequences. I won't go into the endless, blissful hours of bike riding that followed: the trips to the park, the low branches whizzing by my face, the freedom to leave the neighborhood for parts unknown, my eventual familiarity with every smooth route by which to navigate the uneven sidewalks of Findlay, Ohio. These commonplace journeys initiated my own discovery of America. Anyone who ever rode a bike as a kid took the same trip.

Less commonplace, perhaps, is the fact that I owed this brave new world to an ancient Egyptian queen thirty-five hundred years dead. When I got my new-old world history book home and started flipping through it, I discovered some scribbles and geometric doodles and a few Kilroys gracing its pages. The Emperor Augustus had a acquired an eye patch and a handlebar mustache, but to my relief Nefertiti was untouched. She was so beautiful, I reasoned, that not even the toughest high school hood could bring himself to mark her up.

I knew that there were more books about her at the public library, chief among them a moldy old volume about ancient Egypt that I had recently discovered while my mother was returning some books. In a hurry to get to the post office before it closed, Mom had promised that I could check it out at our next visit. As I stared at Nefertiti, I decided that tomorrow after school I would ride my bike downtown to the library and get James Breasted's *History of Egypt*. Or maybe I'd go the next day. I suddenly realized, with a thrill of pure pleasure, that it was up to me.

Jeffrey Hammond, Reeves Distinguished Professor in the Liberal Arts at St. Mary's College of Maryland, has won a Pushcart Prize and Shenandoah's Carter Prize for Essay. His most recent books are The American Puritan Elegy: A Literary and Cultural Study *(Cambridge University Press, 2000) and* Ohio States: A Twentieth-Century Midwestern *(Kent University Press, 2002).*

Mas Fina

Eric Eckel

This story should start with my old man offering me a blue-and-white Corona as he squints to keep the grill smoke from getting in his eyes. I should be saying that I'm limping up the last step onto his faded gray wooden deck, looking to settle into the closest wrought-iron chair I can find as I take the beer, wet with chilly condensation in the humid Kentucky summer evening. I wish I could say I took that amber nectar, gingerly eased myself into the chair, and told him about my worst mountain bike spill to date as he bent over the grill to turn the chicken one last time before coating it with the special barbecue recipe known only to him. But, as you can already tell, that's not the way this story goes.

Instead, I'll have to tell you my tale, as he's no longer with us. He was too fucking stubborn to visit a doctor with a back that'd been hurting him the entire fall of '95 or '96. I forget the exact year, but when your old man passes, you kind of quit paying attention to the dates yourself. At least I have.

Prostate cancer's nothing to mess with. That's one of the reasons I ride every chance I get. My father lived to see fifty-eight. Never spent his 401(k). Never retired. Just worked and worked some more. Don't get me wrong. I'm not bitter. You live the life you're given. For me that means riding as often as I can with a job, a kid, and a wife and mortgage to support.

Sometimes the rides don't go as planned, though. Certainly you've had one of those trips where everything seems to hook up. At least for a while.

You're bombing down a section of singletrack you've always unclipped on in the past, but today for some reason you're just floating along. Bobbing down the trail. The planets line up.

That's how my ride went. A perfect day with a couple of cool fat-tire pals. We head out to a favorite trail and soon separate. I'm alone at the front.

Ahead's a tricky curve, but I've been through it plenty of times before. I've negotiated it going both ways. In the late-summer light and even early on a crisp winter weekend morning. I know the route. It's my home trail.

I blow through that turn. I'm hooked up. Maybe it's the new cross-country treads I've added. Maybe it's my new seat position. Maybe it's my late old man hitching one last ride.

Whatever it is, it feels good. I lean, I roll, I work my way down, up, and around. Through dips, in-and-out-of a crossing, cold drops of water cool my calves as I splash through a creek. Up the other side I begin a long climb. One of those climbs that hurt. My thighs burn, but I concentrate on making the top. A switchback and then more climbing I always try to forget remains. Then I'm at the top. Normally everyone regroups here, but I'm feeling too in-the-groove to stop now. I tilt the front end down over the precipice and begin the descent.

I've been here so many times before. All acceleration requires is relaxing my fingertips on the brake levers. Gravity takes me from there. The wind gets louder in my ears. Again, I'm floating down the trail. My speed increases, I lean left, then right, pushing the rear end out oh-so-slightly to keep my speed up as I slide through another turn.

My fingers let go of the brake levers as the hill's grade becomes even steeper. Leaves slap me in the face, but I learned to ignore that long ago. Rolling along well, now, everything's all right. Work's far away, as are bills, interest rates, insurance payments, and other day-to-day worries.

My speed increases. Up ahead is a fallen tree. It's maybe ten inches high. I've cleared it many times before. My chainrings have rarely even kissed it. It's a textbook bunny hop. Plenty of straight trail on both sides.

Of course, I've never approached it going this *fast* before. But what's a little extra speed. Today I'm in the groove.

Then I learn about vector force analysis. I dropped physics the one time I tried to take it in college. So my lesson is one with ramifications.

I've ridden this trail so many times my mind subconsciously tries timing the jump. But I know I'm going faster than usual. Much faster. So I'm led into a stupid mistake we're all prone to make. I try to compensate for my extra speed, and in the process I overrule my instincts. I have about two seconds before I realize I've calculated wrong. But brakes, even the best disk out there that I don't have, do no good when the wheels are in the air.

Somehow I strike the leading edge of the log square with my front tire. The shock's travel bottoms out instantly. My weight's all wrong.

There are wrecks that are fun, and there are spills that give you chills. I know this one's going to be bad. There's no getting a hand out, there's no rolling to the side.

The next thing I feel, and I feel it sharply, is something trying to pierce the middle of my back. Then my head's in the dirt. My Oakleys peel off, dirt works its way into the gap between my lower lip and gum. My neck strains as my speed, still pushing me forward, tries burying my head under me. Then an arm sends shooting pains from somewhere below me. I get hit in the head with what feels like a brick, but as I'm now unclipped, I see the rear tire that's just struck my skidlid bounce away down the trail. The rest of the bike goes with it.

It's all over. There's some dust, but not as much as I'd expect. Then the shouting begins. A friend behind me saw the accident from the trail crest behind me. They bomb down to where I'm lying, feathering their brakes, as it's a lot harder to rescue two or three riders than it is one.

But I'm already up. The adrenaline begins its energizing rush. It's time to fight or flee, but the battle's already ended. A pedal, most likely, has left a malformed Nike logo on my right shin, and blood's already running into my shoe. The cut probably needs a few stitches, but already I feel proud of the comments the wound will trigger back in the office on Monday.

As soon as everyone realizes that's the worst of it, I hear my companion, a professional photographer, exclaim in relief and probably truth, "That I could sell!"

So, I head home. The wife panics as I'm unloading the bike. How'd that happen (oh, a spill). Do I need to go to the hospital (no). Later that night we head to my mom's for a cookout. All while I was growing up she was overprotective. You know the type. I wait for her to ask her questions, as the wound's still bleeding through the hasty dressing I supplied and I'm limping.

Then, during a lull in the evening's activities, I head out to that empty deck. I grab a seat by the cold grill that hasn't been used in months and pop the top on a Corona. I sit back, put the leg up, and take a long draft as I listen to my shin that's throbbing slowly but firmly, letting me know that I'm still alive.

Erik Eckel works as an author and editor in Louisville, Kentucky. He regularly commutes to work by bike and enjoys road riding, mountain biking, and single-speeding. He has published numerous other books, articles, and columns, including another cycling-themed short story ("Live Bait: Life on the Pinellas Trail") in Dirt Rag *magazine. He is thirty-seven years old.*

It's About Freedom

Roger Deutsch

When I was four years old, I felt a void within myself. Deep thought and a visit to the local department store revealed that only a bicycle could fill the void. Having no job and no money, I decided I would have to get a bike the old-fashioned way. I begged my mom until she broke. "Okay, enough. Let's go buy you a bike."

Later, at the store, I looked over the selection of bikes. When I came to the pale green bike with the hard plastic seat and training wheels, I knew I'd found the one. I climbed on and smiled. The handlebar grips fit my hands as if the bike were custom-made for me. It was more than a bike; it was my future, my freedom. "This is the one."

Mom bought the bike for me and we returned to our apartment. That night, I rode the bike until my legs ached. Every day, after pre-school, I practiced a ritual of riding my bike until my mom yanked me off and tucked me into bed.

After riding the bike for a week, I became frustrated by limitations related to the training wheels.

When either of my training wheels edged off the sidewalk into the grass, the rear wheel would come off the ground and I would stop. This meant that I couldn't keep up with other bikers (older boys) who also rode in the area, around my apartment complex.

I was frustrated. After attempting to remove the training wheels using a hairbrush, a pair of scissors, and a flat-head screwdriver, I decided I should attempt a different method of operation. I begged my mom until she broke.

"Okay, enough. Uncle Smitty will come over and remove the training wheels tomorrow night."

The next evening, Uncle Smitty showed up with his adjustable wrench and liberated me from the tyranny of my training wheels.

He pushed the bike toward me. "There you go, kid. Think you can ride it?"

"Sure I can. Just watch." I had seen the newspaper boy and I knew how to get started. I held on to the handlebars and started running with the bike. Then, as the bike gained speed, I jumped onto the seat. I rode around the court and zipped past my uncle's smiling face. "Not bad, kid. Not bad."

This was freedom. I felt as if I was flying, as if at any moment, my bike would lift off and I'd head for the moon.

Hit the fast-forward button and skip thirty years, to the present.

It's after midnight on an August evening. My two sons are safely tucked in and sound asleep. My wife is reading a book and relaxing.

"I'm going for a ride, honey," I say.

She looks up, nods her head, and goes back to her book.

Outside, I climb onto my mountain bike and head down the street. The night is cool, even a little chilly, but the sky is clear and the stars shine upon me as if they are smiling.

I ride by hundreds of houses. Most houses are dark, with everyone asleep inside. Others have windows that glow with the luminescence of a television lighting up a dark room. There are few cars on the road this late at night and I'm glad.

My mind races faster than my bike. At home, bills are stacking up. At work, my manager is pressuring me to complete my software project early and under budget. Markets are down. The Middle East is a boiling pot, ready to overflow at any moment. What kind of world will my sons grow up in? I pedal faster and the miles tick off. The tension drains out of my body with the sweat.

It's a cool night and the smell of maple logs burning in someone's fireplace drifts on the breeze. I look up again and survey the sky. The twinkling stars, so far away, so mysterious, make me wax philosophical. The brilliant moon, so beautiful and quiet, makes me hope and believe in peace.

I begin to descend a hill and my bike moves forward on its own power; the clicking sound of the gears beating out a tune only I can hear. I raise my hands from the handlebars and the bike continues to gain speed. I'm flying.

Now there are no problems. There is only the bike and me, flying to the moon. I'm free again, just as I was when I was a little boy. This is why I love my bike. It's about freedom.

Roger Deutsch is currently a software developer at a large financial company in the Midwest. But you never know where he might show up. He's worked as a carnie (you know, carnival worker, worst job ever), a roofer, a farmhand, a technical support engineer, and a software tester.

Although he's a married, underweight man, he's used a pseudonym and been published for pay, five times, at a leading online diet workshop as a single, overweight woman.

An Old Bike and an Even Older Man

Louise Blackah

"Eee, now that's a rare sight and no mistake!" came the chuckle from over the wall next door, as Mr. Blow leaned over looking at the spectacle in front of him. I suppose he must have been right too, it must have been very comical, not to mention dangerous, a seventy-two-year old chubby granddad running up the road holding on to the seat of a bike while his thirteen-year-old granddaughter learned to ride.

It's unimaginable in this day and age that a thirteen-year-old would not know how to ride a bike, but back in 1972 that was exactly the case for me. My mother had remarried in good faith when I was six; however, the following seven years had been lost to a physically and mentally abusive man.

We returned from living abroad and moved in with my grandparents, and began to try to establish some kind of normality. As a child my confidence and self-esteem had been destroyed, I had no faith in my abilities, and the only people that I felt I could trust were my immediate family. I soon fell into a familiar routine of spending the days with my granddad.

It came as a great shock to him to discover that I was unable to ride a bike. My stepfather had constantly refused to buy me a bike, regardless of the fact that most of my friends had them. He constantly told me that I was incapable of riding a bike safely and could not be trusted to ride on the roads. On reflection now, I see this as simply yet another controlling tactic on his part.

My granddad decided that I needed to learn to ride as soon as possible, but as we were on a very tight budget a new bike was out of the question. However from the back of his shed he pulled out this wonderful machine that had been my mother's, when she was eighteen, and she had used it for riding to work. After she left home my granddad had used it until he bought his new bike a short while before we arrived home.

Together we cleaned the bike, pumped the tyres, found a repair kit and mended the holes in the tube, and there it was, somewhat old-fashioned, but nevertheless my first bike. As anyone knows your first bike is always special and this one was special for many reasons. Before I had even begun to ride it, it had forged a closer bond with my granddad, helping me to restore my faith in men and in my own abilities as I had helped to bring it back to working order.

Living in a small village, the roads were quiet, and we pushed the bike out in front of the houses. I vividly recall my Nan standing at the front door, her arms folded, watching us struggling as I tried to mount the bike with my granddad clinging on behind. Then as I began to pedal he ran up the road holding the back of the bike for stability. How he never collapsed I will never know; we certainly provided entertainment for the whole street.

It didn't take long to get the hang of it. Soon I was riding up and down the street and was quite competent, if you didn't count the gravel rash on my knees from falling off when turning round in a driveway, or the cut on my arm from hitting the kerb and flying straight over the handlebars.

Looking back I can see that this was a gift from my granddad, the gift of freedom, of confidence in myself, of the realisation that not everything my stepfather drummed into me, relentlessly, was true and that I could overturn these doubts that I had in myself. Most important of all was the gift of freedom and independence. All this from an old bike and an even older man.

From that day onwards I found a freedom that I'd never had before. We went everywhere together, cycled miles. One of the most memorable trips is the day that granddad decided to teach me to fish. We packed up lunch, and he tied rods to our bikes, then put his fishing basket on his back and off we went. It's incredible looking back to imagine that he did so much, cycled so far, but as a teenager I took it for granted.

We cycled over four miles to get to the river, and after this successful outing we returned many times to spend the day quietly fishing together. We cycled to fetch seeds for his vegetable garden and to go to the bowling green for matches. As the years went by I made new friends and as he slowed down, the bike and I carried on cycling.

It's incredible to think that although I rode a very old bike, no one ridiculed me, that I believed that my bike was better than any others, faster (or was that my legs?) and more reliable. We went miles together. It was only when I was sixteen that I bought a motorbike, and the bike became redundant. Even then I couldn't bear for it to be wasted and passed it on to another elderly gentleman whose own bike was very much the worse for wear.

I have four children, and all of them have had their own shiny bicycles from an early age. It was something that seemed important. Something that I felt would alter the course of their lives. But until this year I haven't owned another bike myself.

At the beginning of summer I decided that I wanted another bike, and my husband and I went along to the bike shop to pick a new one for me. Two of my children came too. I was paraded in front of racks of shiny bikes, mountain bikes, stunt bikes, with over twenty gears and amazing gadgetry, and then in the corner, I noticed it, quietly standing there, unobtrusive, totally black.

As my husband was looking at mountain bikes at the back of the shop, he was amazed, and my children appeared to be appalled, when I asked the shopkeeper to bring out the one I spotted. It stood there on its stand, simple, no pretensions, it had "sit up and beg" handlebars, only three gears, there was a rack at the back, and a big black guard over the chain. "But it looks old-fashioned," cried my son in disgust. "Exactly," was my reply.

As the shopkeeper said, it's a "new old-fashioned" bike, and the memories that it brought back to me were worth a thousand brand-new shiny mountain bikes with all their gears, tiny saddles, amazing suspension, and skinny wheels. So now I have my bike, and no one else will ride it in case they are spotted by friends, but me. Well I am happy, I think of my dear granddad, who passed away many years ago, when I ride my bike, and the memories of the days we spent together will never leave me.

I am so grateful in many ways; my sanity, self-respect, confidence, and faith in mankind was restored thanks to an old bike, and an even older man. Thank you both.

Louise Blackah is thirty-eight years old, lives in Lincolnshire, England, and has four children. She makes handmade greeting cards, and is interested in vintage aircraft.

If All the Traffic Were Bicycles

Amy Brunvand

My friend Brian picked me up at the San Francisco airport in a car. "This is so you can see firsthand exactly how miserable it is trying to drive in this city," he said. Brian executed several exotic and frightening traffic maneuvers to escape the labyrinthine airport access roads and merged into the stop-and-go traffic inching toward the city. As we neared our hotel I rolled down my window and scouted for a parking spot. As our car lurched around the block for about the third time Brian explained the situation. "San Francisco has more registered cars than legal parking spaces so it's just like juggling balls. Some of the cars have to be in motion all the time so that others have space to park."

"Is that a parking space up there?" I pointed to the top of a steep hill with a possible empty parking spot at the dead end.

"It's only semi-legal," said Brian. "But I'm willing to risk it. We'll just have to come back and move the car tonight so we don't get a ticket."

We lugged our suitcases five blocks to the hotel and checked into our room. Then we walked across town to the tourist-trap district and rented bicycles.

The girl's frame and extra-soft seat on my bicycle presented a low-performance appearance. Nonetheless, it had small enough granny gears to allow riding up San Francisco's famous hills. The bicycle also came equipped with a handlebar bag containing a patch kit and a map showing the route for a recreational bicycle ride across the Golden Gate Bridge and back by way of the ferry.

"We won't need this," I commented. "We'll just be using the bikes for transportation around town."

The bicycle guy eyed me suspiciously. "Are you riding in the Critical Mass?"

"Yup."

"Don't get arrested," he said with a high-pitched laugh.

In July of 1997 the police started a riot by arresting 250 bicyclists and threatening to confiscate their bikes. After that some people worried that the Critical Mass had become tainted with violence and lost its credibility. However, most people blamed overzealous police for the incident. I wasn't too worried that it would happen again. Nowadays motorcycle cops ride along with the mass. Even though the cops aren't especially supportive, they seem to be under orders not to start trouble.

When Brian, a Silicon Valley software engineer, first told me about Critical Mass he described it with all the evangelical fervor of a convert. "I felt cheated when I found out how much better the bike was than my car, like I had been tricked into driving all that time," he said. "I'm basically lazy so I thought biking would be too hard. But then one week I got over two hundred dollars in parking tickets and it occurred to me that for the same amount of money I could just buy a bike. Even if it got stolen now and then and I had to buy another one, I figured that ultimately it would still be cheaper than paying for parking tickets. Once I got the bike I found out I could actually get places more quickly. Not only that, I could go directly from point A to point B and always get a parking spot right in front."

Critical Mass, he explained, was a demonstration that bicycles are traffic and ought to get the same level of public support. "Four days a week there is a car Critical Mass at rush hour," he said. "One day a week, all the bicyclists happen to be going the same place at the same time. You would love it."

Brian knew he was preaching to the choir. I was already a bicycle convert. Some years earlier my car had broken down. Instead of replacing it immediately I decided to get by with my bike for a while and save up money for a new car. There years passed before I finally bought my car and by then I considered it a luxury, not a necessity.

"The Critical Mass sounds beautiful," I said. "I want to see it for myself."

So Brian had invited me to visit and I flew out from Salt Lake City for the weekend.

Brian and I dodged cars on the narrow San Francisco streets as we rode our rental bikes to Justin Herman Plaza. Then we basked on the sun-warmed pavement waiting for the bicyclists to begin congregating. At first there were just a few, but as people got off work more and more people on bicycles flocked in from all directions. These were not the Lycra-bottomed dual-suspension titanium-framed mountain bike touristic cyclists who vacation in Moab, Utah. They were hardcore bicycle road warriors riding on indestructible utilitarian steel frames. Their bikes were outfitted with urban necessities like luggage racks, anti-rain fenders, kickstands, reflectors, headlamps, extra-loud rubber-bulb warning horns, coffee holders, wicker baskets, and, on one, a welded metal fire-breathing dragon that shot red-hot sparks from its nose. One cyclist tugged a stretchy red dinosaur costume over his clothes and covered his helmet with a toothy T. Rex mask. Then with his long foam rubber tail jutting out behind, he circled his bicycle around the news cameras roaring, "Too many cars! Too much fossil fuel consumption!" Another group was busy decorating the sidewalk with chalk drawings of a bicycle on a bridge before they performed a short play advocating bicycle access to the Richmond-San Rafael Bridge. Some people were handing out copies of the *Auto-Free Times* or a Euro-zine called *Carbusters*. Others distributed little bike-sized stickers that read ONE LESS CAR or WE ARE THE TRAFFIC. I bought myself a black souvenir T-shirt printed with a yellow bicycle icon and the slogan, THE REVOLUTION WILL NOT BE MOTORIZED. Brian bought a shirt with a picture of a grinning anthropomorphic sun riding his bike.

By six o'clock several thousand cyclists had gathered and were antsy to go like marathon runners at the starting line. When the hour struck, those cyclists at the edge of the mass pedaled slowly into the street. The wave of motion began to propagate slowly through the whole crowd. At last the people in front of us began to move and Brian and I coasted slowly out into the street with the swarm. Up and down the street as far as I could see was a mighty river of bicycles and I was flowing along like a boat carried on the current. The city had undergone a startling trans-formation. The everyday urban background of roaring engines was gone, and in its place was the sound of human voices echoing through the canyon of skyscrapers. People were talking and laughing, and play-ing music on tambourines, flutes, clown horns, trilling bicycle bells, and boom boxes that they pulled behind their bikes on trailers. A spirit of courtesy prevailed. Whenever a pedestrian wanted to cross the street or another cyclist wanted to pass, we spoke to each other face to face. My heart swelled with a sentiment unusual to my misanthropic tempera-ment. I felt that possibly I loved humanity after all.

Needless to say, the rush-hour car commuters didn't share this feel-ing of all-embracing love. Locked inside their air-conditioned capsules the carnival pleasure rippling through the cyclists didn't seem to touch them. I suppose that from their point of view Critical Mass must have been just another traffic jam. As we rode past clogged intersections some intolerant motorheads rolled down their windows to shout insults or revved their engines like angry dogs growling in futility at the end their chains. One man stood on his balcony cursing at us. He hopped up and down and waved his fist, purple in the face exactly like "X is for King Xerxes" in Edward Lear's nonsense alphabet.

But many more people, even people who were stuck in cars, smiled and waved and shouted "All right! Critical Mass!"

"Make some noise!" we called out to the stopped cars. They beeped back a friendly shave-and-a-haircut, two-bits. Tourists clinging on the outside of a temporarily blocked streetcar snapped photos as the endless stream of bicyclists parted around them and flowed down the twisted corkscrew of Lombard Street. As we rode on through the city, mini masses of bicycles broke away. The core of the mass grew smaller and smaller until once again Brian and I were riding in the noisesome exhaust of car traffic. In the dusky half-light before sunset, we pedaled back to our hotel. This time we parked right in front. No problem.

Sunday morning I returned my bicycle to the rental shop. I kissed Brian good-bye at the airport and flew home to Salt Lake City.

"I had a great weekend," I told my kaffeklatch at work the next day. "I went bicycling in San Francisco."

"Weren't you afraid of getting run over in city traffic," they asked in alarm.

"Not really," I replied and told them about the Critical Mass. They were skeptical.

"Is Critical Mass really a good way to spread your message?" they asked. "Doesn't it just make drivers angry?

"Why shouldn't they be angry?" I said defensively. "It's not like cars have any legal right to take over all that public space. They just did it by being big, fast, threatening bullies."

"People love their cars," they argued. "They would never give them up."

But I wasn't really listening anymore. Instead I was considering a glorious vision of what my own city would be like if all the traffic were bicycles.

Amy Brunvand, forty-two, is a librarian in Salt Lake City, Utah, who once nearly lost her job by agitating for an employee bike rack. She also writes for Catalyst, *a local monthly magazine devoted to creative living. She owns a touring bike, a mountain bike, a tandem, a unicycle, and a bicycle trailer for baby Charlotte.*

Into the Wind

Christine Brandt Little

I dropped my kids off at school and turned the van toward the gym. Spin class at nine thirty, weights afterward, then the grocery, the post office, pick up the kids. I opened the windows and the wind blew in warm on my face. It smelled of mud and forsythia. I leaned my head back and groaned. Turned up the stereo, Dave Mathews singing about the end of the world. *I can't do this. I've got to go, drive all day, disappear. See no one. Small talk no one.* I accelerated past the gym and turned toward home. In the basement I unscrewed my bike from the trainer. Lifted the top tube onto my right shoulder to keep the chainrings off my shirt. Climbed the stairs to the kitchen and out to the garage. The weight of the bike on my shoulder took me back to grad school in Texas, when I'd ride thirty miles a day, seventy on the weekends, and carry my bike back up the stairs to our second-floor apartment, cleats clanging against the concrete steps. In the garage I put on helmet, gloves, blades, swung my right leg over and clipped in. Pushed off, clipped in the left foot, rolled out the door. With the first pedal stroke the bike leapt forward, and it hit me this was the first time the front wheel had spun in years.

My handling was more than rusty. I wouldn't reach for my water bottle for weeks. I didn't care, I was gone. I rode every day, rain, wind, cold, it didn't matter as long as I got out there. At first I stayed close to home. I didn't know where the loose dogs lived. Didn't know how far I could go before school let out. Didn't know if I could I make it up the steep ridges to the west. It didn't take long to learn. Some days my kids were the last ones waiting to be picked up from school. I'd show up in my jersey and shorts. A smile on my face!

When we were kids my sister and I would pack sandwiches in a backpack and take off for points undetermined, our goal to ride all day and not come home until dinner. We lived in a vast suburban community, the primary benefit of which was miles and miles of bike trails, and we knew almost all of them. Saturdays were for expanding our territory, exploring the outer limits down by the lakes or the park with the nature trail. Stop and eat the sandwiches, get back on and ride some more. Eventually we'd wind up at home, hose down our bikes (we pretended they were horses), stable them in the garage. Mine was blue with a white banana seat. No gears, backpedal brakes. We could pop wheelies and do jumps off the curb; no one wore helmets because no one sold them. Sometimes we'd put up those flags with the long white pole and the little orange triangle on top. I grew out of that bike, discovered boys, and didn't ride again until the summer I graduated from college. The rolling hills outside town called to me and I bought a Panasonic touring bike and felt the world open up again. I wanted to be out there on my own, look around. Pretty soon my sandwich was in my panniers and I had a new riding partner, and we were crossing Ohio, then Colorado. We got married and bought a tandem. I rode in back.

Our tandem got us through some rough patches. Four years of medical school. Five years of surgical training. The ongoing adjustment to parenthood. We used to joke that we could work out any problem—just give us an afternoon on the two-seater. We'd never gone more than ten miles without speaking. But the bike is sluggish, it moves like a draft horse. It does what you ask it, but it plods. It's good training for marriage. Sometimes our pedaling cadence is uncomfortably slow for me. Turns out it's not his cadence either. Somehow we find a cadence and it's influenced by both of our styles. It doesn't feel exactly right to either of us, but we try to adjust. Neither of us is completely in control. And what only one of us wants, we don't get. We've had our best conversations on the tandem, shared our deepest truths and secrets. Sometimes it was happy confirmations of our love for each other. Other times, especially lately, my throat tightened around my tears, and it was hard to breathe.

After years of caring for two small children and a chronically overworked husband I found I'd forgotten how to ask or answer questions like *What do I want to do? Where do I want to go?* It didn't matter—the kids, the husband came first. Better not to ask what I wanted. Just get on the back of the tandem and go where he wants to go while he unwinds. Or get on the trainer and don't go anywhere at all while the kids watch cartoons. I've been riding for years, but you could say I wasn't getting anywhere, and I certainly wasn't steering. Now the kids are older, the husband is settling into private practice, and I find the walls closing in.

So one morning this spring I jumped on my single and rode off. Needed to get a sense of myself in my own skin. See if I could operate on my own without my husband and kids propping me up.

Yesterday I climbed a ridge I'd never climbed before. Each one has its own character and I bend to it, feeling the strength in my legs, taking my rest when I can and breathing in time with the pedal strokes. *This is absurd,* I think. *What can riding teach me about myself? How can it change me? It's a sport, it's fun, what's the big deal?* As I climb, I look up the road toward the next switchback. It's a long climb, steep. There's nothing to do but pedal and breathe. There's no need to rush, just keep climbing. Keep breathing. Eventually I reach the top, sit down, drink. I drop down the far side of the ridge in a tuck, shadows from the trees overhead flowing over my back like water, and finally I burst out into the sun beside a field covered with alfalfa blossoms. My body is covered with gnats and salt, but my mind is swept clean. Farther down the hill there's a long metal-grate bridge. As I cross it I look down through the bridge at the water and rocks below. The grates blur and disappear beneath me and for a moment I'm flying.

But let's not read too much into this. Some are fond of calling the bike a metaphor for life. I disagree. The bike is no metaphor. It's carbon fiber and rubber, cables and air. And yet it's more. For instance, the tandem *is* a kind of metal marriage counselor. Not because you choose to see it that way. No, the tandem really does raise into high relief all the frustrations and joys of being together. On the tandem you and your partner are not metaphorically, but quite literally, *chained together*. And in that crucible the tandem provides the time and space to work things out. Between the endorphins pumping in your blood and the fact that you don't have to meet each other's eyes, the tandem makes it easier to do the work. And there aren't any doors to slam.

And the single? Ride long enough and hard enough, and it *does* make you stronger, tougher, and braver. It requires you to ask yourself what you want to do and where you want to go—in fact, you can't get out of the driveway without asking yourself those questions. And the asking, even those simplest and deepest of questions, is in some way instructive, enlightening. The bike does present you with challenges, and it does set you free, if only for a couple of hours. But those couple of hours may be the best you can hope for—and they may be all you need.

Chris Little is a writer and editor living in Gettysburg, Pennsylvania.

Pedaling in Tandem

Ellen Nordberg

"Watch out for the bus!" and "Don't you see the stop sign?" I used to scream from the back of the tandem to my boyfriend Jon in front. That was in the beginning, when I was hesitant to trust, self-conscious about riding on a bicycle seat once perched upon by his ex-wife.

The tandem was gleaming white, ninety-six inches long, with six water bottle cages and the name CANNONDALE in gold-and-black letters in two places. There was a jagged silver scratch along the cross-bar where I'd leaned the tandem against a no parking sign and it fell, metal scraping white paint.

"Always have two points of contact," Jon admonished me.

This two-wheeled vehicle carried us on rides around the cities where Jon's job took us: Los Angeles, San Francisco, Chicago, and Los Angeles once more. We took organized bike tours through five national parks and along the coast of Maine.

The vistas from the back seat were wide and spectacular, though Jon's rear end and shoulder partially obscured my view, as if I were looking at images in which the photographer's thumb repeatedly cut off the corner of the shot.

Throughout our first year cycling together, being unable to shift or brake, I struggled with control. Eventually, I came to understand the need for surrender. To sit behind him, and simply pedal. Quietly. The landscape came into sharper focus—a dog with his head through the broken railing of a battered porch in Utah, a red-tailed hawk circling the eucalyptus trees in Marin.

The pedals move in unison as you push down on them and then pull up. Single riders asked us if it was hard to coordinate. No, we told them, there are two chains that move simultaneously. No one moves independently. If one rider slacks off, the other has to work harder.

I was sensitive about the implication that I might not be pulling my share of the load.

"She's not pedaling! Ha! Ha! Ha!" old men and teenagers would yell from trucks as they passed, laughing as though they had invented this joke. I worked out with weights, determined to match the giant quadriceps Jon sported.

Over the silence and the miles, we became connected, one unit, legs pumping. Our shadow looked like one entity, one dark amorphous creature silhouetted against the asphalt. Balancing the heavy bike, Jon remained focused, occasionally reaching his left hand back to pat mine.

There was euphoria in reaching the summits, triumph in clocking the final eighty-first mile on our longest ride. Screaming down a familiar hill in the San Francisco Bay Area, we hit sixty-seven miles an hour and laughed like twelve-year-olds in an amusement park. I trusted him to keep us safe.

"Wherever your relationship is going," a retired couple in matching outfits on a yellow tandem told us, "a tandem will take you there faster."

My only jobs were to pedal and monitor the Cat-Eye. I watched our cadence, average and maximum speeds, and mileage. By the seventh year we were together, the odometer read three thousand. We dragged the tandem through six moves in those seven years, beating it up a little more each time, despite the protective case we bought to transport it.

Black padding tape unfurled messily from my handlebars, like loose threads in a heavy hand-knit sweater. I spent hours crouched over those handlebars, trying to crunch my long torso into the section designed for the tandem "stoker," assumed to be smaller than the driver. Being the same height as Jon, my neck would become stiff from trying not to smack my helmet on his rear end, trying to fit the mold, the frame that had not been designed for me.

One Saturday in Los Angeles we went through the usual routine. We put our bike clothes on. Jon pulled the tandem out of the garage and put air in the tires. I filled the water bottles.

"I don't feel like riding," he said, and sat down on the living room couch. Sunlight crashed through the deck door and I squinted to see his face.

He wanted out, he said.

Out?

I knew there were resentments. When we moved back to L.A., I was in better shape and pushed his butt up the hills. In Hawaii, I had flirted with the trip leader. In Canada, he had prepped the bike, packed the lunches, *and* filled the water bottles. But I always expected us to work as a team, to fix whatever was broken, to ride through to the finish.

Jon took off his bike shoes, silver cleats making indents in the gray carpet. He was done, he said.

I begged him to ride with me anyway. I dragged him to counseling, swore I'd learn to be a better cook. Eventually he offered to move out, and I chose to go instead.

I found a temporary apartment, got out my barely used road bike, and hung it on the wall. It would be good practice, I thought, to train on my own and get stronger for future tandem rides.

We continued the counseling and sometimes things got better, some days Jon agreed to go out on the tandem. I impressed him with how fast I could crank, how quiet and focused I could be.

I rode with my girlfriends and went out to breakfast on Sundays. I took a cycling clinic and discovered how to change my own tire. I joined a bike club and learned to shift through three chainrings, and stand on my pedals up steep inclines.

The tandem rides became less frequent, and eventually the counseling ended. We divided the art collection. He bought me out of the house.

By then I preferred the rides on my own bike—the speed I could gain, the responsiveness of the gears to my touch, the self-sufficiency of fixing a flat. I loved the lightness of the frame, and the ease of hill climbing with no one else to hold me back. I could make quick decisions and change course with the flick of a pedal.

He asked if I wanted the tandem, clearly hoping not, already dating someone new.

No, I told him. Just my seat and pedals. I got out my tools and removed them myself.

I went on an organized ride the other day. Made it all the way from Irvine to San Diego—seventy-four miles. With nothing to obstruct my view.

Ellen Nordberg's articles and essays have been featured on National Public Radio, and in the Chicago Tribune, LA Sports + Fitness, Adventure Cyclist, Windy City Sports, *and* Rocky Mountain Sports. *Her fiction has appeared in the literary magazines* River Oak Review, Moon Journal, Kaleidoscope, *and the anthologies* Earth Beneath, Sky Beyond, Take Two—They're Small, *and* Feathers, Fins, and Fur. *She has given readings of her work at Barnes and Noble and Borders bookstores. An AFAA-certified fitness instructor, Ellen teaches aerobics and conducts women's cycling and rock-climbing clinics for REI in Southern California.*

Traveling in Tandem

Amy Kolen

We'd started up the hill, straining on the pedals of our tandem bicycle (a twentieth-wedding-anniversary gift to ourselves, purchased a month before) when my husband, Michael—sitting in front with the gears and brakes—remembered to downshift. Did we think the chain would magically glide into the correct sprocket? The torque we'd exerted on the chain made it jam between spindles, and our feet came down hard on pedals that refused to budge. "Shit," said Michael, as we jolted to a stop for the third time that morning.

Minutes later, I sat in the gravel by the road, arms wrapped around my knees, watching Michael struggle to free the chain with a tire lever, his palms blackening with grease. While his epithets mixed with the chainsaw thrumming of cicadas, I wondered whether I was responsible for this lapse in smooth riding. Maybe my antennae weren't out far enough to anticipate when he'd shift, and I put too much pressure on the pedals. Or maybe I'd been talking when he was concentrating on working kinks out of the cables, and he missed his opportunity to ease the bike into the right gear.

Though he finally got everything working, the tension of his momentary frustration stayed with me. Was a bicycle-built-for-two a good idea after all? Would this open-air tandem experience *ever* be stress-free fun? Would our combined reflexes and Michael's shifting ever improve so that he'd be able to muscle us into the appropriate gear and get us smoothly up a difficult hill? Would we *ever* pass the initiation phase into the delights of this extreme form of cooperative biking?

I may have suggested getting the tandem in the first place. Before, when I rode solo, I never relaxed enough to feel like I could freely circulate through the landscape. I worried about flat tires and parts breaking and being stranded far from home, which led to concerns about the dangers of a woman biking alone. Though it was difficult for me to find compatible cycling partners, riding with my husband—each of us on separate bikes—gave me a companion who didn't mind doing minor repairs on the road. We were too unevenly matched in strength and endurance, though (he surpassed me on both counts), for the ride to be totally enjoyable for him. He admitted gazing longingly at the fluorescent spandexed bikers in their moisture-wicking socks and Shimano shoes with carbon-reinforced soles, hunched over the handlebars of their serious-looking Cannondales or Fujis as they whizzed by.

"I *could* catch up with them if I was alone," he said once, "but not on the tandem."

But a twenty-one-speed, teal, T50 Trek tandem allows us to ride together. Literally. We had the cranks installed "in phase," both pedals on the same side of the bike always in the same position. For equilibrium's sake, I have to mirror my body's movements with Michael's and force myself, when we whiz down breakneck hills, not to lean to the right, say, if he feels we need to lean left around the sharply banked curves on those hills.

During our first autumn with the bike, we rode north toward Lake Macbride to see the leaves of the maples and oaks changing to their fall reds, the black walnuts, elms, and hickories turning to yellows. And it was scary in back with no control of the brakes for the winding, twenty-five-mile round trip, surrendering all control to Michael. The sensation of helplessness combined with indignation from being ordered about by the commands he'd throw over his shoulder—"Lean left. Pedal harder. Coast. Signal right—" dulled my desire to witness nature's colors and stirred issues that I thought we'd resolved decades before. *What's going on here?* I thought. *He decides how fast we're going to go? He says "Lean,"* *and I lean?* And while I never asked any of our married friends who'd borrowed the tandem why they never tried it a second time, or invested in their own, I suspected it had something to do with gender issues and yielding to the power of the one on the front seat.

In our case, though, successfully traveling in tandem does involve a gender division based on strength and size that I had to acknowledge from the outset. As the stronger (to better control steering) and larger (to block the wind) of the two of us, Michael naturally claimed the front, the "captain's seat," with its gear shifts and brakes, a seat sized to fit his body, as the "stoker seat" was sized to fit mine. Everything within my realm of responsibility—signaling for turns and providing muscle power—occurs only while we're cycling, involves little thought, and ends once I slide off the seat. Avoiding potholes, glass, roadkill, and oncoming cars not quite in their lanes, anticipating hill grades and appropriate gears, are among those tasks unquestionably Michael's, but he also (uncomplainingly) oversees the bike's welfare, and by extension, ours.

I don't know exactly when or why my mental shift occurred, why the romantic, fantasy tandem experience of looking "sweet upon the seat" merged with the actuality: me riding behind Michael's sweat-soaked back, catching dollops of perspiration whenever he turns his head, stifling the urge to scream "Slower!" when we go thirty miles an hour down a long, S-shaped hill or to defy orders to "Lean." It must have been a combination of things in the months and miles that followed. Certainly, it involved our motions becoming perfectly coincident. Somehow, we'd harnessed the physical and mental discipline needed for our bodies to work together and power the tandem. And with that synchronicity came an added bonus—paradoxical and unexpected: We were able to experience the landscape, each in our own way. When Michael finally realized his role as avoider-of-road-hazards and captain of our voyages, his earlier frustrations dissipated like dew on a bright Iowa morning in June. He navigated us into the landscape with confidence, which let me relax and become in sync with him and freed me to function more emotionally, aesthetically. Eventually, in the notes I wrote when we stopped, I didn't simply jot *rode by a field*. I could particularize it, embellish that field with details I'd missed before. Allowing myself to lift my head, I finally looked at the land and what was in it.

Today, several years and fifteen hundred miles after we first pedaled the tandem into the world, the landscape unfolds serenely as we head toward Lake Macbride. We speed past immaculate farms and the riding stable with jumps of various heights set up for the class that begins soon. Sailing around the church abutting Newport Township Cemetery, its lawn fuzzy with purple blazing star, we pass fields dotted with sheep, the milk chocolate wool of nursing lambs punctuating the larger masses of white that are their mothers.

A sonorous breath, deep, as if drawn in and expelled by a giant bellows. There. Above the cornfields, the sound of the breeze hitting dry stalks, like rain sticks turned end over end, a hot-air balloon, its primary colors vibrant against the backdrop of cloudless blue sky. There. In the yard with the tire swing on the apple tree, two girls jumping up and down. "What a cool bike," they yell. "Can we have a ride sometime?" There. Along this stretch of county road, pungent smells of hay and manure mingle.

We begin our ascent up "The Hill," an arduous, unavoidable grade en route to the lake, legendary for its extreme verticality, and Michael's helmeted head bobs up and down as he strains seasoned leg muscles. "Good job," I gasp to his damp back as we crest the top of the hill. Then, too winded to say more, I recover in silence, concentrating on the high pitched *ker-ker-cheee* of the red-winged blackbirds in the brush by the road, the low whir of the bicycle chain, and my heavy breathing.

"Bump!" Michael announces news of road conditions that I can't see, and I relax my grip on the handlebars to avoid the jolt. He keeps the pedals rotating at a comfortable speed, brakes well before sharp turns, doesn't take curves too tightly. Without his alerting me, I sense when he'll shift gears, and I ease up on pedaling to help keep the shifting smooth. Today we're synchronized perfectly on the bike.

Now, almost to the lake, we streak past the field, filled with yellow, pulsing butterflies and bordered by pink wild roses, black-eyed Susans over two feet tall, patches of pale blue chicory, and brilliant orange bursts of daylilies thriving far from domestic gardens. An ordinary farm field and the land that bounds it—far from heroic in scale—yet the river of colors, melded into dazzling patterns of tones, light, and shade according to the season, always surprises. On Sugarbottom Road, we fly by the farmhouse where two elderly women, heroic on their own scale, live—Bessie and Betty Shima, hardy women, out doing yard work, taking on the challenge of tending their own home and property. Betty sits astride a power mower, roaring her way across their lot near a crudely lettered cardboard sign proclaiming: BESSIE IS 90 TODAY! Bessie, supported by a thick stick, weeds the patch of ornamental kale around their mailbox. *Osteoporosis or arthritis* or both, I think, while at the same time marveling at her stamina, her ability to move through the world with such patience and grace. "Happy Birthday, Bessie," I holler, waving as we pass. She'd looks up, returning my wave with a dignified nod of her head.

As we reach the last downhill curve, Michael shifts into a higher gear, and we race across the bridge. Releasing the handlebars, I arch my back, raise my arms shoulder high, thrust my chest forward, tilt my head back. Sweat drips from under my helmet into my eyes. Muscles in my bottom and legs ache, and I feel as free as I've ever felt in my life—free and fatigued and grateful for that fatigue because it means I've earned the rest this lake stop offers.

Lake Macbride is a picture-book lake. In the summer, it's filled with motorboats and water-skiers, paddleboats, canoes with fishermen and without, and, on breezy days, sailboats and wind surfers. The lack of aquatic plants near the water's edge makes it easy to see the gizzard shad, food for bigger fish, swarming wildly in the lake just inches from our feet. In schools of what appear to be thousands, they dart frictionlessly through the water, so thickly clumped together in spots, they actually jump out of the shallow areas near the bank and onto the land.

Watching the fish cleave the water, listening to the catbirds mewing in the oak trees, I want to freeze my sense of contentment. The water's surface sparkles hypnotically, and it's not difficult for our eyes to close, for the fingers of my left hand to find those of Michael's right as we lie side by side on our backs by the lake.

"Paddle on the left." A voice booms from somewhere on the water. We bolt upright. A canoe class is maneuvering around the bank, the instructor in the lead, yelling directions through a bullhorn. Of the five pairs of canoeists, only one has finessed the art of gliding over the lake. The others are stuck in an awkward dance that defies lessons in cooperation. *Be flexible. Trust. You can't move any which way and expect to get anywhere.* I speak silently to the people spinning in circles. We wait until the canoeists are out of sight. Then, with a mutual squeeze on each other's fingers, we admit, wordlessly, that it's time to head back home.

Amy Kolen's essay, "Fire," appears in The Best American Essays, 2002 *(Houghton Mifflin), edited by Stephen Jay Gould. Her work has also appeared in* The Missouri Review, The Massachusetts Review, Orion, Under the Sun, *and other publications. She lives with her family in Iowa City and travels in tandem with her husband throughout the countryside around their home.*

Go Hard or Go Home

Chris Fitzgerald

In the heat of last summer, as the mosquitoes swarmed and bred en masse in the still puddles our tires disrupted, when shade offered no more real protection than the blazing sun, and the summer drought we had every year made the ground hard and the riding fast as well as exhausting, Tim and I pushed the boundaries of friendship, physical ability, and gravity itself.

Tim was the only person who pushed me. I followed his lead, watching as his taxi-yellow bike carved perfect turns, crossed steams and ditches, and leapt over logs and debris. His finesse was unparalleled and it seemed that the only things that kept him from bonking on our epic rides were Marlboro Reds and coffee. When he dared to bunny hop a log, I followed suit, garnering confidence from him. When he took a seven-foot drop that led to bridge no wider than my foot, I followed, be damned. I bailed often but he'd wait patiently and urge me on to try again.

As I look back now, our first few rides were short. We'd stay out for a few hours, ride fifteen or twenty miles, and hit a gas station on the way home for sustenance. As the temperature rose, rumors spread of a small team forming that rode like hellions through the woods, breaking trail laws and pushing the limits of biking. The number of people who joined us rose as well and the rides became longer and more intense. We formed a ragtag team of bikers from the most experienced, like Tim, to balls-out riders who would at least try it once, to kids we dropped in under an hour. The team became tight and very territorial.

139

We protected our "spots"—public land that we had ridden, dominated, and claimed. We knew about all the secret drop-offs and switchbacks, the "sand between the lakes" as we called it, where the water parted, leaving a boneyard of rusted cars and forty-ounce malt liquor bottles. When new riders joined, Tim and I played mind games with them, testing them, pushing them to their absolute limit before dropping them or heading back. It was innocent hazing, and most riders came back, donated money, and asked to join the team. The rules were simple:

You ride hard.

You do not wear a team jersey.

You are to be rebellious and risky within your own limitations and accept full responsibility for your actions.

You will apply a sticker to your bike that claims your piece of the pedal resistance.

You will defend trails from abuse and neglect, whether by moto-crosser or state trooper.

If you don't go home bleeding, it wasn't worth the trip.

Team members respected us because Tim and I lived by the motto, "Go Hard or Go Home." There was no gap that couldn't be cleared, no trail uncrossable, no drop we wouldn't fly blindly into only to ride out cleanly or bail magnificently—rolling, flipping, avoiding impalement or a snapped neck by mere inches. I would often stand up with my fist in the air, blood running from my shins and elbows while the other riders looked on in horror. I hadn't made the most beautiful leap of faith, but fate had tried to take me down and I had spit in her face. *You may make me bloody; you may break my arm or worse, my bike; you may bruise my body; but my spirit will forever fight you.* My hand in the air and the grin I became known for, even after the gnarliest of spills, became a trade-mark. Tim understood it but it frightened some riders who complained that we were just cowboys who didn't know a damn thing about rid-ing. They were usually dropped within the first three hours anyway, before the really hard trails came to view.

The team grew, and often we'd stutter the starts because our groups were too large for the illegal trails we were riding. In the end I knew, and I think Tim knew as well, that it would be the two of us, alone, sweating, bleeding, riding hard and fast, pushing each other until the truck to take us home came into view. Often, we'd stop to climb the old train trestle and drink from water bottles and smoke as the sun went down. We saw the skyline, the cars, the buildings, and the chaos of urban life pass us by as we slowed time to a halt and talked about things I could never betray to another human being. This was the midway point, meaning we had another two hours of riding ahead and three to four back.

I learned more about myself and my own endurance on those rides than any other time in my life. Curiosity always pushed me farther. Crashing and bleeding made me get up and do it again. I wasn't fighting nature; I was fighting myself for all I was worth. The bruises and gashes I returned home with were the trophies and purses I'd never win in competition. I'd beaten my fear, I'd earned my red badges, I carved the hip or nailed the drop or crossed the bridge I watched everyone walk across.

On one of the last rides of the summer, Tim and I dropped five other riders and collectively had enough injuries to be medevaced to the nearest ER. We sat for a brief spell on benches built for walkers and rested for the ride back, which always seemed to be through sand and all uphill. I was exhausted, physically and mentally, dehydrated and lightheaded. Both legs were covered in mud and blood and I'd cracked my helmet by landing on my head an hour ago. A cut below my cheekbone told of an encounter with an errant vine. I felt a serious headache developing, I had run out of water, and my legs were rubber bands. We were miles from the truck and amid the heat, bugs, poison ivy, and wounds. I wanted to curl up in the bushes and go to sleep.

As I sat, head hung low, convinced that I couldn't make it, that I had pushed myself a little too hard, for the first time I realized that this was life. To stay where I was would be stagnation. There would be no search party; we were too far into it and on illegal land. No helicopter would take me home; there was no hidden resource drop over the next big hill. To dramatize the incident, I could stay still, give up and die, or push on regardless. Tim was silent and I knew he felt the same. This was life. At our lowest point we had two choices, stand up and grin with blood on our hands, taunt the gods and keep going, or lie down and wait. Lie down and wait for death, for aid to find us as I knew it wouldn't. At the times in my life when I have been there on my mental bench, I never found myself to be so defiant to my own pain and demons, but the change was immediate. I took a small swallow from Tim's bottle and got back on my bike. He followed suit and we trekked back, tired, weary, beaten down, but undefeated.

Tim broke his back on another ride a few weeks later and had to stop riding for two years. The team—what was left of it—donned jerseys and took over the streets, causing trouble and stopping traffic. We were threatened by more security officers and cops than I can count, but we rode hard, ferociously and with impunity, and I came home with a renewed sense of faith in myself each time.

That summer I broke five helmets, got whiplash, blew my knee up to the size of a grapefruit, and had a cadre of scars covering my shins. I tore fingernails off and bruised bones, ribs, and my skull. I loosened two teeth and removed a good portion of the skin from my arms. Tim, laid up and in constant pain, called me invincible because I took the hardest falls and got up laughing. I laughed because I knew that at the lowest point, when all had been drained, the will to survive, the will to keep going as fate rained hell on our heads would always be inside me. I'd found myself and confidence like I had never known before.

I still ride, but without Tim it's hard. No one can keep up, nor is willing to take the chances that I am. Bones heal, scars fade, and muscles mend. The same is true with life, with my heart, my soul, and my will to carry on regardless of the outcome.

Chris Fitzgerald has been an active participant in the underground literary culture since early high school. To date, he has been published in several journals, zines, and magazines, and he freelances copy work as time permits. The Memphis native is currently writing, painting, and drawing with the old-fashioned idea that one can make a living doing what one loves. At twenty-four, his bones are old, but he still goes hard more often than going home.

The Lady of the Ditch

Morgan Coleman

If truth be told, I should never have crossed Route 14, that indelible stretch of pavement that separated my New Mexican town from what my mother called the Big City.

It all started when I received my first *real* bike on my eighth birthday. This coincided with a newly invented rumor surrounding Sleeping Elephant, a deceptively distant mountain that hovered just beyond our backyard. If viewed at the right angle, it looked like a massive beast, patiently waiting for the circus to begin. Just beyond its ridge, my brother assured me, was the ocean, which I had never seen but could faintly comprehend. I imagined myself gliding down a wooden boardwalk and into the mouth of a wave. I could almost hear it, and when I closed my eyes I could almost taste it, the salty vapor in my mouth.

My mother tried every trick she could conjure to keep her son pedaling at home and away from cars. But in the summer of 1982 my legs grew sinewy and impatient. They were like well-taut cords, intimately connected to an insatiable curiosity. They beckoned me to the other side of the highway, where roads stretched on for miles, hundreds of miles, past the twenty-six fence posts, two barking dogs, and dilapidated rain cover that made up our driveway.

"Ever hear of *Ladia Arroyo*," she would ask. "The woman-ghost who snatches up children who walk at night along the ditches?"

I'd nod, having heard the tales in class and on public service announcements between Saturday-morning cartoons.

"Well, she's also out along the highway, roaming for kids on bikes, kids with fancy ten-speeds like yours. Stay away niño, you don't want to ride into her clutches!"

But on one particular day the temptation was too great. If I had known of the concept of inertia I would have used it as an explanation of why I just *had* to break the rules. When I reached the end of our road, there wasn't a car in sight. I looked both ways like a good boy and went for it.

Out of the saddle, I raced headlong into the wind, rocking the bike's large frame (the one I'd grow into) between my legs as I crested the first smooth rolling hill. As I descended the dotted lines on the road began streaming into each other. I could hear the hum of the tires getting louder and felt the velocity in my hands, through my shoulder blades and chest. I could feel a newly discovered speed surge throughout my entire frame like a welcoming bolt of electricity.

And as I turned to look behind me I could see my house, my gravel driveway—the entire valley—shrink and then slowly disappear. I felt like I was controlling a motion picture, and with each stroke of the pedal the movie reel became richer, more vibrant, and faster, faster, until finally, I was amassed in one exhilarating blur of color.

That was until I lost control, starting with my foot hitting the pavement, a move that shot the bike off into a ditch with a short, blunt tumble, carrying my body and my dream of seeing the ocean with it.

I landed face-up to stare at the sky. I could taste blood and sweat, and a gravelly sting on the palms of my hands where my soft flesh made its inaugural contact with the road. In a strange moment of clarity, while lying there in the thorns and gravel, my rational self told me that the boardwalk was not on the other side of the next hill and that the ocean existed only on the maps at school. Strangely, this realization just didn't matter. Shaky and bruised, I got back up, straightened the handlebars, and made the long ride back home.

My mother's lips were trembling in unison with her finger, the one aimed at me as I rode my scraped body back into the garage.

"Where have you been?" she cried. Her eyes were red and glossy and her short breaths hissed between her clenched jaw.

"Get in the house!"

That night my mother scrubbed every inch of skin that had grazed the pavement. She rubbed furiously, scrubbing my knees and cheeks, hoping that with enough force the antiseptic would cleanse not only the marks of gravel and thorns, but the very corner of my brain that led me out on the ride. All of it would drain into the bathroom sink. With tired and restless eyes she scrubbed for what seemed like hours.

I am now thirty years old and have seen the ocean. I live in a house where there are six stop signs, four traffic signals, and one yield sign that separate my front door from a roaring highway. I think of my daughter, her tiny limbs and the vanilla folds of her skin as I strap her six-month-old body into a car seat with its five harness points: each one promising to protect her. I cradle her frame in the crook of my arm and feel the reflexive kicks of her legs, pushing against me and everything that keeps her nestled and close. I look into her eyes and wonder where the bike will take her.

Riding home from work every day in the early evenings (sometimes even later) I am still enthralled by the moving tapestry, the flash of color whizzing by me as I ride behind the violet rays of the sun. This time I watch my road and house slowly appear and become larger, clearer, and more real with each stroke. Sometimes while out on one of those dark rides I think of *Ladia Arroyo;* she has my mother's trembling hands as she crouches behind the bushes, waiting to strike. Sometimes I wonder if she could jump out from beneath the brush and get me; but I dismiss the thought. My wiser self knows that she captured me long ago.

Morgan Coleman lives with his wife, daughter, and two cats on Bainbridge Island, Washington. Between bike rides on the island he commutes to work by ferry and spends way too much time at local bike shops.

Lazarus

Jessica Hutchison

"What is it?" I wonder as my father carefully lifts a dusty metal assemblage from the bed of the truck. He lifts with the back and not the knees, sacrificing body with a certain degree of reverence. Perhaps this time he has brought home some holy relic he found on the side of the road. You just never know with my father. I wouldn't be surprised if he met the pope somewhere and talked him into coming over for dinner, though my mother wouldn't forgive him because she's never convinced the house is clean.

"What do you mean what is it?" my father asks in an incredulous tone, his hurt pride clunking to the ground in all but audible tones. "I found it in Grandma's barn. It's your new bike."

I see nothing new in the teetering heap of badly weathered red paint. I eventually recognize two wheels but the rest remains a mystery. I remind him that I'm a kid, prone to accidents, and usually protected from dangerous sharp metal vehicles of death.

My father brushes a hand across the seat, displacing ancient civilizations of spiders. He's fluent in the language of exaggeration and ignores my comment. "Yeah, it needs a little work but this bike is the best, you'll see."

"Sure, Dad, thanks." I don't want to seem ungrateful. Besides, it's always better to trust my father the first time he makes a wild claim. Saves a lot of time.

He leaves me to pick over the bike and I begin to see handlebars at last.

The can of fluorescent yellow spray paint sticks to the shelf with many layers of hardware store grime. My father jokes that this is because the color is only used in times of emergency, like if someone had no lights and needed to create a nighttime runway strip. Or maybe you could paint the rim of an outdoor basketball goal to play at night. I laugh, but stick to my choice, wondering briefly if there would be any leftover paint, for our backyard was flat and it would be nice to have an emergency runway. At that age, I believed the world could be dominated at any moment by rival spies who lived in the woods surrounding my house.

I browse through the remaining colors and decide to add a bit of red along with touches of fluorescent orange. I'm quite pleased with the colors, though my father only shakes his head and tries not to laugh when the store clerk asks us where the caution sign is going.

A bit of soap and a lot of scrubbing reveals quite a nice-looking 1968 Western Flyer with a curved double top bar, whitewall tires and large chrome fenders. My father reminisces as we tape up the portions of the bike not to be spray-painted.

"You know, this was my first bike," he begins and I sit back and take a break. My father loves to tell stories of when he was young and prefers to have your full attention when doing so. Sometimes, I'm a good kid and indulge him.

"Yep, I was fourteen and working with my father and his brothers building houses. You got it easy, kid, believe me."

I roll my eyes as kids are supposed to do and wait for him to continue.

"Well, whenever we finished working on a house, there was always a lot of stones and trash left over in the yard. So, I got a few extra dollars for raking it all up. I saved the money and bought this bike for fifty dollars at the Western Auto down the road in Palmyra."

He stops for a minute and shows me how to sand down the old paint on the bike in preparation for the new color. His instructions are given in an expert voice though sometimes I doubt he really knows what he's talking about. This is because I'm ten.

"Back then all the kids had these really fancy bikes with a lot of chrome and big wheels and stuff. Looked more like motorbikes really."

I'm unimpressed but he continues anyway, lost in memory.

"I used to get on my bike every day and ride over to my grand-mother's farm. It was probably like fifteen, no eighteen miles away."

I speculate inwardly on the validity of this claim and wonder next if he's going to tell me he rode it barefoot in the snow uphill both ways.

"You get your middle name from her, you know. Your Italian grand-mother, I tell you, she was only about five feet tall but if you were mis-behaving, she could grab you by the ear and still finish making dinner with the other hand. I used to think she was the sweetest lady in the world until I saw her wringing the necks of chickens one day. Yeah, she was one tough lady."

I shake out my sandpaper and watch the old red dust cloud the air. The scent displaces thoughts of dangerous reconnaissance missions through the neighborhood. I realize I'm inheriting not only an old bike but years of family history. That's what that smell must be. Family heir-looms are strange things. They're not so important for the things them-selves, but to remind us of what once was.

We carefully dust the sanded red paint off the bike and apply the vibrant colors, starting with red, then orange, and finally yellow. My mother comes out to survey the work and offers up silent thanks that at least it will be visible a half mile away.

After the paint is dry and the tape removed, the bike looks almost new. A regular Lazarus, raised from the rusty depths of bike death, now stands gleaming in all its fluorescent brilliance. My father pulls out a pair of dark sunglasses for viewing the bike and waits for me to notice his joke. He's still quite a kid.

A new seat, tires, and greased chain make the bike fit for the road. I'm encouraged by my anxious father to try it out. Assuring him I can take it from here, I shoo his hand from holding the back of the seat.

"I know how to ride a bike, Dad, geez."

He relents reluctantly. I think one of the reasons people like having children is to watch them enjoy something they used to do as kids themselves.

Fairly impressed with its appearance, I steer the bike down the driveway. It rides smoothly, its large wheels making easy work of the gravel. In fact, it's so stable that I could ride it with no hands, a trick that quite impressed my neighborhood friends. Life was good.

As I grew up, I could never muster the audacity to replace my reliable Western Flyer. I don't think I could stand the look on my father's face if I ever bought a new one. I always excused the presence of other bikes in my garage as mere backups to be ridden on muddy days. He would believe this or pretend to. Replacing the bike completely would symbolize a rejection of the stories it represented, a rejection of my father. That's just the kind of people we are. A bike is not just a bike, but an autobiography of someone's life. As for my mother, she didn't care as long as I didn't ride it through the living room.

Jessica Hutchison recently graduated with a master's degree in agronomy from the University of Georgia. She now lives in Iowa where she manages to squeeze in bits of writing on disorganized pieces of paper as she and her true love grapple with the bittersweet adventures of owning an older home.

A Return to Freedom

Debora Dyess

I sat in the ophthalmologist's chair, stunned.

"You'll never lose all of your vision," the young doctor said quietly, kindly. He rose, retrieved a box a Kleenex, and put it between us as he returned to his chair. "And it won't happen all at once. You almost won't notice it at first."

I reached for a tissue but sat with it clutched in my hands instead of brushing away the tears that threatened to fall at any minute.

"Later on you'll be unable to read print. You won't be able to recognize friends or family at a distance. It'll be harder for you to do a lot of things you take for granted now. College will be tough because of note taking and studying. There are ways to deal with all of this, of course. You'll learn to deal with it as it comes up. I'm not sure how much longer you'll be able to drive . . ."

"I was going to minor in art," I whispered.

He shook his head. "I'm sorry."

It was too much to take in all in one day. But the good doctor was as accurate as he had been gentle. As the thing in my eyes progressed, some disease with a Latin name longer than my arm, my freedoms diminished.

By twenty-four I made the decision to give up driving. I hadn't had an accident yet, hadn't endangered anyone's life that I knew of, but I drove in fear of doing so. So I turned in my Toyota keys (and the self-reliance that went with them) for . . .

"Are you going to the store? I could sure use a ride . . ."

"Steve's working in the morning. Could the kids and I have a ride to church?"

"I'd love to come! But it's supposed to rain . . . would it be a problem to pick me up?"

Or sitting home, wishing I wasn't.

I hated asking. I knew they all hated being asked. And whether or not that was true I allowed it to put me into a sort of prison of my own making. I stayed home more and more, feeling trapped and claustrophobic. My beautiful new home began to feel small and dark.

We had moved to a small central Texas town when the idea of the bicycle was literally put before me. A friend invited me to go riding.

"That sounds so fun! But I don't have a bike," I explained.

She looked at me as if I'd confessed to being a bug-eyed little green man, but she simply nodded and said, "You can borrow Rick's."

I began to save for a bike the next day.

With four kids, and as a now single mom, the purchase took a while. I mounted the less-than-stylish inexpensive Next with a bit more nervousness than I anticipated and pedaled around the yard. My older kids were in school by then, but the toddler watched in wonder as his old mamma stretched her wobbledy wings first in the front yard and then in the street in front of the house. He laughed as I steered the bike back into the yard and dismounted beside him. I hugged him against me and laughed, too.

Glorious! Independence! Freedom!

I found a baby bike seat at a garage sale and began to explore the range of this new ability. I rode the children to school in the morning and then began to explore. I investigated the neighborhood. I tried my legs a bit more and found that the grocery store, only a mile away, was an easy target for my new independence. The library, our church, Wal-Mart, Hastings, downtown . . . nothing was out of reach in our town! My friend and I, baby seats on both our bikes, became a common sight around Brownwood. Our adventures were innocent and unexciting. But for me they were a release from the emotional darkness that had slowly become my real disability.

I began to realize that as a cyclist I see more every day, even with my imperfect eyes, than many people ever do.

The flirting/fighting flight of a pair of birds goes unnoticed by the driving public but my friend and I laugh about it as we ride to our volunteer jobs.

The pattern of shadow from a live oak tree spreads around me like a dainty crocheted doily on the dark asphalt but no one else notices it.

Clouds whisper across a hot spring sky, offering the blessing of shade to my bike-riding family as we pedal the five miles to the mall (and the closest movie theater) in a neighboring town. "Look at that one," one of my kids, who have all been riding most of their lives, calls. "It's a dinosaur-fish!"

On our family bike outings we comment on the clouds and the color of the sky. We breathe in the scents of the land and the bayou and the cattle we pass. We count how many birdsongs we hear. We notice how many colors there really are in trees, not just one or two greens but a dozen! We experience the most incredible sunsets! My kids notice how much better ice water tastes after a ride, and how much better they sleep. The time spent riding, whether biking to the store or the movies or a friend's for dinner, is talk time. We get to know each other better during those rides than at any other time.

And when the generosity of friends or the hostility of the weather prevents our bike time for a season we miss it.

I will never win the Tour de France. I'll never achieve great acclaim in the cycling world or gain some level of fame as an athlete. My contribution to the cycling world is of no consequence.

But cycling's contribution to my world? The return of freedom.

Deborah Dyess lives in Brownwood, Texas.

Lessons from the Great Divide

Susan Jett

First day out and I was hurting already. It had been more than five years since I'd gone on a bike tour, and I was starting to understand my parents' remembered complaints that the body starts to go to hell after you turn thirty. I was panting as I dragged my bike up that mountain, the first of too many to count according to the guidebooks; so instead I was counting breaths, counting pedal strokes, and finally counting my own fluttering pulse, trying to distract myself from the pain and the impulse to stop riding. We'd gotten on our bikes that morning in a meadow that waved hot yellow sunflowers overhead like a room of kindergartners given their first flags, but had soon moved into the deep forest—fir leaves so dark they were almost black, with green shadows behind the red-brown trunks of spruce and larch. Moose lived there, and around every turn this dirt road took, I expected to see a grizzly or a wolf standing in the road and challenging my right to ride there. Little Red Riding Hood would have looked right at home in this place. We had entered the land of myth, the land of stories from my child-hood, and yet we were only a few hours' bicycle ride from towns and highways and restaurants.

I was trying to see everything and still keep the bike moving uphill. It was just starting to rain and I couldn't decide whether it would stop soon, or if I should dig out my rain jacket. I was deliberating, panting again from the steepening slope (will this mountain never end?), dreaming about soup and my down sleeping bag, when I saw a flash of movement up ahead.

Bears aren't orange, I told my suddenly energized muscles; I was tingling all over with a sudden rush of adrenaline and knew I'd be aching the next day from this chemical buzz. *Maybe Dave is waiting for me?* I pushed on a bit harder, using the adrenaline rush since I knew I'd be paying for it later anyway. Instead of my husband, I saw a stranger, riding toward me, towing a B.O.B. trailer piled high with more gear than Dave and I had brought together. I let my bike come to a stop to say hello to this rider who must be—this June morning in northern Montana—completing the two-month route we were just beginning. He did not stop, nor even meet my eyes, but he managed a nod and continued on down the mountain. I wondered if I'd be so tired at the end of the trip. It was a sobering thought, and I finished the rest of the day's ride preoccupied by his evident weariness.

We planned to ride twenty-six hundred miles miles over rough roads and trails, carrying everything we needed to survive. Most of the route we'd be several days away from towns with the doctors, bike repair shops, and grocery stores we'd need if anything went wrong. We would be going through places I'd never been, and I had no idea what to expect. In the weeks before we left, I found myself poring over maps, trying to imagine where July and August would find me, and in what condition. After reading horror stories of bear attacks and rockslides, we had grimly restocked our first aid kit with everything from SAM splints to snakebite kits and smothered our more intangible worries. Why were we even trying to attempt so much, to exhaust our physical, financial, and emotional resources this way, to leave nothing in reserve for an emergency in order to chase a dream?

At camp that first night, after filtering water to cook with, Dave and I compared thoughts and perceptions from the day's ride. We each rode at our own pace, meeting throughout the day for snacks and meals and rest stops, but our riding days were solitary experiences that we shared each night over dinner. I mentioned the other rider we saw, and Dave shook his head, saying, "How sad that he came all this way and gave up on the first day."

"What?"

"This was his first day out too." Dave said. "I thought you knew. We spoke for a few minutes when I came on him just as he was making a U-Turn in the road. He said he was going to try to hitchhike back to Kalispell. What a thing to see him today, huh?"

I tried to understand that someone could come all this way to begin a ride that must have been months, if not years in the planning, and then abandon that ride on the first day. I was still thinking about it as we got into the tent. The rain had begun in earnest now, and we were listening to it rattle against our tent fly. There was a full moon and I was sure I'd be awake for hours, but instead, sleep came easily. I was exhausted, feeling every one of my years in every one of my abused muscles and tendons, but I remember thinking as I drifted off to sleep that I couldn't wait to get up and do it again tomorrow and the next day and the day after that. It felt good to be out there, good to be living away from cities for a couple of months, good to be on our own with just our bicycles and each other for company.

The next morning dawned bright and clear. The crest of the mountain was just a couple of miles past our camp, and the descent—as steep and long as the ascent had been the day before—was glorious and had us both laughing all the way down. We plummeted back down to earth like a couple of birds diving out of the sky. Cheeks bright red from the cold, flushed with excitement, we rode to our next camp atop a still-snow-shrouded mountain where a bald eagle circled our tent for almost ten minutes, diving low to investigate every time we looked up.

And so we rode. We rode through the sharply angled storybook forests of Montana into the rolling sheep country of Wyoming. Through ghost towns and big cities, sleeping in state parks and KOA

Kampgrounds. We learned to recognize plumy white bear grass, the cloying scent of roadside lupines, and the pelleted scat of big bull moose. Right around Steamboat Springs I finally stopped feeling as though I was asking something unreasonable of my body each time we approached a new mountain range.

We never saw a bear, but we did see lynx, pronghorn, badgers, foxes, coyotes, and eagles. Wyoming gave way to Colorado. There was less grass underfoot, and we even spotted the occasional cactus. Camp robber jays amused us in our high-altitude camps, and we rejoiced when we saw the first lizard skittering along the desert trail in New Mexico. And every day we rode farther south, I thought of that fellow, hauling his new-bought trailer, and wondered where he was, had he gone back home to a job? A wife? Was he regretting having given up his dream or was he rejoicing at having gotten over this bicycle foolishness? Days when the ride was difficult and I was cranky from it, when the weather didn't cooperate, when we were running too low on water, I thought of him and wondered about him, wondered why he'd given up before he had a chance to judge fairly, wondered if I'd have done the same if I were on this trip by myself and had a few bad days—or hours—in a row. Wondered if he hadn't yet learned that things would get better; they almost always do.

As we approached the end of the trip, we kept trying to answer the question that folks in towns asked us, "You know you could ride that whole way in a car in a single weekend, don't you?" I started trying to explain our trip in thoughtful terms, instead of the glib mouthings that came more easily. As I analyzed it, I realized that the glory of a long-distance bike trip isn't in the physical riding. It sounds impressive when you say it out loud, but a twenty-six-hundred-mile tour after all, is just a single day's worth of riding done many days in a row. Your body adjusts, gets strong, becomes dependable; the physical exertion is secondary to the mental exertion of doing something difficult for the *sake* of doing something difficult—and enjoying it.

No, I decided, the glory of a tour like this one is in the private feeling of accomplishment. In facing fears, in riding through them. It is true that pedaling a bicycle all those long, sometimes tedious miles where you might ride passively in a car is a "waste of time" and potentially more dangerous. But if I'd had that same two-month stretch of time to drive the route, would I have ever gotten out of my car to feel trout brushing against my shins as I waded in a cool stream? Would I have exulted in the feel of a late-summer rainstorm driving the desert heat from my skin and making me shiver in August? Would I have eaten huckleberries straight from the warm bear-pantry of berry-lined summer trails? Would I have learned to name all the things I was happy to do without, in order to pursue this dream?

I hope that rider found another dream and that he is pursuing it with all his heart. I returned from my own summer's dream fitter, browner, and quieter than I had been before. Whenever my life seems too crazy, too convoluted to mean anything or to ever settle into anything resembling a normal life, I think about that rider, retreating along the trail he had just ridden. He never gave himself the chance to look back on what the whole experience could have been—the good and the bad. His experience of the trail was based on a single day, and I can think of several single days on this trip that were awful, but I had two months of days to draw a bigger picture from, and the hard work, the discouragement, and the pain were balanced by moments of beauty and wonder. Crossing the border into Mexico was not the reason for our trip, nor even one of its high points; it was a letdown, a harsh ending to a beautiful dream, like an alarm clock sounding too early in the morning.

When we got home and unpacked our bikes from the shipping cartons, I was melancholy, missing the trail, missing the ever-changing scenery, the excitement. I went outside and looked around. If I were visiting here, riding through on a bike tour, what would strike me as wondrous and special? I got on my bike, headed down the driveway and toward the isolated mountain range that heads this valley, hundreds of miles from the Continental Divide. Lizards ran across the road, cottonwoods were just starting to turn golden down by the river, and Castleton Tower was ablaze in the early-morning sun.

It was all right that our great adventure was over; there were things to see right here that could be experienced from my bike. Things to ponder and wonder at, things to remind me how essentially unimportant are most of my problems. Today and every day now, I ride my bike, and I promise myself that I will notice everything, the good and the bad, and try to take it all into account, not just the occasional bad stretches. It's not about arriving at your destination or finishing your trip, or even accomplishing your goals, but rather, it's about experiencing the whole journey and remembering the reasons why you came.

Susan Jett lives and works in Moab, Utah, at Back of Beyond Bookstore, and is currently planning her next long-distance bike tour.

Saddlemasochism

K. Burroughs K.

I thought I'd have problems with my bicycle seat. After a trial run of forty miles, two bones that hadn't hurt since childbirth, the so-called "sit bones," needed a warm soaking and a dust of powder. So, just in case my butt really hurt, I started my five-hundred-mile tour well prepared. Stuffed in my front pack were creams, a little bottle of prescription painkillers, and odd-sized Band-Aids including really big ones for road rash and medium ones for lesser disasters. I had gauze and antiseptic creams. My best purchase, though, was a new kind of bandage that looked like a miniaturized, flattened version of a gel seat cover, translucent and squishy when touched. The palm-sized gel pad was to be applied directly to the wound and removal was supposed to be painless and easy, the manufacturer claimed, because no sticky adhesive tape had to be ripped off the skin. This product felt as if it would provide a cushy, padded barrier between the saddlesore and whatever rubbed or touched it. I was secretly hoping to try it out.

The first day wasn't too bad. My legs and shoulders ached more than my butt so I took two aspirins and performed a strange, but effective, self-administered massage. But the second day was horrible. The inside of both thighs had bruised and two quarter-sized blisters were forming where it hurt the most. My ten-year-old son laughed at my slow, careful descent to my sleeping bag from which I did not, and could not, arise until the next day. In the morning, I knew I was in trouble. The pain was already intense and localized. And there was four hundred

163

miles to go. I took a few prescription painkillers.

Riding wasn't bad that second day, but getting on the bike brought tears to my eyes. Hard riding actually dulled the pain, perhaps because the pain was so intense that it overwhelmed the nerve endings, creating a temporary break in the butt-brain nerve connection. Whatever the reason, the pain seemed tolerable when on the seat—intolerable off it. I dreaded stopping.

When we broke camp that evening, I headed straight for the outhouse with my stash of medicine and Band-Aids. Triple the adult dosage of painkillers hadn't dulled the pain. I peeled off my bike shorts while swatting away the flies and avoiding the huge spiders that lurked in corners and hung from ceiling joists. There was nowhere to sit except the dirty toilet seat. I sat and peered between my legs. Not being a contortionist, I found it difficult to see much of anything . . . the sun was low and there wasn't enough light. So I blindly cleaned my oozing wounds and applied the gel bandages to both sides. Then I walked bandy-legged to the tent and fell asleep, drugged and blissfully unconscious.

The next morning I knew I was in really, really big trouble. The pain radiated down my legs and up to my stomach. I felt nauseous and could barely walk. But being proud, I wasn't going to give up. I'd be damned if I caved in front of my know-it-all son or buff friend who had bragged about effortlessly riding up and down the California coastline. I chanted the mantra of the little engine that could—*I think I can, I think I can.* I prayed with all the faith I could muster. I practiced "mind control." In short, I denied myself the right to feel pain. It wasn't a bad strategy.

I rode all that day trying never to dismount. In the early afternoon it began to rain, first softly, then in torrents, so we guerrilla camped under a grove of trees on the edge of a farmer's field. I took my front pack and sarong and trudged about a tenth of a mile to another outhouse. Again, the light was dim so little could be seen. But it was clear that gel pads were not the panacea for saddle pain. Riding had ground the pads into my skin, merging them into one hard, gelatinous mass. I couldn't pee. My butt was essentially glued across the most private of areas. And I couldn't get the gel pads off. Little tugs were insanely painful. It was stuck to the skin and to tiny, invisible hairs.

This was a situation that called for a tool, some sort of razorlike device that could quickly slice the gel pad from my butt in one, deft movement. My all-purpose bike tool was no such gadget. Perhaps a tiny blade or scissors would have worked but didn't have either of them. I put my sarong on the dirty floor, lay on my back, raised my legs over my shoulders, knees to ears, and assessed the situation. It was obviously me, but unrecognizable. My butt didn't look female. Or even human. Not knowing what to do, I cried.

I obviously needed help, but from whom? I didn't dare ask my ten-year-old son—he was too young for a forced tutorial on female anatomy. It could turn him off to heterosexuality forever and I didn't want that on my conscience. And my male friend would probably enjoy it too much or use it as blackmail or fodder for future social humiliation. But I needed to get the damn bandages off. So I asked my friend for advice . . . not help.

He found a small pair of scissors. And, to make a long story short, after three hours of crying, cutting microscopic hairs, and tugging on what remained of my skin, my butt was finally freed. I couldn't sit, but at least I could pee. We read books and watched my son catch frogs for two days as I healed—my son recalls this as the best time of the tour. I bought a new saddle—my third—and finished the tour.

Strangely, I remember the natural beauty, the laughter and the technicalities of cycle touring far more than the pain. I don't want to sound bizarrely mystical, but there is something about cycling that transcends rationality, common sense, and maybe even the survival instinct. Had my car caused this much pain, I would have driven it off a cliff. When my tennis racquet blistered my palm, I stopped playing for a week.

When my ski boots made my calves ache, I bought new ones. Only my bicycle is given permission to wound me. Only cycling merits self-torture.

I couldn't wait to get back on "lil' red" and do it again.

A year later, I rode the same route with my eleven-year-old son and a fourth, and final, saddle. All five hundred miles of it.

No pain.

K. Burroughs K. lives in Arizona.

Bike-Speed

Susan Burgess-Lent

My "thing" with bikes started early with a cardinal red hand-me-down. For most of my childhood, I was a lone girl surrounded by five brothers. Their rough games, requiring physical endurance and coordination, mattered to me with a desperation only a child facing exclusion can muster. In 1950's suburban Detroit, tomboys like me needed a vehicle simple enough to be any complicated thing: a basic coaster-brake bike. I wasn't fussy about the looks.

Like the guys, I would clip a few Ace playing cards in the front fork where they'd racket against the spokes, and my Schwinn morphed into a Harley. This customization broadcast my arrivals and departures up and down the block, until I myself tired of the constant slappering.

On days when I was excluded from the pack, I tricked up the bike with Reynolds Wrap fins and antennae and flew solo—once to the moon on a mission: to check out the green cheese business. (Mystery later solved by real astronauts, my heroes in an era of now classic science fiction works.) My "rocket" returned me home safely in time for an earthly grilled Velveeta lunch.

In the heat of summer, I rode my lathered "stallion" against interlopers who threatened the sanctity of our scrap-plywood tree fort. My war whoops and the imagined huffing of my menacing metal steed duly routed them. My brothers pedaling hard behind me probably made an impression as well.

When it rained, I skiplaned through rain puddles, legs splayed to

167

catch the spray. In the not-yet-developed fields around my neighbor-hood, I whizzed along dirt paths, scything the tall weeds with my feet. If felt particularly feisty, I raced against anyone willing to designate a finish line. Mimicking the screech of a souped-up Chevy, I signed victories with a slash of skid marks on bright new pavement.

In those elementary school days, I could pedal for blocks with no hands, balancing fearlessly—as though the steel frame was an extension of my body. Sudden dismounts, however, earned me a gallery of new (and renewed) scrapes on my legs. My father duly washed and painted them with Mercurochrome. I wore my "reds" proudly, like merit badges from the Girl Scout troop I never joined.

From my older brother, I learned to thread loose chain back onto the sprockets, secretly reveling in my grease-smeared fingers. The bike was my daily "ride," but, like the guys, I seldom cleaned it of road dirt, much less shined the silver fenders. The bike existed as a necessary tool, giving me a freedom not possible for mere pedestrians. When the wind whipped my hair and cooled my sweaty face, I felt immune to gravity. In my mind, I was airborne. Surface made no difference to an obsessed all-terrain rider.

The ever-malleable tool of my childhood fell from grace around the sixth grade, when I discovered that my male classmates preferred something other than athletic challenges and skinned knees from a girl. I abandoned that Schwinn in the garage like an outgrown toy, with hardly a hair-swishing glance back. In the flush of new hormones, basketball and boys-not-my-brother caught my fancy. However, I never surrendered the T-shirt and cutoffs ensemble of my bike days. The riding obsession lurked quietly in my hindbrain, waiting for resurrection.

It came in a head-slapping epiphany after a nearly twenty-year hiatus. Cycling seemed the most body-friendly way to avoid a fat butt and wimpy muscle tone during my pregnancy. The new bicycle arrived as a birthday gift: a one-speed, coaster-brake Schwinn—this time, pink. I'd insisted on the "simple" model, but the color choice was due to a mistaken notion on my husband's part. In short order, I was readdicted.

My daughter's infancy unleashed a flood of new gear into the household, not the least of which was a child carrier for the bicycle. My girl rode before she walked. Cycling kept me sane through the isolated early years of mothering, those afternoons when lovechild wouldn't nap and I couldn't bear to play her *Sleeping Beauty* drama even one more time.

Frequently, the Schwinn provided my only means of local transport in our one-car family. Running errands required another accessory: a front basket. Mine was wicker, large, oval, and fastened to the handlebars with plastic cable ties. The addition of a bell and lights rendered my bike "fully loaded. " In cold weather, I wrapped scarves over my head and face, wore double layers of clothing. Rain gave me the option of a yellow slicker and/or umbrella. My need for comfort and protection always trumped any concern about appearance, which I suspect may have put some in mind of the classic bag lady with the bulging grocery cart.

My now fifteen-year-old has not been inclined to take up the habit. She tells me it's "cute" to see me riding. I've upgraded to a respectable eighteen-speed Trek, so I can only assume my flowing white hair motivates her observation. Perhaps I'm now an "old lady" on a bike. In truth, I no longer attempt riding "no-hands," nor do I race. I don't embellish the hardware in any way, or make odd noises that would inspire suspicious glances. But I still plow through puddles with my feet deployed. Some secret pleasures cannot be banished.

I ride for the feel of airflow and sunlight and muscles working. Gliding at five miles per hour, I'm at my leisure to check out what's developing in this 'burb. A long-ago vacation area of the nation's capital, this little neighborhood used to deliver up news along simple categories: who had a new child/dog/car, who'd moved in down the street, had problems with their kids, or was remodeling. Most of it's given way in a deluge of change. I see one old house replaced by three modern monsters nestled cheek-by-jowl, a whole woods clear-cut for a new parking garage, a sleepy intersection transformed into a strip mall. I know maybe six neighbors. The rest are passing strangers who, if hailed in a friendly way, usually refuse to respond. Motorists charge past, speed bumps be damned, too close and too fast for cycling comfort. I feel no match for the swell of steel and concrete. Now bike paths offer my only sanctuary.

My most harrowing bike incident, aside from close calls by inattentive motorists, happened at a Metro station. It was a rainy evening. I'd parked and locked the Trek in my usual spot; overnight it had become an unposted forbidden zone for cycles. A Metro cop promptly confronted me. I offered to move my bike to an approved location, stupidly certain that his surly demeanor was just a *Twilight Zone* aberration that would shimmer away. My refusal to produce ID, my eye-rolling take on the situation, evidently set him off. He wrestled me to the ground and hauled me across the station in handcuffs. After shuttling me to the precinct, then cuffing me to a table for twenty minutes, he handed me a fifty-dollar citation. The thrill of riding had acquired a major dent—with more to come.

I've had two bikes stolen: one from my back porch, one locked with a chain at a mall. Another was cannibalized, in my absence, for the rear wheel and seat. Each incident provoked an overwhelming sense of loss, as if some integral part of me had been violated. Repair or replacement superseded any other concern on those dark days.

In spite of the adult disillusionments, my bicycle continues to gift me with its childhood magic. It's given me legs as strong as pistons, and restored my tomboy physical confidence. It's taught me to move through life at bike-speed, a blessed pace for breathing deeply and observing without inhibition. While riding, I sometimes indulge my secret aspiration to be a torch singer, never caring who hears my Etta James wannabe rendition of "Body and Soul." When my legs are pumping and my hair fluttering in the breeze, I surrender to fantasies. The tree forts and the Moon have been replaced by Florentine cathedrals and Tuscan hills blanketed with olive groves.

I'm willing prisoner of this love of bike. I cannot imagine life without this simple, perfect contraption of metal and rubber and dreams.

Susan Burgess-Lent (www.burgesslent.com) is the author of In the Borderlands *(Xlibris, 2000), a novel set during the Rwandan genocide. She has written award-winning short stories and essays as well as numerous columns for* Videography *magazine. Her second novel,* The Slave Tour, *is due out in 2004. She lives near Washington, DC.*

Life Is Short but an Ugly Bike Is Forever

Julie Kangas

My bicycle is plain and old. No one will steal it, and it will not die. It's like a neglected wife . . . temperamental and unattractive but reliable and wickedly strong when she wants to be.

People who do not ride bicycles always take one look at her and tell me what a nice bike she is. For a long time I thought yes, this is a nice bike, and then I realized—*these people have no idea what the hell they're talking about.*

No one who works at a bike shop has ever told me what a nice bike she is. Her frame is bent, not all of her gears work, and she is extremely heavy. She has no brand name, no shiny paint, no sparkling chrome. She's a black eighteen-speed mountain bike my parents bought at Sears when I was in high school. She is dull and solid and built like a brick shithouse.

I have waited years for her to die and fall apart on me, yet somehow she keeps rolling along. Earlier this summer I got a new bike, a flashy green brand-name bike with comfort-grip shifting and shiny everything, and you know what happened? It got stolen.

It was actually embarrassing to have to take my old black beater back out of the garage. I had stripped her of the gel seat, the lights, the basket . . . all of those things disappeared with the stolen bike, and my old bike came back out of storage even uglier than before. It was terribly disheartening.

I got on her and started riding, however, and fell back in love again, that comfortable love of knowing a thing so well it is like a part of you.

I love being on my bike, and after my affair earlier this summer, I have developed a new respect for the comfortable old feel of this one—I know her inside and out, I know what angle to hop a curb at and what angle will send me flat on my ass. I know that she gives me a little extra speed down a hill because she weighs so damn much, but I'm overweight too, and I need the extra exercise when I'm laboring uphill. I know that she's tough as nails and will take the abuse that I heap upon her because she always has and always will. We haven't always gotten along well, but as it is, she is my bike, she is unique, and I love her.

Different folks at different bike repair shops in Wisconsin and Minnesota have told me that there's nothing I can do to fix the frame. One winter in storage she fell from the roof of my dad's barn and just hasn't been the same since. About seven years ago someone at a repair shop told me that it was dangerous to continue to ride my bike with a bent frame. I told my parents this. My dad said bullshit so I kept riding her. I'm still alive.

It's kind of like having a car with two hundred thousand miles on it. She might be in one piece, and might work just fine, but no one's whistling at her as she speeds by, and sometimes I leave the house and wonder if I'll ever get back. There is a special place in hell for folks who steal bicycles, and if anyone ever stole this one I know that I would cry . . . but still, I salivate when I think that I might have a valid excuse to go into the bike shop and take home something sexy and lightweight and expensive.

The memories attached to this bike are at times overwhelming. She took me seven miles into town every day for driver's education the summer I turned sixteen. I was on her the day my boyfriend left town for good and I couldn't stop crying and a bunch of boys pulled up behind me and grabbed my butt. I went to school in Madison, which is a great place to be if you don't like owning a car, and I lived there for six years. I didn't always use her, in fact, I rarely used her, but she was there, collecting dust and just waiting for the day when she would come into her own.

When I lost my driver's license a couple of years ago, I rode her three miles to work every morning and three miles back at night. She came into her own as a utility vehicle—a grocery getter, an errand runner, a solid and reliable thing that gave me the freedom I had lost when I got caught driving drunk.

That recklessness in me extends to the way I ride my bike. I am not the model cyclist. In general, I obey the rules of the road, riding on the right shoulder and signaling my turns, but I ride aggressively and I am not shy about taking a lane when I want to. I cuss and swear at folks who cut me off or tell me to get off the road, and let me tell you, animosity toward bicyclists is rampant where I live, even though the signs at the edge of town say that we're A BICYCLE-FRIENDLY COMMUNITY.

I really don't care anymore. I've gotten my license back. I'm sober and working on becoming a little more responsible. I don't own a car anymore by choice. I love going to the grocery store on my bicycle and getting just as many things as will fit in the basket. I love not having to pay for insurance, parking, and oil changes. I love being able to work on her myself—adjusting her brakes, changing her tires, lubing her chain. I don't pretend to be a bike mechanic; once in a while I take something apart and have to walk my bike to the repair shop to have a professional help me fix it.

When I am flying down the road on my bike, the wind filling up my lungs so I can't breathe and the street flying below me in a blur, I am sublimely happy. When I fly past cars stuck in traffic, I laugh. I am free and in the world—I feel the air, the rain, the wind, the dust, the sun, the dark, the smells and sounds and sights that people in cars do not and cannot see. Yes, occasionally I get wet or tired or sunburned or I get a bug up my nose. These things happen. They are part of being in the world.

Last summer I tried to dress my ugly bike up by making her an evangelist. I got a sticker that said LIFE IS SHORT—PRAY HARD and slapped it on the frame.

In a few weeks, having been rubbed to pieces by getting locked up against stop signs and trees, the sticker said only LIFE IS SHORT.

She's just a bicycle, I know, but I still think she finds that kind of funny.

Julie Kangas lives in Oakdale, Minnesota.

One if by Land, Two if by Sea, and Nine if You're Like Me . . .

Martin Criminale

"But son, why do you have so many bikes? You can't ride more than one at a time . . ."

And so it goes.

It all started when I was in college. Not having much luck with my schoolwork or with women, I started to notice that some guys I looked up to rode bikes. *Cool,* I thought, *so will I.* In college—and elementary school and grade school and high school for that matter—it's quite important to be part of the "in-crowd." Not having many options, I decided that bikes were going to be my "in."

So off I went on my first road bike. Vinyl saddle, super-narrow bar and short crank arm, toe clips scraping the pavement when I couldn't flip the pedals fast enough, top tube short enough to give me constant neck pain, high-tensile-steel-throughout road machine. But hey, even then certain stuff was cool. I had Suntour power-ratchet downtube shifters (smooth as silk baby, no auto-shift here) and a Winner six-speed freewheel. Nothing but the best. Any trained eye could tell that this bike was serious because I had removed the pie plate/spoke protector!

And I liked it . . .

Invariably, as people get into a sport, they start to get "in the know," and as more time went by, I realized that my bike was not so cool. An upgrade was required. Say hello to the Performance mail-order catalog!

I mean, how great was this. They had everything from (Italian looking) frames to components to some very American-looking clothes. It was a turnkey solution right there in my hands.

This time it was all about Columbus chromoly, Shimano Ultegra, and Cinelli. And that six-speed freewheel . . . ? Gone. *This* bike was all about ultra-seven, baby.

It's a slippery slope for sure. One day you are riding in jeans shorts and the next you can't go out because your matching jersey is still in the dirty clothes pile and needs washing; or because it's raining and you haven't given your "rain bike" the once-over yet since you hung it up last spring. And stuff starts to get nostalgic so you don't just "upgrade" your ride, you make an addition to the stable.

Soon you have separate shoes for each bike, perhaps even—dare I admit this—separate outfits. Here in my garage, it has deteriorated to this:

Race Bike—This is the full meal deal. All the stops have been pulled out here. It's the light frame with the light parts group, your own blend of your favorite custom, after-market stuff, trick wheels and a few odd Ti and carbon bits to top it off. Years ago these things weighed in at just under twenty-five pounds. Now you can't show your face in the group ride if it's more than eighteen. Of course I don't race anymore but that isn't going to stop *me* from spending more cash. Why just the other day I got the full carbon fork and handlebars. I'm pretty sure it's down to 17.5 now . . .

Rain Bike—That's right, you wouldn't want to sully your cherry, summer machine in the harsh elements; this bike is crucial in the Northwest. Mine has permanent fenders. And for most people, you end up logging more hours on this ride than your nice one. Too bad . . . But hey, it gives you the perfect excuse to throw money at another piece of equipment. I mean, if you're going to be on it for half the year, it might as well be something of substance, right? For instance, why suffer the inconsistency of caliper or cantilever brakes in the rain when you can get some really trick mechanical disk brakes? I can think of no reason . . .

Track Bike—It just happens. All of a sudden you are racing except there are no corners, just banking. These bikes are *supposed* to be simpler and cheaper but if you (like me) decide to get the full compliment of cogs and chainrings you quickly put the kibosh on *that* theory. Sure, you could get rid of it but what about the memories . . . So every once in a while you dust it off and tell some stories about how you were right in there bumping elbows with [drop your favorite name here] as the last lap bell rings. Ah, those were the days.

Mountain Bike—Man does not live by blacktop alone. And a good thing too. What fun, it's like hiking only much faster. And people talk of *epic* road rides; well try adding the possibility of a fifteen-mile hike while pushing your bike (in the rain, uphill, over a technical trail) and the definition of "epic" takes on new dimensions. But when it's right it's *so* right. As you Zen your way down a trail, taking the corners faster than ever before, you come alive! You can hardly contain your whoops of joy but you bite your tongue because you can't bear to break the beautiful silence. The only sound is the high-pitched hum of your cassette as you fly down the trail.

Town Bike—One of my favorites. This is something with platform pedals so you can actually ride the damn thing without changing your shoes. I use it to go to the movies in the summer or to run the occasional errand, like going out to have some pizza and beer. Mine is my old hardtail (after I discovered the unadulterated bliss that is full suspension) with riser bars and a Singleator. That's right, only one speed. I guess I needed to try to relive the BMX childhood that I never had. Plus, it makes it pretty hard to have anything go wrong with this bike. I say bring back the jeans shorts and the Vans shoes!

Single-Speed—Yeah, I know I already have one, but this bike is different. It's a fixed-gear road bike. So not only can't you shift gears, you can't coast either. Why? Some people will never understand. It's so basic, so pure, so simple, and it would be so light too if mine wasn't built with some old, salvaged steel frame. After a long summer of riding bikes with eighteen and twenty-four speeds, it's amazing how much of a mental relief this ride is. To not ever have to worry about what gear to select for the upcoming climb is such a load off. And for those that tend to not be able to ride easy, this is the perfect governor.

Touring Bike—Surely you can't go on a tour without the proper equipment you say . . . I can, I have, and the right bike makes such a difference. Longer chainstays, all the braze-ons, it just works. Your feet don't scrape the panniers, the bike inspires confidence on descents, and you have room for fat tires *and* fenders. I just want what I want when I want it, is that so bad?

Tandem—Okay, in my case it's *two* tandems. One is a fast road tandem and the other is one I ride with my eight-year-old son. Surely you can't expect one tandem to perform such divergent duties? No way, I *need* both. And in my experience, there is nothing quite so effective at keeping a couple together on a ride as a tandem. This can be a huge bonus. Think about all the times you have fallen off the back like a blind roofer or the times you have been fully juiced up and unable to hold back your superhuman strength and annihilated the bunch—now imagine adding twenty pounds to your bicycle frame and sticking another rider of similar weight to you on it as well. Isn't that better? Truly, a tandem can be a phenomenal thing to ride. Once you get coordinated with your riding partner you can get these things positively humming along. And still carry on a conversation. How cool is that.

There you have it. I have just enough bikes to do everything that I like, on a bicycle that is. And isn't that what this is all about? When I grab my messenger bag, throw a leg over my town bike, and hit the park for an ice cream and a read, nothing could be finer. When I crest the summit of some fabulous mountain pass on my race bike, and feel the utter joy of accomplishment, my spirit positively soars. I love them, all. *That's* why I have them.

I gotta stop typing now, I hear there is a sale on Vans and I need a new pair . . .

Martin Criminale, born 1964, is currently living in one of the greatest cycling cities in the United States—Seattle.

He says: "I didn't really start cycling until I was in college. Up until then my riding consisted of going off of plywood ramps with my friends on our single-speed kid's bikes. So in college, I got my first 'racing' bike because what I had up to that point just wouldn't do. Then I started racing cyclo-cross so I had to get a cross bike. Then I started racing in the dirt so I had to get a mountain bike. Then I started racing on the track so I had to get a track bike. Then it was time to see the world so I needed a touring bike.

"Then I had a son and stopped racing. Of course this meant I had an early midlife crisis so I had to get a BMX bike to relive my childhood. And then I had to get retro so I got a fixed-gear bike. And then my son got older so I had to get a tandem so that we could ride together.

"Now I'm thinking of doing a little racing again. Man, would you look at all those shiny, new racing bikes out there? I might have to get another one . . ."

Bicycle Bliss

Shaunna Privratsky

M y dad smiled down at me and said, "Shaunna, Mr. Jorgenson has a mountain bike he wants to sell. I was going to give it to you for your birthday tomorrow. What do you think?"

I drew in a breath of pure amazement. I nodded yes so hard my long blond hair bounced. Mr. Jorgenson unloaded the most wonderful bike in the world. It had extra-wide tires, shining gears and levers, and bright red handles. I'd never dreamed I'd own a bike like that.

Dad handed him a check already written out.

"Thank you. I have something for your daughter, if it's okay with you," Mr. Jorgenson said and pulled out a new leather wallet. He looked at my dad with raised eyebrows. Dad nodded.

I danced from foot to foot. Mr. Jorgenson dropped to his knee and held out a twenty-dollar bill. A huge smile lit up his heavily freckled face. I took the bill, awed and a bit frightened. It was more money than I'd ever owned at one time.

As Mr. Jorgenson turned to go he said, "I remember when I was nine all I wanted in the world was a bike and some money of my own. Happy birthday, Shaunna."

I thanked him from the bottom of my heart. That bike opened the door to freedom. I spent the next four summers riding it up and down the narrow two-lane road that snaked through the thick forest. Huge eighteen-wheel logging trucks thundered up and down the road twenty-four hours a day, a constant threat. I was always careful to keep one ear tuned for their approach so I could pull my bike well into the ditch. I didn't want to become one of the "unfortunate statistics" that never seemed to slow down the speeding trucks.

My sturdy bike carried me up and up as far as my legs could go, then I turned and started down the mountain. I can't describe the incredible lightness of being and the joy that filled my body as I sped dangerously fast, my tires singing on the black pavement, my hair streaming back in the cool wind of my own making. I held tightly to the brilliant red handles, feeling as if I was flying, tethered to the earth only by my strong grip. My dad always said I went too fast, one pothole or pebble in my path and I would've crashed spectacularly, seriously hurting myself. I knew this at the time but I couldn't stop myself. The feeling was too breathtaking.

That bike was my friend, my companion that I trusted completely to deliver me safely back home after one of our wild rides. I knew every inch of my bike, the exact place to sit most comfortably, the amount of pressure to apply on the brakes, the balance point to ride without hands.

I sometimes revisit those days in my dreams. The feelings come back, fresh and exhilarating as if I was back on the seat of my splendid bike.

We moved all the way across the state of Montana when I was four-teen. My bike made the trip as well, but somehow it wasn't the same. The gravel road in front of our house was difficult to maneuver and the heavy traffic made it quite dangerous. I rarely rode my bike since it was so much easier to catch a ride from my parents or a friend. My life became busier with friends, school, and eventually work. I had less and less time to ride. My fantastic bike found a place in our storage shed and began gathering dust.

When I moved away to attend college, I cleaned out the shed and got rid of a bunch of old stuff. I came across my bike, still faithfully waiting for me to ride it again. I smiled at the many happy memories I'd created on my bike, and then common sense reared its practical head. I ended up selling my bike for ten dollars to a young girl down the street. Her shining eyes and breathless thanks lightened my heart. I'm sure she enjoyed that bike as much as I did.

Today I own a sensible, regular ten-speed. I take my children, Alex (age six) and Erica (age nine), on the bike path near our home. We always have a great time, going up and down the gentle hills and curves.

I still love bike riding, but somehow the adventurous thrill that used to grip me is missing. Maybe it was the true danger of flying down that steep mountainside that got my heart pumping so fast, or maybe the fear of encountering a huge log truck on the narrow twists and turns.

I like to think my old bike is still racing up and down roads, making a young girl happy. I can always revisit those days of bicycle bliss, in my dreams.

Shaunna Privratsky authored the award-winning The Silk Robe *and* Bypass Blunders, Improve your Prose *along with over one hundred articles and stories. She lives in North Dakota with Wade and their children, Erica and Alex. Join the free Writer Within Newsletter at http://shaunna67.tripod.com.*

War Bike

Ben Grubb

Tales tell that Knights of the Round Table could sometimes call a great steed to help them on quests, a War Horse of strength and noble bearing.

Well, my red Giant mountain bike's not noble—in fact, it's a street fighter—but a War Bike it is. It's gone on journeys in the Sierras and withstood the cold of the Appalachians. It's raced along midnight streets to the sound of nothing but its own wind.

But no, the Giant's no spoiled princess but a grizzled veteran, spattered from sweating and battling and flashing its red grin. Though it has proved its mettle on track and trail, the War Bike truly shone on one muddy day years ago that involved no travel at all. The story will make lovers of cycles and cycling cringe, but that occasion is why I clean the damn thing so often, and why my calf still bears the scar of being punctured by a spoke. Here's what happened:

Oberlin College in Ohio hosts a bike derby. Intermittently banned and tolerated by the college, this orgy of destruction takes place in the mud of spring. Ohio in March turns from being merely cold to cold and mushy, a vast, chill swamp. On the chosen day of this season, the derby organizers build the arena.

Twenty yards in diameter, marked with a blue-chalked string, the arena sits between two dormitories: the posh, turreted Talcott Hall, and the patchouli-fogged, organically crunchy Harkness. Spectators lean from windows of both buildings, and hundreds more ring the arena

187

itself, their pants dirty to the knees before the bikes even appear.

Enter the derby combatants. *Contestants* cannot describe these armored riders. All wear kneepads and boots, plus head protection of some kind. Some sport goggles, others spiked elbow pads. Many bear weapons—wooden cudgels, coat hangers bent into long hooks, rope whips. Ostensibly these are to be used only against opponents' bikes. Most riders know better. Everyone carries some variant on these armaments.

All this, of course, does not apply to Maddog. Maddog, biochemistry major, materializes hefting his signature implement, an agricultural scythe. I am pleased to note the organizers have ordered the scythe's blade wrapped in foam. Maddog's curly bronzed hair stands up in all directions, and he wears nothing but crimson swim trunks. Apollo might look like this, riding down to quash some mortals. Beneath Maddog rolls Ironsides, an amalgam of salvaged bike parts with tires wider than my thigh. This experienced derbyist has fitted his bike with an obscenely small chainring and grotesquely large freewheel cog, giving him a tiny bottom gear. Nothing stops Maddog.

It is thirty-eight degrees. At the sight of Ironsides and its rider, many combatants, including me, begin to sweat.

Maddog takes his place in the ring of riders. One of the organizers, an asthmatic named Shelly, calls out the rules:

"The Bike Derby is an all-out contest. She or he with the last functional, mobile bike will be the winner. Upon each mobility-kill, the rider of the deceased bicycle will exit to the side with all possible speed. If needed, the medics will give assistance [two bio kids with boxes of triangle bandages, Neosporin, and an Automated Electronic Defibrillator wave cheerfully]. NO *ad hominem* attacks, though vehicles are fair targets. NO retaliatory strikes by dismounted contestants. Exiting the arena, i.e. crossing the blue line, merits disqualification. So does enlistment of outside help. [Shelly glares around at the slavering fans.] Are the rules clear? Any questions?"

There are none. Shelly steps to the side. She removes a whistle from her trousers pocket.

"On your mark!"

Heckling actually ceases among the spectators. Through the quiet, we hear a couple of first-timers click their shoes into pedal locks.

"Get set!"

Silence piles up like frosting on a cake. Georgette, my lab partner from physics, pulls a kid's baseball bat from her backpack. Next to her Roisman pulls down his ski mask, but you can still see the shaking in his hands over the brakes. A couple of others bounce their front tires in the mud. Maddog sits totally still, eyes half closed. Every spectator leans onto her toes, not breathing.

The whistle blows.

Have you seen the movie *Henry V* by Kenneth Branagh? In it, there is a horse charge that is never shown directly. Instead, you see the soldiers' faces and guess what is happening from their reactions. Imagine my face in a like situation and its expressions: my look of wonder at three dozen bikes charging to control the center; flinching as Roisman's tire pops in the collision and he goes down; wincing to see Maddog ride over the fallen rider to hack at a sophomore's derailleur with his scythe, which immediately loses its padding; sadness to witness two women, roommates, ride about the arena's edge, bashing in each other's fenders with clubs and hurling cuss words; finally, my ferocity when the first attack comes, a bearded Jesus-type looking to ram my rear wheel.

I plant my front wheel and pivot the back out of his way. The hippie flies from the arena and out of the contest, a casualty of inertia. My feet on the ground, I swing around to face a trio of soccer players who are maneuvering as a team. Dimly thinking, *this is unfair,* I speed right at them. Hitting nothing, I stop short of the blue line, only to see two of the soccer players have fallen anyway. One of them loses momentum and tips trying to pull his foot from the pedal clip. Ironsides gets the other, grinding right up and over the front tire.

In fact, Maddog has demolished most of the field, stomping, slicing tires, and kicking in spokes with steel-toed boots. As I watch he rides Georgette right out of the arena, finishing her off with a shoulder shove. Her face lands outside the blue string, and she is done.

That leaves only the remaining soccer player (Chris something), the Dog, and me. We pedal slowly about, eyeing the others' conditions. Chris's right ear leaks blood. Dog and I watch him. The instant his hand leaves the handlebars to wipe the cut, we're upon him. I slam into his back wheel. Maddog reaches in with the scythe to try to cut the gear cords. He succeeds a little too well, incidentally nudging Chris off the saddle.

Even before he hits the mud, Chris shrieks foul play. Leaping up, he lurches for Maddog, who has removed himself to the far side of the arena. Shelly and two heavies run out to stop the fallen rider, but Chris's fellow soccer players join him in the assault. Soon ten or fifteen people are shoving and slipping in the center of the circle. I sit and rest. Maddog actually puts out the kickstand and eats a carrot he had taped to his handlebars.

Sooner or later the brawlers remove themselves and their muck from the arena. I square off my Giant opposite Ironsides. To this time, my red War Bike has seemed solid. Brakes are soft from the wet and the front wheel wobbles a bit from hitting Chris, but everything works. Ironsides appears unperturbed from my vantage point. All, Maddog and I, spectators and organizers, seem at rest, relaxed, waiting.

Maddog lunges.

The upshot of Ironsides' customized chainring and freewheel, of course, is a 20.8-inch low gear diameter. This means that, while it takes Maddog about thirty-four pedal rotations to reach me, his feet move faster. He accelerates sooner and faster than I, and his inertia is much greater than mine upon impact. Which means, "Whether Ironsides hits the Giant, or the Giant hits Ironsides, it's going to be bad for the Giant."

Luckily, Maddog does not simply ram me. He flicks to one side. I attempt to swerve, but his boot staves in three spokes of my rear wheel. One of them spears my left calf, which I flung out to keep from falling. It hurts, but I do not stop to pull out the metal, instead wheeling on the departing Ironsides. Riding up behind it, I pull a stunt I've never before tried.

I pop a wheelie. Maddog flings himself forward to avoid my wild tire but fails to clear his bars. All his weight falls on the front tire, which blows out. The Giant crashes down, my metal hub screeching against the side of Ironsides' seat tube. I almost fall, especially when my left leg lands. Grimacing, I walk the weakly rolling Giant free of my opponent's mangled remains. Blood seeps into my sock, every breath a knife cut.

Then I grasp the situation. I yell for a long time, then turn a slow, rackety victory lap, showing off the Giant to one and all.

That was the Giant's finest hour. Later, in the evening after the derby, the organizers piled all the wrecked bikes in a heap and set them ablaze, a kind of funeral pyre. I reached into the bonfire and retrieved the handlebars from Ironsides. They hang now on the north wall of the kitchen, my one and only hunting trophy. Every once and a while, I'll see those bars, then wander over to the Giant and just spin its tires a while, thanking god for my War Bike.

Ben Grubb is a carpenter in Berkeley, California, where he lives with two impossibly funny sisters and a touring bike named Boxer.

Ma Kettle Biker

Peggy Newland Goetz

"When I rode across the country on my three-speed Schwinn, I wore a bathing suit," Mom says looming over me, her face full throttle as she tells me about her 1956 bicycle trip. I know this story, I've heard this story, I'm about to hear it again. I have no choice.

"I know, Mom," I say.

"We didn't have fancy suits like you wear today." She points at my polypropylene, my padded shorts, then bangs on my helmet.

"I know you went bare." Meaning just hair, no hat, no protective device.

"Just when I went skinny-dipping with the cowboys." This is my mother, the wild Ma Kettle of bicycling, when girls and especially nice virginal girls like my mother of the fifties didn't do these sorts of things. Decide to ride a three-speed Schwinn bicycle across the country because she wanted to see surfers. Break up with the fiancé, Charley the Chest—a man who wanted to pave highways. Quit job as a school teacher. Pack one duffel bag with a buttondown blouse, some Bermuda shorts, saddle shoes, bathing suit, sleeping bag, cocktail dress, pearls, red lipstick, and Bible. Convince a Girl Scouting friend to come along for the ride. Train for the trip by riding around the blocks of her Brooklyn, New York, neighborhood exactly two times. Get on a bike and just ride. She was the "just do it" girl before all the advertising.

"You little hussy," I say. I wonder what skinny dipping with cowboys means when you're a fifties girl bound for California. Do you use the cocktail dress as your shield to the water or just wait for a cloud to pass across the sky?

"I hope you'll find adventure." And she means this. She always means this, because adventure is her middle name. Going on adventures, making up adventures, those were the bylines of my childhood and everything about growing up meant hearing about her bike trip. How it felt to ride so early in the morning, that the road was still wet with dew, hearing the sun set and watching the embers glow after a campfire in some city park. "Where's your tent?" she asks.

"I'm staying in motels. I've told you that." I've told her everything about my trip. About this cross-country bicycling adventure I'm taking because of her. In spite of her.

"I camped," she says as the streets of New York City fill up with businessmen with cell phones, women in tall, clicking heels, children in uniforms holding nannies' hands.

"I know."

"In farmers' yards, in city parks."

"I know." I push my bike along the sidewalks, stopping at all the crosswalks, waiting for the flashing GO signs to illuminate, my mother's hand on my handlebars causing me to wobble off center, almost crashing into pissed-looking people on their ways to jobs, meetings, affairs, schools, subways, home. Everyone going places, faces down, quick feet, as we trudge/trip down the street, my mother and I, with my silver 24-speed Schwinn. "I'm not as adventuresome as you."

"Sure you are. You're going, aren't you?"

I am going. For reasons I don't even understand. To discover my mother in a different light? To get to know myself? To make her proud? To make her see me? To finish something for the first time instead of haphazardly or not at all? "Well, I'm packed."

"Overpacked."

I have to bring my laptop, my cell phone, my Palm Pilot. I have to keep my job. My mother just quit, told the school where she worked at to go to hell and left. But I'm a wimp, fearful of losing the paychecks to pay for my new car, my racing skis, all these toys I've accumulated but rarely have time to use. Because I work. And work. And never take time off. Until now. With this trip of my mother's. I have neoprene, polypropelene, spandex, elastane, CamelBak, words my mother can't even pronounce. I'm not washing my face in streams or eating steaks cooked on fires or spreading a bedroll in a city park. I'll be in Motel 6s with my Neutragena and Burt's Bees, my astringent packed in tiny plastic bottles. "I need all of this," I say.

She just shakes her head.

We get to the start of my trip. Rockefeller Center of all places but this is where she started so this is where I will be. At the start of Mother. In the crowds, with the stares, as my mother tells strangers what I'm doing.

"She's riding her bike across the country," she tells the Sabrett hot dog man. He shrugs.

"Big deal," he says.

"I did it in 1956," Mom continues.

"Now that's impressive. You get famous?" He gives her a free hot dog.

They talk as I check my tires, check the brakes, the mirror, adjust the Camelbak nozzle, put on ChapStick.

"She's just like her mother," she says to the hot dog man next as she walks away from him, back to me. This is a lie but a lie I'll keep.

She pushes my back tire and blows on my back right before I start. For good luck, I know. "You be careful," she says, her usual soft voice has a threatening edge. She can't be there to pick up my pieces like she has all of her life, the disastrous love affairs, credit card bills. I've depended on her all my life and now I'm taking her story and she's depending on me to make it my own. Without her.

"Good-bye," I say.

"Don't say that," she says shaking her head.

I take off through traffic and turn once, my saddlebags tipping me left then right, and see her. This lone figure waving in her Hawaiian muumuu, her hair flattened down by city breeze. But I can't stay backward long because what's in front—garbage trucks, taxis, a messenger biker in black with goggles—demands more.

To take a trip is to release something. Let it go. But at the same time it is a taking on of something else. Something outside yourself that may or may not be filled with parts of life you still carry, still push deep. For the first few days, I kept her there. I read her journal from 1956, with her many descriptions of rolling hills and beautiful vistas and friendly people giving her canteens of water and barns to sleep in, a kind of Nancy Drew happiness to her words, with each day full of surprises! Full of joy! All with exclamations! Her trip was a trip, in her head, to herself and she couldn't believe it—that she was actually riding the bike. The bike was her ticket to someplace outside her life. As I read and kept my pace, I called her each night. I sent postcards.

But sooner than expected, I wanted the ride to be closer to my own and less of a history between mother and daughter. I'm seeing through my eyes the roads she'd pedaled but what I pass through is in a prism completely different. There are the fields of corn she slept in but I now ride past in the dim light of early morning. There are the ponds she swam and drank from but I now ignore because is the water safe, are there microbes, where's my Poland Spring water? There are the strangers who no longer wave at, give keys to, bicycle riders passing through. But at the same time, there are the sunsets, the taste of cold water in my mouth, the hill done, the hill coming, the howling winds, the broken asphalt, barking dogs, welcome meals, and welcome beds. Just like my mother's. There is the time up when my legs are just screaming and the time down when my legs are humming. Just like my mother's. There are the friendly strangers with open houses once I tell the story of my mother and there are the songs I remember, the Girl Scouting ones she sang, the hiking and boating ones she taught. There are the cowboys. There are the mountains and there is the sun and everything most days is beautiful for at least one minute or more. Just like my mother's.

I take it all in and take it all on, this trip being colored and made into something my own, but not quite my own. "Her"story overlapping with my story so that a mother gives back to a daughter going on. A true beginning.

"You're almost done," Mom tells me the last night of my trip on the phone. "You'll see the Pacific tomorrow. I'll be waiting for you."

"I don't want it to end."

"But it won't. It's just beginning."

The stories, she means. What you take from a trip and keep as you release the actual road. I remember her stories but I'm also collecting my own to tell her. I'm thinking, remember the time when I hit that storm in the Rockies and they closed Independence Pass right after, eight inches of snow on the ground? Remember the cattle drive in Utah? The Winnebagos with the video cameras? The thrown beer bottle at your leg? Remember the rain in Nebraska, the dead towns in Nevada? How your biking shoes filled with sweat in the Poconos? My voice, an echo keeping track of the what I saw, how I felt, where I was, why it was, when it happened like a mantra. This calming place now rather than the static one where the focus was off, the picture so unclear. Of me, of my mother. Of us and what it meant to ride.

When I get there, with the Pacific flowing over our bare feet, Mom holds my bike as she has held me all of my life. One hand on the handlebars and one hand on the seat, steadying yet pointing me away. To this. Our two faces, this one bike, facing west, to the sunset, the bicycle our diving board.

"What was the best part?" Mom asks as we lift plastic Holiday Inn cups filled with wine.

There is no other answer. "This."

And a wave crashes against both tires, sending us off balance again.

Peggy Newland Goetz has just completed a novel. She writes from New Hampshire and rides her bike every day.

Kneeling at the Altar of Schwinn, 1966

Samuel R. Irwin

Free. Absolutely free. There are a few moments in life when one feels completely free. For me, the driver's license, high school graduation and my first apartment were not true freedom, but responsibility in disguise. My only true and lasting freedom was discovered at age five when I learned to ride a bicycle.

Early on, when I started grade school, Momma felt safe enough to allow me, a towheaded little boy in khaki uniform, complete with black tie and Perry Como cardigan, to walk the few blocks to school. As the year progressed, Daddy and sisters taught me how to ride a bike. The Murray fat-tire I learned on was a girl's model; I could not sit on the seat and touch the pedals at the same time, but ride it I did. Momma let me wheel down the street and soon I was the only first grader riding a bike to school at St. Joseph's in New Orleans.

It was complete freedom—smoothness, rolling wheels, speed, the sound of the wind in my ears, wind I had created. I felt godlike.

After Daddy retired from twenty-three years in the navy, my parents were ready to return home. We rooted in Breaux Bridge, a small town right in the middle of French-speaking Acadiana where I continued to pedal myself to Catholic school and home again.

Breaux Bridge is the kind of small town in which every bike-riding kid should live. It was just the right bike size. Honing my cycling skills by learning to negotiate the curbed sidewalks and the metal grating on the Bayou Teche drawbridge, I soon learned everything in town was within riding distance. I could ride my bike to the store. I could ride my bike to school and church. I could ride my bike with my chums to baseball practice, to the bakery, the Tastee-Freez, Tiger Inn, Western Auto, the public swimming pool, football games, the Jeff Theater, and Johnny Hebert's Sno-Cone Stand. We did not even have to lock our bikes. Freedom.

When I turned nine Daddy bought me a twenty-four-inch Schwinn to replace my sister's hand-me-down. I loved that bike so much that one time, when I had lost my brand-new football, Daddy locked up my bike for two weeks as punishment. I was grounded . . . my wings clipped. Seeing my bike jailed up was worse than a belt spanking. I rode that bike for two years until a new love turned my head.

When I saw the first Schwinn Sting Rays, I had to have one. Sting Ray—the very name created a yearning so deep, so powerful . . . I knew this was more than puppy love. This was the real thing. I did not feel right asking my folks for a new bike when I had a perfectly good, if boring one under the carport. If I were to get a new Sting Ray, I would have to earn it, so I asked my grandfather for a job in his grocery store.

Poppa owned a country store in Henderson, a tiny, hole-in-the-wall fishing community nestled against the western levee of the Atchafalaya Spillway in St. Martin Parish. Amy's Grocery, with two Citgo gas pumps and a coal oil hand pump in the front, was located on the clamshell shoulder of Route 352. The gas pumps were the kind with the little balls in the bubble you could see moving as the gas flowed. It had everything: penny candy, *pop rouge,* rope, plumbing fixtures, fishing tackle, nails, shoes, rubber boots, belts, canned goods, corn feed . . . all the basics. Near the back of the store, shoppers were greeted with the smell of boiling crawfish from my grandfather's seafood market.

I spent eight weeks of the summer of '66 working in that un-air-conditioned country store stocking dusty shelves for the princely sum of one dollar a day. Mind you, as a sixth grader who was small for his age, I weighed only about seventy-five pounds. The bales of sugar, rice and flour I hefted were 60 pounds a piece. I struggled.

My Aunt Hazel, or *'Tit-soeur*, (pronounced *teet-suh* and means "Lil' Sister" in French) as we called her, wasn't much bigger than me. And she didn't feel like lifting those heavy bales either. Smart *'Tit-soeur* had a way of making me feel big and strong and guilty all at the same time.

"Sam, bring your strong muscles over here. It's just me, by myself, and I can't do dat, no," she said in her Cajun accent.

So I'd go to help *'Tit-soeur* lift the bale and invariably end up lifting it all by myself, not minding the effort because there was a Sting Ray at the bottom of those heavy loads.

There were several fringe benefits to working in Poppa's store as all the ice cream, candy, and pop was mine for the taking. Ma-maw fed me a delicious dinner (we call lunch *dinner* in South Louisiana) every day and we always had catfish *courtbouillion* (pronounced *coo-be-yahn*, a Cajun smothered tomato-based stew with big chunks of catfish served over white rice) or crawfish stew on Fridays. She seasoned her Cajun dishes so much that my lips burned when I washed it down with a six-ounce Coke in the little, glass returnable bottle.

Finally, after two months, I had saved forty-eight dollars. I knew I was close to having enough and I got Momma to take me to Johnson's Bicycle Shop in Lafayette. There were rows and rows of Sting Rays, so bright and shiny, so beautiful . . . so sacred. I knelt down in prayerful thanks; hooded monks with bike chains wrapped around their robes instead of crude rope belts appeared, lifted me up, and placed me on a golden Sting Ray.

"Sam, Sam?" Momma said, shaking me. The monks had disappeared, but in front of me was the golden Sting Ray with a matching metallic banana seat. I ran my hands over the high-rise handlebars, put my foot on the rattrap pedal, raised my leg over the seat, and rode it the few feet to the door.

Trying to sound casual, I said, "I like it."

"Samuel, are you sure it's the right size? It looks a little high."

It really was, but I knew I would say anything to get that bike. I was prepared to create any mendacity to claim this treasure, but no words formed in my mouth. Mr. Johnson saved me. "Oh, we can just adjust the seat a little, and it'll be perfect. He'll have room to grow. What are you, eight?"

"Twelve," I said defensively, but I shook it off. Here was the Holy Grail of bicycles under my butt and I was not going to be prevented from riding it for being sassy to the Schwinn salesman.

I was short fifteen dollars, more than two weeks' wages. The thought of spending valuable summer bike-riding time earning more money in that hot, dusty country store, free ice cream or not, was unbearable. Momma loaned me the extra fifteen as I made one of many solemn promises to pay her back. Returning home to the streets of Breaux Bridge, I rode my bike tirelessly, Gump-like, to the ends of the earth and back, my debt forgotten, my guilt absolved.

I loved that golden Sting Ray.

At age forty-seven, I have six bikes hanging in my garage: two mountain bikes, two road bikes, and a commuter (a converted Schwinn Varsity). Still hanging there is the twenty-dollar pink bike I bought secondhand for my daughter when she was six. When I notice it hanging there in the corner, I cannot help but be reminded of the cavalier days of my boyhood and a melancholy longing for my Sting Ray fills my soul. Riding my mountain bike on trails through the lush, green woods of the Cypress Bayou swamp my freedom returns. I am whole, renewed, free—godlike, even if it is only for an hour or two.

I pity my wife and her poor riding skills. She grew up in the country along a gravel road unpaved still to this day. She thinks it great accomplishment to retrieve her water bottle without having to stop or fall down. Oh, what happy, glorious fortune growing up in a paved paradise like Breaux Bridge. Roads, flat and smooth, paved with concrete and asphalt and Louisiana's ride-year-long climate, all that was good accessible by two wheels. How different would my love affair with my bike be had I grown up on the hilly streets of San Francisco or in the harsh winters of Minneapolis?

I may never have known real freedom.

Sam Irwin has been "a puppet, a pauper, a pirate, a poet, a pawn, and a king" during his thirty-year work career. Currently he is a journalist for the Louisiana Department of Agriculture. When he is not writing about cows, sugarcane, chickens, and cotton, he is riding his GT-I Drive at the Comite Trails in Baton Rouge.

The Downhill Stretch: An Elegy

Judith Strasser

My father is dying, and all I want to do is ride my bicycle.

My father is dying. He fell and fractured his hip, coming to visit me. Now he has a staph infection. He lies in his hospital bed, unable to walk. Unable to sit. To stand. A doctor checks his chart. She says, "I know about you. You're a physicist. You've been to Antarctica. You've even biked in Holland."

My father, by his example, taught me to exercise. He walked to work, several miles each way. When he retired, he started to swim. He bought a bicycle and taught himself to ride. The morning he fell, he'd walked to the gym and spent two hours there, working out with weights, swimming laps, riding an exercise bike. He entered triathlons. In a picture I keep on my dresser, he's surrounded by trophies; two or three medals hang on ribbons around his neck. He says he always won because he was the only competitor in his age category. He has a fine sense of humor, but the picture's not really a joke.

When he came back from Holland, he told me, "You can't lose weight by biking. You should see the fat people there, men and women, all of them on their bikes."

I said, "I bike to eat. After sixty or seventy miles, a hot fudge sundae's okay."

Which is true, but not the whole story. I bike to relax. To calm down. To dispel anxiety. An old boyfriend once said, "You work harder at relaxing than anyone I know." It was not a compliment. I was training to ride from Boston to New York.

"It's not hard work," I said. And it's not, though maybe it was at first. I rode an old ten-speed; I wore moccasins and regular unpadded shorts. I got very sore, and I walked a lot of hills. But there was something compelling about it. I would leave work completely exhausted, hang my bike on the trunk rack, and drive out of town to the start of the Wednesday-night ride. On the first gentle rise, my friends would vanish, leaving me struggling up the hill. But after a muggy day, the air was clear and cool. Holsteins gathered at the fences, mooing encouragement. The barns glowed in the low golden rays of the sun. I loved the Wednesday-night rides; they gave me energy. My friends waited for me at the turns. And afterward, we all went out for pizza. We were the Biking Babes.

I bought a Trek 520 and rode it for more than ten years, on Wednesday nights, on weekend tours, and on GRABAAWR, the five-hundred-mile organized ride along the Wisconsin River from its headwaters in the north woods to Prairie du Chien, where it meets the Mississippi. I conquered the Wright Stuff Century and all its short, steep hills. I shipped the Trek to Boston for the AIDS Ride to New York. Hurricane Floyd grounded us for two days, but the third was one to savor. First I changed a flat for two helpless and grateful men. And then little boys doing wheelies on stunt bikes led us through the Bronx— and stopped short, near the tops of the steepest hills. We scattered and braked; we managed not to run into anyone. Triumphant, we crossed the bridge and rode into Manhattan, coasting down Riverside Drive.

And then, about a year ago, on the first balmy evening after a snowy winter, I went for a Wednesday-night ride. The sweet, soft air smelled of fresh-plowed earth. Overhead, great Vs of geese honked each other north. Crocuses pushed through the farmhouse lawns; yellow-green willow whips swayed in the breeze. After the ride, I put my bike on its new rack, on top of my new car. I turned the key, switched on the radio.

A glorious Beethoven concerto carried me into town. I met the Biking Babes at a Chinese restaurant. We ordered garlic string beans, moo shoo pork, cups and cups of tea. My cookie promised good fortune. After dinner, I drove home, high on biking, and spring, friendship, and food, singing along to Mozart—straight into the garage.

And totaled my trusty Trek. I replaced it with the bike I hope will last the rest of my life, a very expensive Gunnar with a custom-fitted frame. (Friends said, "Check your homeowner's policy." Who knew insurance companies covered stupidity?)

Now my father is dying, and all I want to do is ride my bicycle. He has fractured his hip. He's tied to his bed. He has a fever; he's pulled out his feeding tube and all of his IVs; he's often delirious. A doctor asks, "Who are those people?" and he looks across the room at his wife and at me, his firstborn, his biking daughter. "The Taliban?" he says.

My father is dying, and I want to ride my bike. I want to swing a leg over the top tube, clip in to the pedals, and head out Seminole Highway—past the trophy homes, the tennis courts, the pools, past farms and villages. I want to see hawks soaring, possums and coons in the cornfields; I want the sharp black-and-white smell of manure. I want to read the wind in the grasses, to pump hard and gain the summit, to keep an eye out for potholes, to stretch out for the downhill run.

My father is dying and all I want to do is ride my bicycle. I want to ride it for him. It's not hard work; it's what I do. Like seeing. Like being. Like breath.

Poet and writer Judith Strasser lives and bikes in and around Madison, Wisconsin. She's the author of a memoir, Black Eye: Escaping a Marriage, Writing a Life (*University of Wisconsin Press, 2004*), *and of* Sand Eye Succession: Poems of the Apostles (*Parallel Press, 2002*).

Pedaling Pregnant

CJ Lockman Hall

It was my first mountain bike race and I was pumped. The course was familiar, its long climbs spoke to my strength, and I was ready to tackle the technically challenging sections. I started the race at an easy pace but soon was exhausted, uncharacteristically walking doable climbs with labored breathing. I struggled with the simple act of clipping into my pedals. I had ridden this course so well so many times. Frustration and disappointment mixed with the sweat pouring off my body.

A few weeks later, I discovered that I had not raced alone—I was pregnant! I chuckled as I reflected on the race with new eyes—the bone-rattling, shin-gashing, asthma-laden bike race was quite a welcome to the world for the baby!

Although I quickly got over my disappointing performance, it took longer to adjust to pedaling pregnant. The gentlest hills left me winded. My fine-motor skills (which were not so fine to begin with) decreased along with my kinesthetic sense, dampening my desire for technical riding. I admit that secretly I was glad to skip the trail with the two skinny trees, where, on a good day, I would barely squeeze my bike between the trees before turning sharply onto the short, narrow bridge that shot up into a gnarly rooted, rutted hill—complete with drop-offs on both sides.

But deep down, I missed the thrill of attempting obstacles and riding trails that leave no time to think because you've got to be in the moment. I stuck to trails where I could bail if I failed, eventually moving to smooth dirt trails and finally (gasp!) paved paths. As my riding options dwindled, my midsection increased; I discovered true meaning of *fitted jersey*, but I cherished the changes for what they represented.

Riding kept me in good physical shape and soothed hormone-injected emotions. The sense of release, accomplishment, and mind-clearing powers that bike riding provides alleviated the stresses caused by the unexplained waits and snarly staff at the (now ex) doctor's office, the (now ex) sonogram office's clinical emphasis on my "advanced maternal age," false positive blood tests, and health insurance snafus.

After a particularly unproductive conversation with the insurance company, I yanked my shorts over my belly, pasted on my shirt, and bolted to the lake on my bike. Along the way, a bee crashed into my helmet and flew off silly. A crow screamed at me so forcefully that it broke its perch. I realized that getting my dander up, like the bee and the crow, would help neither the baby nor me. That moment, I decided to change doctors and sonogram offices. I then focused on the beautiful cool breeze on that hot day, the sounds and scents of summer, the soothing rhythm of my cadence, and how much I would enjoy mountain biking with my child. Thanks to biking, I had a calm, productive afternoon.

I also had humorous moments while pedaling. One day, I recalled how my sister-in-law walked two miles daily up to the day she gave birth. For months, her kid wouldn't sleep unless he was moving. They'd push his stroller around the neighborhood at night until he fell asleep, but he'd wake up the moment they got home. What if my kid wouldn't sleep unless I was biking? I pictured myself pedaling through the woods in the black of night, baby in tow, singing lullabies while riding over logs. I giggled at this new image of "night riding."

I took my last ride on a picture-perfect day, my biking days temporarily over due to discomfort and doctor's orders. I still yearn to pedal to the lake. I miss evening and weekend rides with my husband. I will miss riding in the snow.

But in return, I am looking forward to the most wonderful gift in the world. On days when I wondered if I could be the mother that my child deserves, I'd often find my answer on a ride where I'd watch mother ducks showing the ropes to their fuzzy ducklings; admire spotted fawns, shadowed by alert, protective does; and surreptitiously root for mother turtles laboring to bury their eggs. One day, I met a woman joyfully exploring nature with her kids—inspecting moss patches, collecting rocks and watching turtles—and it warmed my heart.

I'll gladly trade a few months on my bike for a beautiful child whom I can introduce to nature and biking. But I can't wait to attach the baby trailer to my bike and head to the woods, mother and child biking together once again.

CJ Lockman Hall writes in Rockville, Maryland, where she lives with her husband, Micky, who introduced her to mountain biking, and with her beautiful little girl Torrie.

"Who Wants to Marry a Bicyclionaire?"
or,
Bicycling in Search of the Erotic in an Ekpyrotic Universe

Peter Gelman

1.

Let me be the first to admit that I do not suffer from Penile Numbness. I make this courageous statement in the hope that it will be helpful for others not as bold as me.

Not only is my plucky, cheerful minipump still functional and operational, chronic bicycling actually helps my Master Blaster thrive.

According to my research, the bicycle may actually promote Genital Sensation Syndrome. To research, I pedaled uphill and I coasted downhill, yet I found nothing but peppy, perky, nimble effervescence in my member.

You know what I mean if you have ever felt the surprisingly erotic and scrumptiously semi-scrutable nether-fondling and gripping of one's bicycle seat. *It is for this reason that we must never, ever ride a bicycle,* unless we want to be sensitive to the erotic bumps of life.

Never! Never, not even once! It is too dangerous! Dangerous to the body, worse to the soul! Biking leads us to wonderful, playfully erotic tickling, prickling, and zickling. It zickles in an especially delicious manner when bumping over a speed bump. The sensuality of cycling returns the pagan spiritual fire in our sense of being-alive-in-a-body.

Riding a bicycle gives such a soulful completeness as to suggest the Round Rolling Being of Yore. By *yore* I suggest the old Platonic myth, the strong, happy creature that Zeus sliced in half to separate Rider from Wheel.

I love the Wheel. While gazing at the come-hither curve of a handlebar, my chest heaves with heart pangs of desire to cardiovasculate! A fever to *go, go, go* grips me when contemplating the capacious rake of a touring fork!

2.

Every once in a while I find in the bike magazines a wistful male expression of desire for a woman who knows how to repack cup-and-cone hub bearings.

This is healthy, an erotic interest in a woman's skills and companionship in sweaty, dirty bicycle adventures. Such women exist in increasing numbers, to their credit. Yet for some reason—so far—women refuse to parade in fragile wisps of bathing suits, one by one demonstrating their ability tighten brake cables and realign derailleurs.

Having admitted the personal and private fact that bicycles don't make me numb, I can admit that a TV game show did. In this contest, fifty female contestants competed in a pageant in which victory meant marriage with a millionaire.

Drowsing after the show, I mentally digested this brazen, broadcast proof of the minuscule strings that hold my values together are no stronger than the strings that hold a bikini into place.

I was not shocked—rather the opposite (which I found shocking).

I woke up feeling pretty sure that as a result of that silly show, something was wrong with my body's participation in reality. I floated in a seemingly insubstantial state. My member reported no sensations to my brain. My brain itself had nothing particular to say to my member. Both were unusual. I felt a sort of ghostly, insubstantial numbness all over and through me.

After drinking a cup of coffee I glanced out the kitchen to find that Mount Tabor floated on an ocean of mist. The light somehow created a reflection of the old volcano upon the mist like an old Chinese painting.

Standing at the balcony of my back porch between the teal plastic recycling shelves and the bicycle pump I was so inspired by the sunlight on Mount Tabor that I gave forth a little warble in the form of a whistle.

I climbed down the moldy and mossy stairs (all three of them) with such alacrity in my eagerness to open the garage with my bikes that I was able to hear a whistle from behind.

The odd thing was, this was the same whistle I had given forth but a moment ago.

That was not possible, I realized. There was something vacuous about the moment. It was hollow. It lacked substance. I realized I would never reach my bicycles. I realized I had merely dreamed about it. I was in fact dreaming about the dream.

In the dream I told myself to remember to write: *"It was then that I woke up."*

It was then that I woke up.

3.

I woke up. Humbled, I started over. I drank a cup of coffee. I looked outside: It was raining hard in that gray, forbidding, shadowy way. Mount Tabor was but a gray smear, a hint of sliding bulk in the general drippiness of Being.

Lying in bed, I contemplated the insubstantiality of such things as volcanoes, bicycles, light, sound, wooden steps, and aluminum cans. Although this was a gritty reality, there was a softness and humility to it.

I considered the kind of reality promulgated by television: Fifty women paraded in bathing suits for a millionaire. Each had three minutes to reveal her personality. Each asserted her self-respect, her happiness with her career, her independence, and her utter lack of interest in money.

Something about this didn't make sense. Can love so easily fit financial requirements? Are these women real? Are these the long-promised sexy robot women from Mars? Probably not, but if not, what's going on?

What is reality? Sadly, we don't know. Just kidding! We do know: The universe began as a Schwinn Varsity ball bearing. Heated to ten billion degrees, it exploded, and in one second, became a cosmic velodrome. But what caused the ball bearing to heat up? I'm glad you asked.

The latest theory states that before the Big Bang was a Big Splat coming out of a parallel universe.

Polite circles (which don't invite me) call the Big Splat "the Ekpyrotic Model." I understand that this model is the most super of all supermodels because it is so super it is actually cosmic.

What's this about a Big Splat? Let's start at the beginning. Remember those little bikini strings that are stronger than my values? They are no surprise, because physicists say that the universe is made of teeny-weeny teeny-tiny vibrating strings—strings smaller than atoms holding up the bikini bottoms of the universe.

As everybody knows, there is more than one universe in higher-dimensional reality.

These are like ball bearings, rolling around in a cup-and-cone hub bearing. One of these ball bearings was ours, known as Space-Time. Another one was, needless to say, invisible, and known as [ ].

Space-Time and [ ] were imperfect ball bearings in a Ten-Speed universe; no grease filled the recess between cup and cone. Instead of grease, the manufacturer used those handy little vibrating strings.

As a result, Space-Time and [ ] rubbed against each other, causing friction. The friction melted [ ] and splatted it onto Space-Time. This instantly created an unwieldy ball-bearing glob. It overheated and exploded.

That's the Ekpyrotic story behind the creation of this excellently bikeable universe we've all come to know and love so well.

With this in mind, now we can answer: What is the purpose of life? What does a thing look like when no one's looking at it? What is subjective and what is objective? What is Missy "the Missile" Giove doing right now? Why do bicycle magazines have so many automobile advertisements? Why do so many bike wrenches belong to this guy "Allen"? And why would these women want to parade on national TV exposed to the marital scrutiny of a smirky bachelor millionaire?

We broadcast this squalid view of humanity not just to millions of enthralled viewers, but to the stars in their whirling bike-wheel constellations. It was embarrassing to my sense of reality, and it was embarrassing to Space-Time.

It made me wonder: Should I bother getting out of bed? The sense of reality conflict depressed me. Why get out of bed? Reality was so tenuous. As my numb member indicated, the stability of the universe seemed a little too tenuous just then.

I could not permit Space-Time to end its embarrassment by destroying and replacing Earth. Space-Time could do this by running over Earth with a top-heavy Black Hole much in the manner of a giant SUV running over a Styrofoam package peanut.

What was the key to release the U-lock of this angst?

Lying in bed, I thought about it. I called forth the usual torrent of fiery intelligence from my mind. Whether they appeared or not is another matter. In fact only one feeble would-be idea appeared. Giving it the benefit of the doubt, I assumed a familiar manner and called it "smarts." (It was a sort of confidence booster, just between you and me.)

These "smarts" struggled to find their way up from the depths of my brain stem. It was like Lance Armstrong charging up the Alps on a K-mart Huffy bike in a sort of Tour de Gelmo-Brain. Racing against him were all sorts of worries, fears, and anxieties. Which idea would win the polka-dot jersey worn by the King of the Medulla Oblongata? I was curious, but as soon as I turned on my mental ESPN to watch, the TV went blank.

Suddenly something kerplunked into being in my mind. It hit, bounced, and rolled, for it was a wheel. In fact it was a cerebral bicycle wheel, printing a message in my dirty mind with its tread: *You're not a millionaire, true. But you are a bicyclionaire.*

4.

I slipped into my streamlined bike shoes with growing excitement. Now quite awake (or so I believed), I proceeded trippingly down the mossy steps, mincing across the grass, and leaping once, twice, then fluttering into the garage. There my harem of three bicycles greeted me with their plucky spokey-ness and firm frame geometries. Which one should I ride?

"*Pick me,*" cried the hybrid. "*I have a two baskets that can carry your groceries. I may be a bit heavy but that's because I'm strong and stable. I can bring home the tofu bacon and fry it up in a pan. And I can wink—I have a generator light.*"

"*Pick me,*" urged the recumbent. "*Sure I'm slow uphill, but don't the kids cheer you on? Don't you feel like you're flying a plane when you ride me?*"

"*Don't pick me,*" the road bike teased, "*unless you want to fly like the wind without hardly any effort at all, unless you want to conquer the miles liberated from fealty to that single-minded tyrant, Gravity.*"

I did not wake up, because I was already awake. I was in a reverie, smiling, and having imaginary conversations with my two-wheeled lovers.

Yes, in fact I was talking to myself loud enough for my neighbor to hear.

She asked me, "Are you talking to your bikes?"

That was the question she asked but the way I interpreted it is: Do three bikes, instead of one, make up just more material clutter in our material society?

"I'm not talking to my bikes, they're talking to me," I told my neighbor.

To her puzzled look, I explained, "I'm a good listener."

She returned to washing her car. "He's talking to his bikes, can you believe it, Boo-Boo?" she asked her Subaru.

Confounded by all the questions I had asked myself, I rolled along on my road bike, picking up speed. The slope of Mount Tabor grew steep and I labored to keep up the speed. Behind the castle wall of the reservoir, the water was full of clouds.

I rode on up the spiral road. There was a pungent steam coming out of the park compost heap. As I reached the top, I could feel the great firs breathing.

It may have been an illusion of Mount Tabor mist, but at that moment I felt nothing but a sense of good fortune and general worthiness to be alive.

Nothing seemed important but the fact I was happy. On the top of the park I gave myself a victory lap. I felt such gratitude to have bikes to ride and a beautiful wet city to ride them in.

Peter Gelman, a novelist, also writes for bicycle magazines. Some of his humorous bicycle stories appear in Traffic Life *(Buckmaster, 2003). Look for more to appear in the future. Peter lives in Portland, Oregon: petergelman@yahoo.com.*

The Secrets of the Love Affair

Varick L. Olson

My second most prized possession is my weather radio. Most people give me a funny look and just say you are weird. Some ask, "Okay what is your most prized possession?" My bike and the love we share, but most don't ask.

The ride, it is all about the ride. A few pedal strokes and I am away from the ordinary. The ride is time to be free, to be myself without any encumbrances or expectations.

Love affairs have origins. My affair has great credentials. You talk about the love affair people have with cars. Well, cars originated from the bike. Louis Chevrolet worked in a bike shop before recruited by GM. Early cars had bike wheels, chain drives and other bike parts. The effort to build roads in the USA came from riders of the bike. These early lovers of the bike wanted good roads. And almost everyone recalls Orville and Wilbur Wright; they took their love affair with the bike to the air at Kitty Hawk. And you Harley lovers, your bikes had pedals until the 1920s. Madison Square Garden was built for bicycle racing. Bicycle racing was more popular as a spectator sport than baseball. Races were held in many major U.S. cities. So what is there not to love about the bike? A love affair with roots like these makes for a great genealogy.

In the fall I see the woolly bear caterpillars crossing the road. A winter ride is good when my water bottle doesn't freeze. In the spring I see tundra swans and geese on their migration and smell the soil as the farmers prepare the fields. The aroma of dirt lets me know I am alive on this earth. In summer I smell the fresh-cut hay and see the ring-necked pheasant, red-tail hawk, and deer. On the bike I am able to be free to listen, smell, and watch. Yes, the ride lets me be part of the world.

My bicycle, such a peaceful machine offering countless hours of free therapy. Sometimes my neighbor will ask, "Where are you going?" I say for a ride—just a ride, I will know when I get there. How far? When I feel tired or the sun goes down. I rest at night, as does my bike. The ride is health and healing through movement. Efficient too, it runs on bananas, peanuts, and water.

I recall a marathon ride. I was riding two hundred miles in a day by myself, just because. I stopped in at a convenience store to replenish my fluids just hoping someone would ask this sweaty cyclist "how far have you ridden?" I just wanted to say a hundred miles so far, and maybe get a "wow that is something!" Nobody asked. Maybe just as well to keep my love affair a secret. I know and God knows, and that is enough in our world of competition and constant emphasis on winning.

With a secret like this it is hard to understand why I haven't had the tabloids at my door. Of course mine is true love, until death do us part. The tabloids don't usually deal with the true stuff. So as with most true loves, which bring happiness not accolades and press, I will keep pedaling and enjoy my secret love affair. At about age one hundred I will be riding up one of those 2% grades on the prairie, you know, one of those hills, which are really not hills but the grade seems to go forever, and at the top I will just tip over and leave this world. Someone will come along, get on my bike, and the love affair will ride on.

Varick L. Olson, P.T., Ph.D., is a physical therapist clinician, researcher, and educator who has learned from his wife, children, patients, and students that life is to be lived well. At present this Iowa Hawkeye resides in Wisconsin and serves as a missionary converting Badgers to the truth and the light of the Hawkeye—very difficult work!

If Ever There Were Warriors . . .

Tim Noakes

Perhaps it was a calling. I honestly don't know, but when in high school I found myself patiently waiting for class to end so I could go out and ride my bike, I sensed that something was different. Different enough that I knew *calling* was written all over it. The attraction to the bicycle was just too strong to be dismissed. Consequently, during those impressionable years as a postadolescent kid, I began a lifelong journey into the realm of cycling and all it had to offer and all it had to teach. And I am still learning.

The first race I did was when I was ten years old. I was thrown into a race with all these eighteen-to-twenty-two-year-old men who were, like myself, just starting out. The only difference was they had leg muscles, arm muscles, facial hair, and deep voices. I remember being at the starting line looking to the left and to the right and seeing nothing but huge shaven legs staring me in the face. Was I nervous? Yes. Was I scared? Yes. Was I excited? More than ever. And as the race began all these "older" men effortlessly rode away, leaving me to do the entire eight miles on my own except when I was lapped and, for a few seconds more, I became part of the race again. It was without a doubt one of the hardest rites of passage that I ever had to go through, leaving me so exhausted I could hardly make my way over to the car after the finish. It took me four years to gain enough gumption to race again. Callings, I realized, never go away, so it was inevitable that I would return to the starting line again.

It is now more than twenty years later, and I have raced throughout the country and throughout the world, but it was in Europe where my

223

eyes were open to the higher meaning of cycling. I was lucky enough to spend six months in Belgium, an experience that all cyclists, no matter what their ability, should try to experience, if for no other reason than to be a part of a society that reveres and respects the cyclist. The most important lesson I learned there, however, was not how to suffer and how to persevere during a race. Rather, it was what I learned about the glorious machine that I had taken for granted for so many years: my bicycle.

Being fresh, young, and naive from America, I would show up to races with my bike completely filthy from the incessantly harsh Belgian climate. My "excuse" was often that I was just too tired to clean it. This, I soon discovered, was sacrilegious. The bicycle, you quickly learn in Europe, is the purest personification of the bicycle racer. If you choose to show up to a race with a bike covered in dirt and mud, then you are viewed as a racer who is undisciplined and lazy. However, if you show up to a race with a pristine bike, even if it is absolutely pouring down rain, then you are a true racer, respected because you respect the bicycle. Consequently, no matter how tired you were, no matter what the weather was, you spent time cleaning the bike, making it shine and glisten, realizing that the bicycle ultimately is your weapon, your tool, your means to victory, and should always be treated with the highest regard. To this day I have not forgotten that lesson.

Now that my bike was, and is, perpetually clean before every race, there still was the actual race in which to compete. And that is an entirely different story. If the training goes well, and you feel like you have done nothing else in this world but dedicate yourself to the sport, then it became very easy to assume races would go easily. Reality, though, always offered its harsh and bitter lesson. A race, simply, is never easy. And even if you win (which, in cycling, is a rare occurrence), the race is never a walk in the park. The race is grueling, hard, discouraging, and painful, but it is above all wonderful and spectacular. The race becomes your only focus and your only care in the world. Nothing else matters once that gun goes off. Whether it is on a hot, summer day or on a cold, wintry day, nothing will distract you from the fact that there is a finish line somewhere off in the distance, and you will try as hard as you can to make sure you are the first to get there. I cannot tell you how many races I have participated in, how many start lines I have seen and how many finish lines I have crossed, or how many miles of roads I have raced, each one of them capturing that element of racing that made it great in its own way, whether I won the race or was dropped within the first few miles.

Still, some races stood out above others, and many times these are not the races where you came across the line first. Sometimes the most memorable races are the ones where, against all odds, you happen to survive to the end, where you found the inner strength to grit a little longer and push a little farther, even if the grandstand at the finish line was being taken down when you finally got there. Such a race for me took place in Holland on horrendously gray, windy day. We (a group of seven of us) were all told that within five kilometers we would be riding back to the hotel after being quickly dropped by the Dutch cyclists. When told this, we all looked at each other and said, "C'mon, who are they kidding?" Within five kilometers the Dutch cyclists did in fact drop all but two of us. The other five, broken by the carnage and completely discouraged, slowly rode back to the hotel. The two of us remaining, though, kept on fighting. Then, after fifty kilometers more of this blistering pace, I was the only one left of the original seven. The pace simply never let up, and I was in agony. Finally, we reached a town that I assumed had to be the finish town, for I had already suffered too much not to be near the finish. I quickly looked down at my odometer and saw that only eighty of the total 180 kilometers had been raced. I still had a hundred kilometers to go. If there was ever a time to wonder what in this world drove me to do such a crazy, difficult sport, it was right at that moment when I was hoping to see the finish line around the next corner but realized that I had covered less than half the distance of the race. Needless to say, I made it to the 150-kilometer mark before it was my turn to be dropped by the Dutch cyclists. But in my career that was one of the highlights. I came across the line proud of what I did, although the winner was already collecting his prizes and receiving his accolades. Strange how "getting dropped" can be one of your most memorable races, but it was there on those windswept roads of Holland that I learned how to reach deep and go that one step farther.

But perhaps the most important lesson cycling was to give me was learning to trust others. Cycling, or the act of riding a bike, is a very solitary experience, and typically draws strong, individualistic athletes. But bicycle racing is entirely dependent upon the idea of team, of riders sacrificing themselves for other riders, of selflessness that can possibly propel others to victory. It is an extremely difficult concept to accept, particularly for individuals who were attracted to the sport for its inherent solitariness. But sometimes a team appears that that does just that: It acts as one, with all the riders coherently working together in order to produce a win that, for everyone involved, is just as rewarding as the victory itself. There are few images in cycling that I value more than that of a rider coming across the finish line with his arms up in the victory salute while far in the background one of his teammates, just as happy and excited, also has his arms up in the victory salute. It is not a lesson easily grasped in our country where individualism is the essence of our national creed. Yet if riders can embrace a more selfless attitude the rewards will be extraordinary, even if the team doesn't win. In all my years of racing on different teams throughout the country, I have to say that only one team has worked in such a manner, and I cannot tell you how fondly I look back at the riders and the races from that particular season. It was truly magical.

Ultimately, though, cycling goes beyond lessons. It is a sport about courage and suffering and perseverance. It is a sport that requires the individual to reach deep into himself or herself and go beyond the normal boundaries of pain and hurt. And this is not only felt at the Tour de France level; on the contrary, it is a requirement at all levels of the sport. Yes, we marvel at the strength of Lance Armstrong or Eddy Merckx or Miguel Indurain, but in any race, from the local beginners' race to the Tour de France, the need to reach deep in order to push through the pain is, amazingly, the same. The grimaces, the sweat, the burning legs, and the aching lungs are suffered by every single racer who is striving to win, or even finish, a race. It is here that I find the sport full of courageous individuals, modern warriors, so to speak, who have trained their bodies and their minds to deal with the hardships of the sport. More than any other athletic endeavor cycling harks back to those honorable days of heroism and chivalry, where there existed a sense of nobility and pride in one's skills, along with inherent dangers and obstacles that are essential to victory. Like medieval knights upon their horses (and I do not use this metaphor lightly), bicycle racers enter the battlefield flying the colors of their loyalties in the guise of their jerseys, ready to risk all the dangers necessary to, hopefully, carry away the spoils of the day.

We live in a soft age, an age dominated by hours sitting in front of the computer, sitting in the car, or sitting on the couch mesmerized by television. It is an age lacking in many of the hardships that, ironically, touch deeply into what it means to be fully aware, fully alive, and fully human. But one sport throws the individual headfirst into those essential experiences that makes one appreciate life to its fullest. That sport is cycling.

Tim Noakes lives in Charlottesville, Virginia. He says, "I spent most of my racing career in the beautiful roads of Northern California near San Francisco. Graduated from the University of Notre Dame with a philosophy/literature degree, which ironically taught me to race my bike instead of pursuing a lucrative job. I have learned that a proper education will always make you follow your passion, which is why I still love to ride my bike."

A Rusty Old Memory

Carlos A. Sintes

We were clearing out the basement—recovering my memories from yesteryear—when she spotted the rusted Colnago. Cobwebs clung to some of the front wheel's twenty-eight spokes.

"Want to throw this old thing out?" Sophia asked. "It's been sitting here forever."

Campy small flange hubs held DT spokes laced three-cross using aluminum nipples and dust dulled the finish of Super Champion, Medaille D'Or rims. The bicycle was state-of-the-art equipment back in the late seventies and early eighties—a time of friction derailleurs and itchy wool cycling shorts.

I skimmed dust off the top tube as if the bicycle were a treasured bottle of wine. Miraculously, my silver companion had survived numerous crashes and even carried me to a state championship victory. But that isn't why I kept it. Once, that Colnago and I received the leadout of a lifetime from Greg LeMond.

In 1980, I entered a local points race held a few days before the Olympic trials. Many of the hopefuls stopped in town on their way to Lima, Ohio—including the man who would win three Tours.

It was a typical Chicago criterium: a mile course with four corners and two overpasses masquerading as hills. Late in the race, I fought my way into a breakaway group of ten or so spearheaded by none other than LeMond.

We flew around the course. I was fit, felt great, and was in a move that would stay away. Now that I was in a smaller group, and with the final sprint counting double, there was a realistic chance for a top ten finish.

With two laps remaining, a hotshot broke away from our little pack. As we crossed the start/finish line on the bell lap, he maintained a two-hundred-meter gap.

Our first corner turned left onto the incline of an overpass. To have a shot in the sprint required coming out of the final corner no more than fourth. I was near the back of the group and needed to move up. LeMond passed along my right, accelerating. Not an explosive jump as if he were attacking, but a move intended to get him to the front. What better wheel to follow in a sprint? I latched on.

LeMond just kept picking up momentum and by the time we reached the top of the overpass he was at warp speed. I managed to hang on. The next corner was a downhill left we hit so hard I'm still amazed we remained upright. On the long straightaway, LeMond put his head down and scorched the earth. The world around me was a frantic blur and I felt as if I were fighting to stay behind a motorcycle. Regaining some composure, I glanced back . . .

Whoa! We had a gap and I was getting a major-league leadout by one of the best in the world. LeMond didn't view me as a threat—probably sensed I wouldn't have been able to pull through if my life depended on it. He was flying and rapidly closing the gap on the rider ahead. I concentrated on LeMond's rear tire. Suddenly it occurred to me: I could win the final sprint!

I tried to remain calm as we streaked into the third left-hand corner and charged up another overpass—the breakaway rider was just ahead. He glanced back at us before the last corner and I recognized disappointment in his glazed eyes. I knew he was trying to quickly recuperate for a final gallop to the line against Greg LeMond . . . and some local yahoo.

I never even daydreamed of being in the same league as LeMond, but that day I was positive I could beat him. I was a decent rider and possessed a sprint that had served me well. Besides, I had just received close to a mile leadout—at warp speed—and all I did was sit on. LeMond was probably hurting, and "Mr. Breakaway" looked cooked too.

We swept onto the final straight. LeMond was behind the other rider, both of them looking at each other, oblivious to me. I had the element of surprise and planned to blow past them with 250 meters to go. I'd put everything into my final sprint—use every fiber of my being, burning off every drop of energy I possessed.

We cruised toward the line. Three hundred meters remained . . .

How good was LeMond?

As I timed what was to be my explosive acceleration, LeMond dropped down a gear and, like a bottle rocket, took off. With a *whoosh* he instantly shot two or three bike lengths ahead of me and left me gaping. I jumped, knowing I'd never catch him, but tried nonetheless. As LeMond crossed the line, I stopped pedaling, mesmerized. Several riders blasted by me on the left, but I didn't care. I was in awe.

Normally, it's humiliating to get a whole lap leadout and be beaten in the sprint, but not at the hands of Greg LeMond. It was an amazing and rewarding experience.

LeMond went on to trounce everyone at the Olympic trials and, from there, continued his journey to becoming one of the greatest cyclists of all time. I raced several more times with LeMond in the peloton, but never had a picture taken with him.

I gazed at the dusty relic of a bicycle and floated in my cloud of wonderful memories. The feel of Sophia's hand caressing my shoulder brought me back to reality. She was looking at me with understanding green eyes, as if she knew what I was thinking.

"Sweetie," she said, "we'll keep your bike forever."

Carlos Sintes and his family live in suburban Chicago. His cycling career included winning the 1981 Illinois State Cycling Championships, but he is most remembered for his credited role in the Academy Award winning film Breaking Away, *where he played the part of an Italian cyclist.*

Leaving the Sport You Love

Bruno Schull

"A rider who leaves his sport is the loneliest person in the world."
—Eddy Merckx

It is late night in the spring, and I am in the small town of Shasta City, California, north of Redding where the Great Central Valley fades into the high country of the Trinity Alps. Alone, I am surrounded by the anonymous comforts of a small hotel: heavy drapes that open onto a parking lot, a bed with coarse blankets, a television above a mirror on the wall. I am lying on the bed flipping through the channels on the television. As the images flash past my attention is suddenly captured. There, on the screen, is a professional bicycle road race in Europe. The race is the 2002 Amstel Gold in Holland, one of a series of races called the Spring Classics, which define the early part of the professional season. A breakaway of four riders has escaped from the main group, or peloton, which follows closely less than two minutes behind. The riders in the break are working together, exchanging pace at regular intervals. My eyes follow the riders, noting their posture and pedaling action, calculating their chances, measuring the gap to the peloton. The world is familiar to me. I used to work against the wind in similar breakaways. I used to be a bicycle racer.

I began riding bicycles in New York City where I was raised. Soon I began racing in a high school series, where I won a simple gilded plastic trophy. Eventually I moved to California and advanced through the

233

ranks until I reached the level of Category Two. The minor leagues. I raced with riders from the National Championships, the Olympics, and professionals. Even now, years later, I am still measuring my worth, rationalizing my performances, trying to place myself in the world of bicycle racing. In the final estimate, I was an average bicycle racer with a good sprint. I had the intelligence to know my strong points, absolutely no fear of danger, a great fear of failure, too little confidence to be a champion, a romance for the country, and a consuming passion for racing. I was respected by some riders, though not by all, and I won several races, though I lost many more.

Eventually my knees succumbed to the debilitating effects of thousands and thousands of revolutions, and I left the sport. My legs were supported by knee braces, and I was unable to pedal a bicycle. I confronted the choices I had made in pursuit of bicycle racing. In no particular order, I had abandoned a career in a biology (which lasted one week), a career in graduate school (which lasted one semester), and a career in medical school (which lasted five years), as well as several relationships with women. To support myself while racing, I worked as a mechanic in a bicycle shop. I also wrote about my experiences bicycle racing, a project that consumed several years of my life and had no foreseeable end in sight. The irony was obvious: I was a bicycling writer who could not ride a bicycle.

I was left with the feeling that I had not accomplished all that I could have on the road. I still had races to win. I still had points to prove. But as the years passed, I began to suspect that the chronic injury to my knees, which refused to heal despite the attention of various doctors, physical therapists, acupuncturists, hypnotists, and pharmaceutical aids, was not an accident, and that on some deep level, which I had not yet acknowledged, I did not really want to race at all.

Years later, following two knee surgeries, the book finished, having found a rewarding career and a wonderful partner, I realized that bicycle racing no longer attracted me with same gravity. Sometimes weeks would pass—incredibly!—during which I did not think of bicycle racing at all. And when I did remember bicycle racing, with distance and perspective, I was proud of what I had accomplished.

To understand the significance of leaving bicycle racing, you must understand why I began racing. My parents, while committed to healthy physical activity, have always cultivated a haughty disdain for organized sports. My father, for example, has visited the local swimming pool to perform his lap-by-lap ablutions almost every day for thirty years; however, I suspect that he has never in his life thrown a ball or swung a bat in a contest with another man, and the most he has ever said about racing is, "When are you going to stop riding that damn bicycle?" Perhaps my choice was guided by pathos, an Oedipal attempt to defeat my father. More likely, I began racing as a natural attempt to develop in my own direction.

I also began bicycle racing out of fear. In New York City, I spent a large portion of my childhood living in terror of physical confrontations. In retrospect, I was not afraid of commonplace scuffles between boys; rather, I was afraid of the beatings and brutal violence I often witnessed.

Attributes such as strength and bravery are important to young men, and I searched for a place to prove myself that was not as exacting as the streets. Bicycle racing is a very hard sport, and I discovered that I was not a coward, as I had long believed, or that even if I was afraid I could conquer my fear.

Also, I believe that within certain people there is a streak of pure independent character that defies explanation. The desire to express this character, more than anything else, fueled my love of bicycle racing.

What did bicycle racing give me beyond the obvious rewards of victory? At first bicycle racing gave me freedom. As wrote famous French champion Bernard Hinault, "By letting him travel further from home, a bike gives a child a greater sense of space and a new freedom." On my bicycle I explored the neighborhoods of New York City, and in the summer I rode on long excursions through the Catskills, the Adirondacks, and Canada. When I moved to California bicycle racing gave me community. The great majority of my friendships were forged on the road. Finally, bicycle racing connected me to country, seasons, and nature.

Through bicycle racing I learned about the world. Every bicycle race contains enough stories to fill several books. There is a difference, for example, between winning a race by working hard at the front, and winning by concealing yourself in the pack. There is a gesture in giving, or not giving, a thirsty competitor a drink of water. Character is revealed by the way riders deal with success and failure. As Italian professional Maurizio Fondriest said when he retired, "Cycling is the most difficult sport in the world but it teaches you how to live." Most of all, bicycle racing taught me to recognize my dreams—to win a bicycle race or write a book—and work hard for those dreams.

So, then, how do you leave the sport you love? Italian professional Brambilla, famous for losing the Tour de France on the last day of the race, dug a narrow grave in his backyard and buried his bicycle upright in the ground when he retired, because he no longer believed himself worthy to ride a bicycle. Another retired rider, over beer and a cigarette, reflected that he planned to join the French Foreign Legion, that mysterious fighting force composed of misfits and outcasts. Not all riders suffer when they retire. The American champion Andy Hampsten, who won the Giro d'Italia, hung his bicycle on a large golden hook and retired to the hills of Tuscany, the site of his former triumphs, where he runs a small winery and leads leisurely bicycle tours through the countryside.

In the local community there are riders who cannot leave the sport, drawn downward in a slow spiral of oblivion, and there are riders who regulate their passion, balancing racing with family and career. I suspect, however, that riders who have truly given themselves over to bicycle racing find that while they have received much in return, even more as been taken away, leaving a hole that can never be filled.

Even now, it is enough to simply turn a corner in the sun, see the road rising under the trees, or feel the season in the air, and I am immediately reminded of bicycle racing. When I travel through the country I imagine the routes of bicycle races. And when I leave the San Francisco Bay Area, I remember all the mornings that I drove away from the city before dark, heading for distant parts of California to compete in bicycle races.

Traveling to Shasta City, I passed a series of rolling hills in the valley. Here I recognized the site of one of my first bicycle races in California.

The memory of the race was still clear in my mind, the burned brown hills, the hot dry air, the dusty gravel roads. I got a flat tire and rode to the finish alone. As I passed the site of the race, I was overcome with a great feeling of nostalgia, as if I met a former lover after many years.

Why did I travel to Shasta City? What had I become? In the hotel I was filled with a mixture of excitement and fear that I recognized from the night before bicycle races. Above loomed Mount Shasta, a fourteen-thousand-foot volcano bounded by glaciers and peaks. At the foot of the bed was my backpack with ice ax and crampons lashed to the outside. The clock was set for a alpine start the next morning, and on my helmet was a headlamp to illuminate the seven thousand vertical feet of snow and ice and rock that lead to the summit. I had begun mountain climbing, as if driven to those heights by my love of bicycle racing. This was the first mountain that I would climb alone. And the night before my climb, while I had not seen a bicycle race for many years, I found myself watching the Amstel Gold Spring Classic.

The sport had not changed. All of the elements that I remembered were still there. The smooth working break, the roar of the crowds, the concentration of the riders. Each of the four riders in the break had a chance of winning. Lance Armstrong, from the United States Postal

Service team, three-time winner of the Tour de France, and probably the strongest rider present. Michael Boogerd, a Dutchman who raced for Rabobank, twice winner of Amstel Gold. Michele Bartoli, leader of the Italian Fassa Bortolo team, riding behind his Russian teammate, Sergei Ivanov, who was pacing his leader, and appeared strong enough to win the race himself.

As they neared the finish the tactics gradually unfolded. With strength in numbers, the two riders from the Fassa Bortolo team attacked, one after another, to wear down the others. They turned the last corner and came down the long boulevard before the cheering crowd. Then they began to sprint, with all the riders out of the saddle throwing the bicycles back and forth as they approached the finish. Finally one rider crossed the line first.

The sprint left me thrilled and excited the way I always felt after racing. The next day I would translate that feeling into the climb on the mountain. I was free. And yet, I would always be riding the same race.

Bruno Schull is the author of The Long Season: One Year of Bicycle Road Racing in California *(Breakaway Books, 2002). He grew up in New York City, moved to California, and raced for over ten years as an amateur in the United States and Italy. He now lives and works in Berkeley. He no longer races, but rides for pleasure in the hills and countryside.*

Riding with the Big Dogs

Bob Cook

Head down, legs churning, lungs heaving, under a still-overcast sky, oblivious to place and time. Third in the paceline, concentrating on the rear wheel not three inches from my front tire, my only thoughts: *Keep spinning, make it to the next rest area.*

Blowing past a road to the right, a sharp whistle pierced my concentration followed by a shouted "right turn," "right turn." Ceasing my cadence, I raised my head as the rider in front of me veered sharply away, only to find myself just inches from plowing through the red, rear wheel of the lead bike as it decelerated directly in my path. A quick jab of my handlebars averted the wreck and now gliding, I mechanically rose up to check traffic, made a quick U-turn, and, with a couple of hard, standing pedal strokes, turned left at the missed road. The chase to regain the pack was on.

Bearing down hard to accelerate, savage spasms suddenly electrified and tied up my quads. The pack was hesitating, waiting for us to rejoin them. They were just ahead, but with my momentum broken and legs now cramping, my will finally cracked and the desire to hustle back disintegrated. Sixty point nine miles from the start; for me it was over. Reluctantly, sheepishly, I informed the closest rider of my surrender, told him to rejoin the group, tell them to go on, that I would finish on my own. Before speeding off and abandoning me he asked if I was sure. I nodded, looked up, managed a smile, and said, "I am the weakest link—good-bye."

239

My ride with the big dogs at the front of the pack was over. Groups like that had passed me many times before. Sometimes I'd see them approaching in my mirror. Fast files of fit riders in bright cycling jerseys, eyes shielded by technically cool, expensive frames and lenses, rapidly pedaling slick, tricked-out cycles and reeking of excess testosterone. Often they seemed to appear like magic, sometimes shouting a warning: "On your left," more often not deigning even to acknowledge my labored cadence, middle-age presence decked out in an end-of-the-season-sale, terminally-out-of fashion jersey, outdated "bargain" helmet, and no-longer-chic emerald green frame as they blew past. But for the past nearly three hours I'd been an active cog in one of those predatory pelotons. Flying along like real cat riders, gobbling up uncounted roadkill of recreational cyclists, and casting them aside in our wake.

Some younger, faster friends had invited me to join them on this century ride. Early, eyes puffy from lack of sleep and high pollen count, we drove off under thick gray clouds, but far to the west the sky was bright and I asserted confidently we'd have good weather for the ride. I tried to look self-assured and calm as we unloaded the bikes and pinned on our ride bibs at the start/finish area, but was acutely aware of my mismatched, dated riding togs, middle-age spread straining the Lycra, and skinny, unshaved, pasty, pale white legs.

The easy, invigorating, compelling sounds of conversational chatter and gear shifting attended us as we eased through the brace of riders getting under way and wound our way to the main road. But as soon as we turned onto the main road the race was on! In no time, I was gasping for air. It took all I had, more than I realized I had, to keep pace. No time for taking in the sights, thinking about the route, or any of my usual musings. Just spinning like a madman, at a higher cadence and in a bigger gear than my norm. We passed scores, maybe a hundred or more riders before we'd covered even ten miles. It was exhilarating to be part of a fast paceline, but I wondered how long I could keep up. Never fully catching my breath, all the bright colors of the bikes and jerseys and emerald green of the countryside dimmed monochromatic. My world became a completely gray blur. Gray pavement, gray ghostly shapes of riders all moving under a dense gray sky.

Everyone helped me along, encouraging with words from time to time, lagging back to let me catch a wheel when I caused a gap. Someone rode up beside me to ask what pace I liked. I was utterly speechless, couldn't think, and didn't know what to say. Did he mean speed or cadence? Uphill, level, or downhill? Was the right answer faster or slower? I tried to say the current pace was okay, but feared my reply didn't make any sense.

When I faltered and a gap grew, someone would whistle or yell to the lead to back off and suddenly I'd be back in the line. As the miles sped by it was gently suggested that I needn't keep taking a turn at the lead, I should just stay in the middle of the pack where the going was easiest. But how was that done? As each rider in turn broke off after a short lead my spot automatically rotated forward. Should I pull out of line and crowd back to the middle with each turn? Should I take a brief lead at the front, or just stay at the rear? I wasn't sure what the etiquette was, didn't know who to ask, and was unable to clearly formulate or pose the question! Things got even more complicated when we'd pass a rider or small group and they would try to hook on to our paceline. We invariably dropped the outsiders, but the muddle of passing was confusing and worsened my already faltering confidence.

In an hour we reached the first checkpoint—mile 23. No sooner had we arrived than everyone was in a hurry to get going. I rushed to the port-a-potty, refilled my water bottle, gulped down half a banana and cookie, and then we were off, heading for "The Hill." I was barely managing the rollers with them, by hopping out of the saddle and crunching bigger gears than normal; I feared that on anything referred to as a climb, I would be toast.

Meanwhile, I rushed to keep pace. No scenery for me, no easy conversations; I barely noticed the intermittent light sprinkling of rain. Legs ceaselessly churning, faster and in a bigger gear, for longer than I could ever force myself to do on my own was the sum total of my existence. I had become an engine.

Our speed gradually slackened and I noticed groups of cyclists clustering up along the rising grade. Riding through increasingly rugged terrain, slowly gaining elevation, I gradually dropped behind the pack. Curt stayed with me. I told him to go ahead, but he seemed satisfied to lose ground to the others with me. The incline kept increasing, then, rounding a bend the road climbed visibly up.

"The Hill." I geared down and as the road switched back and forth lost sight of the others. I felt like a snail and stood up stomping on the gears trying to maintain some semblance of a respectable pace. Then, gasping, I resigned myself to the saddle, my granny gear, and just spun. Eventually, the grade eased, I caught my breath, geared up, and gained a little speed. The climb continued; steep, then flatter, steeper again, always upward through tall, dark, dripping firs.

Around the middle of the last climb Mike came speeding downhill to pick us back up to the others who were waiting at the top. The course map read: "View Point—enjoy entire valley." I never got a chance. I saw neither valley, nor view; just the familiar forms of my fellow riders. The race was back on as soon as I crested. Speeding downhill along the bumpy road I'd just caught my breath when a stop sign loomed into view; vacation was over. Someone yelled "Busy road—look out, get going and we won't be on it long."

We got going; we weren't on it long.

Our core peloton swelled and shrank as we swooped past cyclists and spewed them out the rear. I flexed my ankles, strove for pedaling perfect circles, anything to keep up with the wheel in front of me. Miles whizzed past. Mike and Pat rode from time to time by my side, shielding me from the wind, creating more draft. Passing a town Mike mentioned his parents grew up there. I wanted to reply, to tell him I had a friend who grew up there too, but having trouble speaking, I just nodded my head and kept spinning.

Outside town we overtook more cyclists bunched up along some rollers. As we swept past, again and again I rose out of the saddle and sprinted to keep pace. In my mirror I glimpsed those we passed, some struggling to join us, none able to keep up. Even without making any effort to rotate to the front I was barely holding the last of the line. Then in the distance I saw a congestion of cyclists and my unuttered prayers were answered: checkpoint 2, just shy of mile 54.

Pulling in, the sky was still thick with heavy gray clouds, my perception of color still flat. Drenched in sweat, yet chilly, I couldn't fathom how I could keep going. Choking down an energy bar and filling my bottle, I saw two friends. A chance to talk and delay the stop! I told them I was with a serious group and in over my head. I considered riding the rest of the way with them, but didn't want to delay my ride back at the finish and still held out some minor hope that our group might back off the pace just a bit. Noticing the others already standing over their bikes looking restless, I dared dawdle no longer. Jumping back on the bike, again we rolled.

Leaving the rest area I felt better, and the pace seemed a tad easier. There were eight of us now, two riders having joined with us somewhere along the way, and on a very rural road we fanned out across both narrow lanes, forming a compact, wide peloton. Swept along inside, enjoying the "whooshing" noise, I stretched and felt endorphins firing! Pat rode up and told me to consider removing my jacket—he felt it was too loose and its flapping was slowing me down. Though too chilly to ride without it, I was delighted to blame my struggles on poor jacket aerodynamics! Just beginning to think I might possibly keep up the rest of the way, we came off the back road, remorphed into a single paceline, and sped up. The race was back on, the endorphins off, and my whole essence became again to be the pedal. Within a couple of miles there was the missed turn, the cramping, and my ride with the big dogs was history.

I hung my head, found an easier gear, and tried to spin the cramping out of my quads. Once more I accelerated; again cramps cut me short. I was just too spent. Ahead, Mike veered out of line, looked back and reached his arm skyward. My head was down again before I realized he was waving good-bye to me. When I looked up to return the wave, he was back in line, growing smaller as the pack inexorably pulled away. Thirty-some more miles to go—but at my own pace with a chance to gently spin the cramps from my legs, listen to the birds, take full measure of the newly plowed fields and fruit blossoms. I relaxed and for the first time in hours caught my breath while on my bike. The sun was ready to poke out from the clouds and again I noticed colors. My big-dog day was done. But, man, what a ride it had been!

Woof, woof!

Bob Cook lives in Portland, Oregon.

The Face of the High Desert

Rachel Sutton-Spence

According to the badge on her chest, the dealer's name was Janine and she came from Elko. Our tour had stopped for the night at the Win Luck Casino in Winnemucca, Nevada, and now I leaned against a one-armed bandit, watching Tim and Bruce playing blackjack at her table.

Elko is like Des Moines, Iowa, or the small town of Pontypridd, back home in the Welsh valleys—it's somewhere to come from. You wonder why anyone would move to Winnemucca until you see Elko. Elko County is bigger than Wales and has a population size to match Pontypridd. Nevada is an empty state, with its endless hot desert plain, and it makes for splendidly solitary cycling. I'd thought Pontypridd was a backwater before I rode in the High Desert. This morning, we'd cycled through forty miles of scorching wilderness to get to the town of Puckerbrush—population 28. Then another thirty miles of sod—all to Winnemucca.

At least in Wales there's a village every few miles, with a pub and a post office. And even in the wildest parts there are plenty of sheep for company. All we'd seen today had been a roadkill coyote, two soaring turkey vultures, and a small, self-absorbed snake sunbathing on the pavement.

Janine had a face like Elko County. It was an empty expanse of no reward. Not barren, exactly, but nothing to offer human comfort. Win or lose, blackjack or bust, her expression never changed.

It was the original poker face. Her eyes were blue and hard. I was sure I could see a steely gleam. Crow's feet narrowed her eyes permanently in suspicion. Her nose twitched slightly, as if in dignified disgust. Everything about her exuded disapproval and disappointment.

Casinos are the Devil's work, and gamblers are Satan's spawn. The Lord shall wreak His vengeance upon long-distance cycle tourists who spend an evening in this sink of depravity. Janine didn't need to tell us—you could see it in her face. At the Winnemucca Baptist revival, you might expect that look in the minister's wife. In a blackjack dealer, it was plain weird.

Her mouth barely moved. In this land of the free, it was giving nothing away. I wondered if she ever smiled. I doubted it. After all, she came from Elko. *Puckerbrush* and *Winnemucca*—don't those names make you want to smile? *Elko* sounds like a brand of furniture polish. You could hear the slide guitar tuning up, just for her. *Sometimes,* her mouth implied, *it's hard to be a wo-man.*

You wouldn't want to kiss that mouth.

Or would you? I thought about it. She licked her lips. A tiny, barely perceptible gesture. Whoops! I've been too many hours pedaling across the High Desert Plateau. Is it just me, or is it hot in here? But, yes, you could kiss that mouth.

Luckily Bruce interrupted my improper mind games.

"Come and play."

"I don't know how."

Janine smiled. Smiled?

"I can help you, honey."

Help me? Honey? Excuse me, but aren't I a member of the Congregation of the Damned?

I sat at her table and Bruce gave me two chips.

Her poker face was just a professional persona. The coldness vanished like a mirage. Her eyes weren't steely—they were twinkling. And those were laughter lines, not crow's feet. That twitching nose was not disdain, but economy of effort. Players set in for a long session don't talk, but they communicate through twitches and glances. She did smile but her smiles were precious and she wouldn't waste them. I worked hard to earn them and treasured each one she gave me.

Janine's face was the face of the High Desert. When you first look, it's barren and unwelcoming. Your one thought is to put your head down and pedal like crazy to get out as fast as you can. Get to a land of plenty where the life is easy. Even Pontypridd looks like the Promised Land when you've spent a day in the Nevada desert. But if you stop and look, and stop fighting it, you can start to love it for what it is. If you try to understand, you'll see the beauty. It's subtle and it's hard-won, which makes it all the more precious. It's in the resilience and in the perfect adaptation to a hard life where nothing comes easy but if you play your cards right, you can still win. You probably won't win big, but you'll get through.

I played for half an hour. I turned that two dollars into twenty and then lost it all. The whole thing was strangely satisfying. That's what long-distance riding is all about. You ride your heart out, just to get back to where you started. If you don't understand it, you never will. If you do understand it, there's nothing to beat it.

When I left the table she said, "Come back and see us again, now."

Yeah, right, like I'll be riding through Winnemucca again this lifetime. But now, as I haul my way up the steep Welsh valleys in the icy rain, I think of Winnemucca and the High Desert. And I do see her face.

Rachel Sutton-Spence is a British cyclist, but she loves riding in the United States. She has ridden across it west to east, and north to south.

Did Someone Mention Bicycles?

Barbara Ashworth

Well, since you brought it up, let me tell you my tale of the two-wheeled contraption that has brought such pleasure and such pain into my life. I wanted a bike, oh how I wanted one. I begged incessantly for months. To get a bike would liberate me from the territory known as my yard, and it would also mean that I had become accepted by all of my classmates. The answer to my pleas was repeatedly: "no." Bicycles were too dangerous. You see, I was a city child who lived on a main thoroughfare with heavy traffic most of the day. Also pointed out to me was the fact that the city was filled with evil and violence, which no child should ever have to be exposed to. And topping the list was the number one argument: I was a girl. My mother, who had been born and reared in the country, and who had not seen a bicycle until she was grown, kept insisting that the city was not the place for riding a bike. Come to think of it, the country must not be a place for bikes either, since she had not seen one until she came to the city. But I didn't dare say that, for it would have been sassing.

At any rate, I hung in there. I begged and my parents refused. It was the pattern of my days until the day my grandmother came to live with us, and grandmothers can be good for some things. This one took my side, and by my ninth birthday I got a bicycle: a bright red-and-white Schwinn equipped with fender rack, basket, taillight, and bells on the handlebar. I was in seventh heaven, but only briefly. Immediately I was told that to ride my bicycle I had two choices: I could wait for my dad to take me to a side street where he might walk beside me while I rode, or I had to ride my bike in my own backyard. Now I am here to tell you that it wasn't much of a choice. First, to be caught riding one's bike with one's dad walking shotgun is the kiss of death with the other kids. I was aghast. Besides, to ride so slowly would never let me feel the wind blowing through my hair and would never allow me to feel that marvelous sense of freedom that appeared to be present when other kids rode their bikes past my front door. At any rate, the second choice had it all over what the alternate plan presented.

I was to ride my bike in my own backyard, a space of fifty feet by fifty feet, which meant in order to ride I must go in a continuous circle. This might not have been too bad except part of that space was taken up by rose beds that lined the yard, a set of outdoor furniture, and a small shed in the back left corner. Amused? Wait until I hit you with the next object that I had to dodge. My mother held that sunshine and Clorox combined made for a wonderfully white wash. So installed also in the backyard were poles at either end of it, from which were strung wires on which clothes could be hung to dry. You got it. I had to ride and duck, ride and duck, ride and duck and dodge. If I missed one beat of the rhythm I could decapitate myself. I was accused of being oblivious to the world when I was riding my bicycle. Hell, I was just trying to keep from committing suicide. This wonderful red-and-white bicycle soon became the enemy, and was holding my prisoner. How could I get out of riding it and not lose face? I didn't dare tell my parents that I no longer wanted a bicycle, so I came up with a plan.

One cool Saturday afternoon in November I aimed the bike at the shed in the back of the yard. I came up temporarily out of service with a broken leg. The bicycle came up permanently out of service. With a great sense of relief and defeat we donated the bike to the old fix-it man who picked up on trash day any parts that he might be able to use, and I resigned myself to never knowing what it was like to feel the wind blowing through my hair as I zoomed down a long road with no turns. But somewhere way down deep inside the desire for a bike of my own never quite dissipated. My children all had bikes, and I never once tried to sneak a ride. Along came the grandchildren, and they too all had bicycles. And still the desire grew. So one day I made an announcement: I am going to get myself a bicycle. Now I had thought it all through. I explained what good exercise it would be, and how it would save gas for me to run to the store and the library, and be a great way for me to visit all my friends. Absolutely not. Was I hearing correctly?

Both my children and grandchildren all explained just how dangerous it would be to ride a bike out in traffic and in a world filled with violence and evil. Had I not heard this story before?

"I'll just ride on the sidewalk."

"Nope, you can't do that," they explained.

"I need the exercise," I pointed out.

"We'll buy you a membership to the spa," they countered.

I gave up. It was just not to be. I was doomed forever to a car. I did not bring it up again, and probably would have given up on the idea, but I went garage-saling one afternoon, and there right in the middle of discarded treasures I saw it. It was bright blue with a basket on the front and the back, a rearview mirror on the left handlebar, and an ooga horn on the right bar. It had a large padded seat that more than handled my grandmotherly girth. But best of all it had the thing that put it over the top: three wheels. The seller told me that senior citizens could ride a three-wheeler on the sidewalk. I paid the asking price and left my car parked in their driveway while I rode my new purchase home, making a stop at the store. I bet you can guess the reactions of my family members. Right, I had committed a cardinal sin. But this time I was not to be denied, and since I had seniority at my house I demanded the right to set the rules for my bike riding. What could they do to me?

It became my favorite way of travel to friends' homes, the store, the library, and the park. I even rode it to church one Sunday morning when my car had a flat tire. And most of all it has become an escape for me and my little dachshund. When all else fails and the family is too much with me, I just put Muttley in the back basket, don my sneakers, and jump on my bike where I can ride with wind blowing through my hair. (I'm telling you, those three-wheelers go faster than you think.) And best of all, I no longer have to go in circles.

Barbara Ashworth lives in Tampa, Florida.

The Revolution Evolution

Rich Beattie

It wasn't much to look at. Blue metal. Black seat. Yellow tape on the handlebars. Sears logo affixed to the front fork. But to a four-year-old who had yet to master anything but a Big Wheel, this 1972 hulk of a ten-speed was dazzling. The gears were golden pistons, the pedals enormous ottomans, the spokes blinding rays of sunlight.

Most importantly, the bike was my brother's.

Eleven years older than me, Bob was the kind of brother who patiently sat through matches of the endless card game War, held me on his lap through countless episodes of *Sesame Street,* played with me and my Fisher Price garage, even remembered the names I had given each figurine. He was my friend, but he was also my hero. I loved the music he blasted. I craved the sports he played. I saved the magazines he discarded.

But his bike was the quintessential symbol of everything my hero represented. It required size and strength, it offered freedom. It was the vehicle that took Bob off to his camp-counselor job every summer day and the mystical world of high school the rest of the year—or at least when the brutal weather of Rochester, New York, allowed. I admired and coveted the two-wheeler merely because it was his. Yes, it weighed a ton. Yes, it had the world's cheapest components. Yes, the paint was chipping off. But the bike was him and he was the bike. I wanted to be him. And that meant riding his bike. Someday.

I grew into my own Sears bike: a small red thing with a banana seat and streamers on the handlebars. Bob took me out for my first spin on that bike, supervising as I balanced my way on training wheels and ultimately running alongside after he took the balance assisters off. Eventually I was good enough to set out down the street—a journey of enormous proportions. I'd shakily pedal my red two-wheeler and he'd confidently pump his blue machine. We'd ride past the suburban homes with their barking dogs and fresh-cut grass, out to a narrow ribbon of creek where we'd stare down into the trickling water. We'd return to the driveway, fill the family's ancient slop bucket with soapy water, wash down the frames and wheels, then turn the hose on the bikes. I don't remember what we talked about during those golden moments of spring and summer, and it never really mattered. I was out showing off my bike and my hero brother. And I had him all to myself.

I was eight when Bob went off to college. The bike stayed behind, settling into a semi-permanent groove against the garage's wood-paneled back wall. My brother had graduated to four wheels—a white Chevette in which I imagined him tooling around campus. I never cared much for the car: my eye remained trained on his bike. The area of the garage where it rested was sacred territory. I didn't even want to touch the bike, for fear of disturbing something in the cosmos.

Through the cold upstate New York winters and the humid summers it would sit there sprouting rust. But it was still the most beautiful thing I had ever seen. My brother came home for vacations, but he had new friends, more demands on his time. Even his work required new measures like wearing a tie and driving clients around. The bike just sat there.

When I was eleven, my folks bought me a ten-speed for my birthday. It was my favorite color: red. It was my size. I rode it because it fit me. But it wasn't Bob's. His was the bike I craved, and though the blue frame seemed Brobdingnagian, one day I decided I to give it a shot. I hefted it away from the wall and clambered aboard. I couldn't even reach the pedals. It didn't matter. I balanced myself against the wall. I felt like a king.

Eventually I grew into his bike, and when he finished college and set off for Colorado without the ancient machine, I asked if I could co-opt it. He said yes. Not that I would have listened if he had told me otherwise—the rusting hulk of metal was the only two-wheeled chariot I was interested in driving. I took it to school, around the block, out to see friends. It was practical, but it was also my way of preserving my brother and our special relationship. And that became my mission: I refitted the tires and brakes. I rewrapped the handlebars. I washed away the effects of the weather. I still worshiped its original owner, but he was thousands of miles away. Though we talked often, I knew our relationship was changing.

When I went off to college myself in Washington, DC, the bike was at the top of my packing list. I didn't care that it was fifteen years old and the frame was practically melting. I took the bike everywhere: to class, on the bike path out to Mount Vernon, over to National Airport to watch planes take off, through gorgeous Rock Creek Park. One place I couldn't ride was the dirt path along the C&O Canal—terrain reserved for the nobby tires of a mountain bike. My friends rode it and I had to make do with hearing about their adventures. That was fine: I resolutely stuck with my skinny-wheeled bike.

That summer, Bob got married. I went to Colorado for the wedding, and something very unexpected happened. We went out drinking together for the first time, and right then I realized our brotherly bond had profoundly changed. Growing up, bars were the structural equivalent of big bicycles—the hallowed ground of the aged aristocracy. I was never old enough or big enough for either. But I coveted the bike and I craved going to bars not only because they gave me a chance to be close to my hero, but because they represented the freedom of adulthood. I already had the bike, and here I was with him on the turf of maturity. Suddenly, Bob was no longer this mythic hero who could do things I couldn't. We now had the same privileges. We were contemporaries. I had grown up.

The day after I returned to DC, I came out of my apartment to find someone had wrapped the bike's front wheel around the post it was locked to, warping it into a perfectly rounded U. I was in shock. I was upset. But I knew right away I wouldn't replace the wheel, that I would never ride the bike again. Preserving this little piece of my past didn't seem to make sense anymore. In fact, I saw the bike in a whole new light: One pedal was falling off, the frame was more rusted than ever, the chain barely grabbed the gears. Why was I holding on to this aging giant? More importantly, why was I holding on to this piece of my brother? He had moved on from our youthful suburban innocence and I had to also.

I couldn't bring myself to throw the bike away, but having it take up space in my tiny apartment made no sense. Not knowing what else to do with it, I dragged the mangled piece of metal to the center of campus and locked it to a bike rack. Here I was in college and still showing off my idol. Then one day I walked by to find the lock snipped and the bike gone, taken by who knows: drunk students, campus security, a scrap metal dealer. It made me sad, but it was a good sadness, a liberating sadness.

Two weeks later I bought a mountain bike, jumped some curbs, rode the C&O Canal path, and never looked back. But I still think of the bike—the magical hand-me-down that transformed my life—and its hero owner. And it always makes me smile.

Rich Beattie is a freelance writer who lives in New York City. Formerly an editor and writer for Travel Holiday Magazine *and the adventure-travel site* GORP.com, *Rich now writes for* The New York Times, Travel & Leisure, Frommer's Guidebooks, Boating, *and others.*

It's Not About the Bike

Cathy Donaldson

Brand consciousness is specious. I consciously try to avoid imbuing inanimate objects with emotions or meaning. A new bike is very nice, but it won't make me smarter, more handsome, or win me a dream date. Sadly, I've noticed that today's consumer bike magazines are mere sales catalogs for overengineered products ridden by daredevils who like to jump off cliffs, or for Euro-snobs who wear their bikes as some sort of stylish and expensive metal accessory.

I'm much more interested with what's in the road than with who's watching me as I ride on the road. When I pull my bike alongside a rumbling eighteen-wheeler, it usually scares the living daylights out of me. So, if you're expecting this piece to be a panegyric to the 2003 platinum series double-butted chromoly steel with carbon forks, rah-rah components, and a butter-filled suspension system, you're out of luck.

Actually, I did buy a new bike six months ago, selecting last year's model over this year's, because I couldn't care less about the headset upgrade but did prefer gray as a frame color. This bike was the first one I'd ever purchased for myself. I've had bikes before, but all of them were either hand-me-downs from a brother or a cousin, or selected on my behalf by my more machinery-savvy father or a former husband. The only reason I bought a new bike at all was that some lowlife stole my twenty-year-old bike off the rack outside work last December. The bike I'd lost wasn't anything special: an inherited early-1980s mountain bike that I'd retrofitted with slick tires, full fenders, and a rack with foldaway carrier basket. But losing that bike still hurt. I was furiously angry for days, because it meant I had to go back to the gym and take spin classes, where I spent most of my time bouncing up and down on a stationary bike, staring at the behinds of various narcissists.

Shopping for an adult bike in December isn't ideal. I was too late for this year's sales, and much too early for the new bikes, which don't show up until February or March. It was Christmas, but I wasn't shopping for something with training wheels and pastel streamers on the handlebars. My choices were limited to a few unloved orphans with various failings. What's worse, I had no one around to shield me from that semi-civilized creature, the bike salesman.

Now, bike stores are hardly hives of activity during the dark winter months, so it surprised me greatly that the store employees could still be so arrogant. In one store after another I was treated with disinterest, because neither my budget (too few dollars), nor my requirements (not easily slotted into the MTB/roadie paradigm), appeared to match the expectations of the bike store employee. No, I didn't want an armored extreme mountain bike capable of climbing the sickest slopes. Nor did I want a feather-light bicycle that forced me into a riding position that would have launched me over the handlebars like a javelin. I do remember saying that I was looking for a year-round commuter bike. But I definitely got the feeling that my presence was some sort of warm-up act for Lance Armstrong. Apparently Lance was about to walk in at any time and drop several thousand dollars on a bike so space age that it was tethered to the floor with guylines. I had precisely fifteen minutes to accept whatever the salesman was offering, pay up, and head for the door.

Perhaps if I'd worn formfitting clothing, I'd have gotten more attention from the gearheads in sales, but I'm not Lara Croft. I'm just a normal woman with a job, a life, and a credit card. I did wonder a few times what it would have been like to work with a saleswoman, but I never did find one.

Well, I wanted a bike too badly to give up, so I skipped all the self-styled "Best Bike Shops of Seattle" and finally found my bike in a messy place down by the airport. This dealer cared enough to stick with me while I fitted my somewhat adaptable body to a somewhat adjustable bike. We worked out a comfortable stand-over height and shortened the reach, switched out the seat, and he helped me put on various after-market gadgets that served some actual practical purpose: repel rain, measure mileage, audibly alert pedestrians.

My new bike is a venerable touring model that could take me to Timbuktu, if I was so inclined. I'd learned from the dismissive salesmen that such bikes still existed, though they're so unfashionable these days that they aren't even exhibited at the annual trade shows. "No one buys them anymore," sniffed one, without a hint of irony, "except in Seattle."

It's a great bike, with a relaxed fit, and that nice upright seated position of the mountain bike minus the teeth-rattling effects of knobby tires. My daily commute is 15 miles, not 150, so I don't need suspension. A new bike meant I had the excuse to upgrade from shoe cages to clipless pedals, and I got a new wardrobe to match: fluorescent yellow jacket for eye-popping visibility and black pants to hide the grease. The bike has also introduced me to several new friends: Mike, a recumbent riding computer guy, Jeff, a scientist, with the same model bike as me, just a few years older, and Carl, an eighty-year-old bike-riding retiree. Now I get friendly nods from bony bike messengers, a woman who wears furry clogs while riding, and the man with drywall bucket "panniers" and a broken ski tip, mounted downward, as a back fender. I visit daily with the local wildlife: blue kingfishers and gray herons that live in the Ballard Locks, and a homeless woman who spends part of every day at the waterfront park, staring out at the bull kelp floating inshore.

In June I took my bike on a road trip to the Canadian Rockies and rode four days on the Ice Fields Parkway. By day's end my leg muscles felt like they'd really done something and I got to meet cheerful long-distance cyclists from Vancouver, Ottawa, and San Diego. I learned from these cyclo tourists that the French like bikes too, so next year, I've decided to put my bike on the plane and go. Everyone seemed to know that it's not about the bike; it's about the ride and about the rider. It's the chance to go wherever you can imagine. It's about passing through a lot of fakery, and indulging in the pure joy of whirring wheels, wind, mist and rain in the face, and meeting all the others out there who choose to do something both energetic and spiritual each day.

Cathy Donaldson bike-commutes in Seattle, a generally bike-friendly town. Everyone important to her is a rider: husband Joe, daughter Lauren, a bike-commuting grad student in Tokyo, Japan, and dad Frank, winner of the hundred-mile Brisbane, Australia, bike race in 1933.

The Inside Spin

Charles Adolewski

That the bicycle is the most efficient tool ever invented to transfer energy into motion is a widely held and long-standing belief. The usual meaning associated with this remarkable appraisal of the bicycle is that, compared to the automobile, which has wreaked havoc upon our planet like no other invention ever has, the bicycle is a gem of creation.

Contemporary American society has been structured around the automobile. It is now a necessity for many people in order to get to their workplace. But Americans are not only dependent on their motor vehicles; they are infatuated with them. Americans have become spoiled rotten. How many of us have thought nothing of the long-term cost to the environment from hopping into our cars and hying to a convenience store for some milk or a loaf of bread, or driving across town for an ice cream cone, a cup of coffee, or a newspaper? Yet the number of people who commute by bicycle versus the number who commute by motor vehicle is paltry. The enormous potential for commuters to make a difference becomes apparent in the light of only a few statistics: More than half of all Americans live less than five miles from work; the easiest automobile trips to avoid, the short ones, contribute heavily to pollution because of unburned hydrocarbons released into the air from cold engines, which do not fire effectively; and if each American driver were to save only a quarter of a gallon of gasoline daily, America could eliminate the need to import oil from the Middle East. Also, bicycle commuting could alleviate tremendously a big headache in many places—parking—as at least eight bicycles can be parked in the space required to park a single automobile.

Although the bicycle's capabilities are myriad, one of its nicest features clearly is to offer riders the ability to combine transportation, exercise, and recreation all into one activity. Taking this feature to heart with unbridled enthusiasm, my friend Ellen and I once parlayed this winning combination into a two-and-a-half-year-long journey. Our bicycling odyssey brought us eighteen thousand miles around the United States, through western Canada, and into northern Mexico.

In this fast-paced, regimented world, emphasis is placed on accumulating possessions, gaining security, and stacking up accomplishments, yet people yearn for the freedom of a simple lifestyle. On our slow-paced, open-ended journey, we kept matters simple by carrying everything we needed to be self-sufficient, and we loved spending most of our time outdoors. We never found the landscape boring, and we could not help but meet people—they came to us, asking question after question and offering us friendship and hospitality. When we set out, we planned to travel for about a year. However, our trip became much more than a bicycle trip, as it broadened in scope mile by mile and day by day. Traveling by bicycle was a fun and environmentally responsible way to explore the big backyard of the United States. It was also a great way to promote bicycling. The longer we adventured, the more we loved it. Our goal was not to cover a certain number of miles or to reach a certain destination, but to live each day to the fullest.

While en route, we often thought about a dear friend of ours who had died of cancer prior to fulfilling his dreams. We thought of other people we knew, too, who were waiting for that special day—retirement—when they would then do all those wonderful things they had been putting off. And we pedaled. We thought about careers, the meaning of success, and the emphasis placed on the secure life. And we pedaled. We thought about our own lives and how they had changed.

We looked ahead, too, but usually could see clearly only as far as the next mountain or to the desert horizon. And the pedals kept going around. We're not sure when it happened, but there came a time when life before the bike trip seemed like an old dream, life beyond the bike trip seemed like it could be anything we wanted it to be, and the life of each and every day—we cherished for its own sake.

The wonderful transfer of energy for which the bicycle is noted is therefore far from limited to the realm of the physical transfer of energy, as the power of the bicycle is equally evident in what it can do for the workings of the mind.

One hot and steamy afternoon Ellen and I pedaled up yet another long steep hill along the Blue Ridge Parkway, and from that day on, my perspective on hills was changed forever. During the intensity of the cycling, I realized that the climb is really a dance. It is also a tightrope walk, or a combination of tightrope walking and dancing. As a form of art, the climb is bounded by neither stage, studio, nor end of rope; it is fluid, linear, one-way. Required are strength, agility, and a certain mental composure. For this particular performance, 150 pounds of yours truly, along with 80 pounds of gear and supplies, rode 30 pounds of bicycle and accessories. All this was balanced upright upon two narrow tires, which formed the only earthly contact.

Looking down while climbing, I gazed at two finely toned, compact and strong legs that, after seventeen thousand miles so far of this trip alone, were thin, brown, and like pistons. Sweat poured from my body, even as I worked in the lowest—and easiest to pedal—of eighteen gears. Up and down went the legs, driving pedals that made cranks go around, to drive chain and chainrings in order to push the wheels themselves. These "pistons" pumped at about one revolution per second— and *they never stopped*. The dance always moves. It has to.

Without forward progress, bicycle and rider cannot remain upright for long. The bicycle wants to lean over to one side or the other and lie down. Unless gravity was countered, my body would have complied with the bicycle and gone down with it. Here the front wheel came into play. Provided there was momentum, its pivoting helped maintain balance. During the climb, it pointed a little bit to the left, then a little bit to the right. The bicycle never traveled in a perfectly straight line. Making tiny snakelike movements, it crawled uphill along the side of the road.

The bicycle seemed to *steer itself.* My hands only rested upon the handlebar: now on the top section, sometimes down lower over the brake-lever hoods, and in various combinations in between. Never needing to bend over completely and grasp the handlebar dropouts, from where I could have virtually *pulled myself uphill,* I remained upright and steady while climbing at three miles an hour. A dip of my shoulder, causing a slight change in center of gravity, and the bicycle traveled in the direction my body leaned. A gentle push on the handlebar, from the side the bicycle was turning toward, and direction of travel changed. *I never consciously steered.* And so went the dance: The body weaving left and right; bobbing up, bobbing down; feet made one with pedals by toe-clip stirrups; buttocks pressed into the saddle; "pistons" *never stopping*—up and down, up and down, around and around. The climb is the dance, the constant flow through nature, the balancing act supreme.

Without a doubt, energy that most efficiently becomes motion is the bicycle's most salient characteristic, but it is when we internalize that energy that the experience of bicycling becomes most rewarding. Consider how the wheels spun on the inside as Ellen and I approached the tail end of our phenomenal journey.

On our way north across the Merrimack River, in Lowell, Massachusetts, I automatically looked downriver, toward where I was born in a small hospital around the bend. On the other side of the river we turned west for Dracut, and I showed Ellen the tenement house that is the first place in which I can remember living. To this day I still relive experiences from there in my imagination.

Then the thing happened. Right there in the Centralville section of the city, between the location of those early memories of mine and the house in which Jack Kerouac was born about a mile away, I looked down at my odometer, and it read 19.50. However, on display was far more than the number of miles we had traveled so far that day from Walden Pond; *1950 is the year of my birth!*

As the wheels turned and the numbers mounted, episodes of my life played out in my mind and corresponded with the numbers. Every hundredth of a mile was a year; every tenth, a decade. My mind acted fast, keeping up with the pace. Memories of Lowell during the early fifties led to memories of the mid-fifties, when I had moved to the adjacent town of Dracut. The next time I looked down, I saw the early sixties. There I was in junior high school during the advent of the Beatles. An intense period of war opposed by a peace-and-love movement ensued. Very quickly I went through high school, then tried and failed at college. I had to go to war, both externally and internally, before I could find my own peace. I saw myself in the army, serving in Vietnam, then returning to college for a true introduction to the study of literature and philosophy, which led me to the green mountains of western Massachusetts and beyond, all the way to the eye-opening glare and fare of San Francisco.

The odometer kept turning, and my psyche continued reflecting. The years I did not see were represented as a void—indeed there had been some dark times. Pedaling toward the Dracut of my youth, the seventies and eighties flashed before my mind's eye. I saw myself as a cub reporter in Kansas and as a forestry worker in the high country of the Colorado Rockies. The eighties also brought me to Cape Cod, where I had met Ellen, discovered healthful living, and begun the *real* pleasures of cycling. Now the numbers read 1989, the year we had begun our trip. A life compressed into minutes was flicking before me; 1990 and 1991 flew by. Now I was no longer in the past, but projecting into the future. When the numbers turned 20.00 and beyond, the projecting mechanism began to muddle. Although the wheels and numbers turned steadily, the form of the digits was too strange to represent years of my life. But I did not mind—I did not want to look too far ahead anyway.

More amazing than being led into the *future* by the numbers while bicycling *back* to the place where we had started was my regarding *past, present,* and *future* at the same time! *Over there* remained what little was undeveloped of an old cow pasture in which I had roamed as a child; *here* stood the emptiness where once the branches of a majestic elm tree had soared; and the *future* portrayed me coauthoring a travel-adventure book with Ellen into the nineties. *There* went the road on which I had walked, bicycled, and driven automobiles countless times on my way through the Collinsville section of Dracut; *here* I was on it once more, as a traveler returning in a manner I had never done before; yet the *future* showed me to be bound for distant countries. Back to the *here* and *now* once more—*I felt like a stranger in my own hometown!*

Having finally come full circle, Ellen and I both were sad. Still, a surge of happiness found its way into our warm embrace.

"Well . . . we did it!" I said with a great big smile.

"What a crazy thing to do—bike eighteen thousand miles around the country for two and a half years," Ellen replied through tears of joy. "Who ever does anything like that?"

Charles Adolewski lives in Tempe, Arizona.

The Yellow Huffy

Paula R. Hagar

The best bicycle I ever had was my very first one—a cheap, glossy yellow Huffy ten-speed that I paid sixty-five dollars for with my own hard-earned cash. When I wasn't living in Lake Ontario during those muggy northeastern summers, I was living astride the hard seat of that flying machine.

Even once I could drive, there were many silent places, dark nighttime places the bike could take me that the big boat of a 1960s car could not. The blurred journeys on my Huffy freed me in summer, the same way skiing did in winter—flying, soaring, the wind so cold tears froze on my face. Night after night I flew through the streets of that stifling dying little mill town from which I wanted nothing more than to escape. As if maybe, if I flew just a bit faster or a little farther, I could pedal into another life.

Down South Indiana Avenue I flew toward Huntington Street, toward the Black River, my heart bursting in my throat, pedaling so fast my braids blew straight back from my head and unwrapped themselves. The rotting black tannins of the cold river seeped inside me as my lungs pumped until I could barely breathe. I had been warned to never go near that fierce river, whose swift currents gave power to this town and would suck even the strongest swimmer into the deep limestone caves submerged along the banks. But the musty faint sewer smell of the river gave me a strange comfort; somehow it pulled me closer to the earth to which I was so bonded.

I wanted to fly, and did on those nights as I flew through the world that was mostly black: the sky; the river; the night; my mood. Though long ago converted to electric, I still heard the century-old gaslights sizzle in the damp night air and welcomed the dim golden glow that mingled like magic with the starlight above. I tasted the salt of my tears mixed with the river dew, a faint metallic burn on the back of my tongue. Hot-cold pockets of air hit my skin like strobe lights. The air itself burned moistly hot in spots from the slumbering meadows, and dankly cold in others from patches of air sodden with the breath of the cold river. I tasted whiffs of pork chops frying and hamburgers grilling as I sped past the homes of happy families. The clank of plates pulled from cupboards and set on the table, the distant bass laughter of a man, his wife's soprano tones, and the shrill cries of hungry children ready for the meat-and-potatoes dinner Mom was dishing up filled me with a Norman Rockwellian longing.

I pedal faster, my quads and butt muscles straining against the delicate stitches of the thin patches in my jeans. My neck is taut as marble as I thrust my figurehead out in front of me, as if that will raise me off the road and then I'll really be flying, high above the lights of this worldly prison. Wheee-e-e-e-e—I am flying! I follow the dark shimmering curling ribbon of river as I flee through the night. I follow the river by the humid fishy iron smell I taste as I lick my lips. I follow the murmur of the river's heart as it tumbles over the ledges of limestone, and swirls and swishes in and out of hidden caves. I soar through swirls of bats that dart for bugs above the holes to their cave homes, their squeaky radar *cheeps* guiding me onward. I drink the night air that tastes like iron, limestone, chalk, and fish, and fills my belly with the promise of morning, even though I am never ready for the blaze of morning's brilliance. I swathe myself in the comforter of starlight, a kaleidoscope of warm-cool air patches, the golden squares of light from other people's windows, the charcoal and pork chop drippings of their suppers, the ache of my silent bedroom whose walls whisper sad poems of adolescent angst, and I stop to let the river speak before I turn to go home.

After my beloved grandma died, the yellow Huffy was my best friend during those lonely teenage years, until it was stolen right off the front porch, the lock picked. I'd paid for the bike myself, and knew every square inch of it by touch and by heart. I had taken that cheap bicycle apart time after time, lovingly oiled the chains and brakes and gears and derailleurs, and put it back together.

Heartbroken, I became a vigilante. Determined to find the thieves who had picked the bike lock, I spent days driving around the seedy neighborhoods north of the tracks. One night I saw some hoodlums dismantling yellow bicycles on a dim front porch, called the police, and soon thereafter the yellow Huffys stopped disappearing around town. My investigative quest to find my beloved bike helped break up a burglary ring that was stealing dozens of the identical bikes purchased by every kid in town that year. I never did find my own yellow Huffy.

With the insurance money, I bought what they told me was a better bike, a gleaming orange Sutton English racer, sleeker, more streamlined, and twice the cost. The orange Sutton took me on many flights too, but it was never the same.

About that time boys with fast cars became more appealing, and for years afterward the Sutton sat in a rusty pile behind the garden shed before I could bring myself to put these pieces of my life out with the trash.

But now, thirty years later when I pedal my sleek Trek twenty-one-speed, it is still the yellow Huffy I remember, with the serious girl in granny glasses and braids hugging for dear life the handlebars of the bicycle that set me free from the agony of being sixteen.

Paula Hagar is a forty-eight-year-old writer, photographer, artist, naturalist, traveler, seeker, and yoga fanatic who can be found bicycling her way around Denver, Colorado. Her writing has appeared in The Sun, The Diarists' Journal, *and* Somerset Studio.

Phat

Amanda Stone

My mountain bike had a thick chromoly frame, handlebars you could grip with the muscles in your back, and fat tires. I had bent the turn-crank on my last bike, an aluminum ten speed. But this one was built of stronger stuff. When I pushed hard on the pedals, they pushed back. I could feel the tires grip firm on hills I wouldn't want to walk up.

The bike shop guy had not gotten what I'd said when I walked in.

"There are some nice hybrid models that are more appropriate for street biking," he said, glancing from the bike rack to my waist. The bikes were two high, with a rack suspending half of them in the air.

I repeated myself. "I'm here to get a mountain bike. I am looking for a Bridgestone BB100 with an eighteen-inch frame. Like this one right here." It was red.

As I lifted it out of the line he said helpfully, "I can let you take it for a test ride. Wouldn't you rather try these hybrid bikes first?"

I wrote him a check and rode it home, oily stains soaking into the right calf of my favorite pair of jeans. I didn't wear those jeans again for the rest of the summer. I took all my other pairs and cut the legs off.

I hadn't worn shorts in five years. When I was fifteen and lost sixty pounds, I took up whitewater kayaking and spent every minute at the neighborhood lake in my purple boat, practicing Eskimo rolls. On weekends, I hit the Youghiogheny, the New, and the Gauly. It was just me and a paddle. I felt like an amphibious centaur, water exploding, carrying me fast. I skirted holes and rooster tails and plowed through river waves I couldn't see over. In the eddies, I flirted with raft guides whose eyes went from my face to my boat. If they could have seen under my spray skirt they would have seen shorts.

Over the winter I gained back forty pounds. I no longer fit into my wet suit, my life jacket, or my kayak. I was going to get everything in a larger size except there was no larger size.

But on my bike I fit fine. I let the battery go dead on my car while I rode my bike to work, to friends' houses, and to buy groceries. The main road outside my neighborhood was also the main tourist drag to the ocean. On weekends, the cars moved maybe fifty feet every ten minutes. Tourists sat baking in their cars. The lucky ones rolled up their windows, turned up the air-conditioning, and barked at their kids. I rode past them all, leaving them to watch my butt disappear down the road.

I lived in a student co-op. Between all eight of us and our friends and our friends' friends, there were always people in the kitchen. While making a cup of tea, I could overhear discussions about the quality of last night's punk show or the ethics of wearing wool. One night I went in to make dinner and a roommate had some new friends over.

"I just mostly feel sorry for them because, like, what kind of sex life can they have?"

The woman who said this had her back to the door. Those who didn't were looking at me with wide eyes. I smiled at them and opened the refrigerator.

She continued, "I mean, otherwise, I don't have any problem with people being overweight. But what about like ever finding someone who would want to have sex with you?"

I shut the refrigerator door already laughing at what I was about to say. "I feel compelled to say that I have a divine sex life." The woman swung around and saw me, or rather my body. While the rest of the kitchen howled and she bugged her eyes out in horror, I left the room laughing.

Because it was divine. Every night I took my boyfriend to where he couldn't talk, to where he couldn't move. His body soaked me in like I was butter. Our breath was still and then peppered with moments of hyperventilation. In the morning, my housemates asked if we could keep it down. We tried to but you know how it goes.

But when things got serious, he left me because of my weight.

"You fucking know you're attracted to me," I told him when he said why he was breaking up.

"It's not that," he said. "Do you know what people say about me? It changes the way they look at me. It's embarrassing just to be seen with you. That's not what I want in a life partner."

And you're not what I want in a life partner, either, I wanted to say back to him. Unfortunately, by the time I meant it, weeks had passed and he was long gone.

I didn't ride my bike for a while after that. I spent a lot of time reading and baking bread. Winter came. Rain lashed at the windows while I sipped tea and waited for the second rising. In the spring, I pulled out my bike and lubed the gears. I found a group of women and we road fifty miles up Highway 1 to camp out near a waterfall. I was the last one to make it to our lunch stop, the last one up the five-hundred-foot climb at Scotts Creek. But I got to the campsite before nightfall. We all talked about how exhausted we were and watched bats catch mosquitoes.

A little while after the camping trip, I was riding down Ocean Street. Ocean had a bike lane but it disappears without warning in front of the 7-Eleven. A white truck on steroids and tractor wheels came up behind me as the lane narrowed. The truck was full of men, three in the cab, three in the bed, all in white muscle shirts with baseball caps on backward.

"Get off the road, you fat cow." As I heard the words, I stood up on my pedals and pumped hard. I was trying to catch up with them before

I had even registered the insult. They took a right and I took it hard, staying on their tail. The driver's eyes were on his rearview mirror. The guys in back banged on the back window. "Dude, she's following us."

They took another right, then a left. I stayed with them on the turns. They got to a straightaway and gunned it and I couldn't keep up with them. But then they stopped at a red light. I put everything I had into my thighs. Everyone in the cab turned to watch my approach. The men in the bed pressed their backs against the cab. When I was ten feet away, the driver shot straight through the red light and I let them go.

I stood there at the red light not knowing exactly what I was feeling. I leaned on my handlebars with my feet wide apart. The light turned green and I stood there trying to figure out why I was so happy. I felt my heart pounding hard and firm. I felt my breath long. My legs stung as wind tickled the sweat off. I thought, *You don't know what you've got until you have to fight for it.*

My bike took me up dirt roads, down fire trails, through meadows and winding switchbacks. On a trail that followed the coastline, I came upon a bobcat in midair pouncing on mice. I rode to an alcove and found a beached gray whale, offering his belly to the sun. I climbed up a thousand feet through meadows and redwood forest to look down on the ocean stretch out like the stomach of a faraway lover.

This is me at 250 pounds. This is what my doctor calls grossly obese. This is what others have said is the definition of ugly, of wastefulness, of sloth. My clean, sweating body offering pleasure and resistance and laughter and desire. This is what I had climbed a thousand feet for.

Amanda Stone lives in Santa Cruz, California.

Dalton Highway

Tom Snyders

It was a preemptive strike on a midlife crisis. I found myself on a horrendous gravel road, pedaling out of Prudhoe Bay, Alaska, on a fully loaded touring bike. That's Prudhoe Bay—as in at the Arctic Ocean—as far North as you can go in North America by road. I use the term *road* very loosely—as in loose gravel. There would be five hundred more miles of it before I even reached the luxurious pavement of the Alaska Highway. My destination was Key West, Florida—sixty-one hundred miles to the south and a world away.

My mind kept asking the same question, *Tom, what the hell are you doing here?* In addition to the gravel, the weather, the mountains, and the remote wilderness, there were also the grizzly bears.

Of course, I knew it was all part of my deeply hidden brilliance. The plan was to survive a daring adventure, to arrive in Key West lean and mean, and to turn forty uneventfully two months later. As an added bonus, I had contacted the Guinness people—as in world records, not beer. I figured with a recent world-record feat under my cap, turning forty would actually be a source of pride. There were a lot of things I didn't know.

As my thighs started burning from traversing the steep grades of the Dalton Highway, another thought kept popping into my mind, *Who the hell built this road?* I also shouted the word *bastards* quite frequently. It was only the first day of the journey and I was already talking to myself. By day three of the trek the mosquitoes were driving me crazy. They were joined by these unbelievably big and aggressive horseflies. Because of the painfully slow going on the gravel, those bastards could keep up with me. The word "Bastards" now applied to the mosquitoes, the horse flies, and the drunk engineers who had built the road. On this same day, at the top of Antigun Pass, I literally almost passed out. It was only 4,739 feet, but it was another of their trademark steep grades—an almost impossible climb on a touring bike loaded with a hundred pounds of packs. *Bastards!*

While catching my breath, I noticed a glacier alongside the road. In my delirious state I hadn't even paid attention to it until then. It was incredibly beautiful, and helped to calm me. There was a stream seeping from this glacier. Out of water for the past three hours, I anxiously dipped one of my three water bottles into this glacier stream and gulped many refills of this fresh, ice-cold nectar of the gods. It was awesome.

Day four started badly. I was struggling against a rugged wind. It was raining. The road had turned to soup. My chain and gears were clogged. The hills started up again. I was fighting hypothermia. Just another day on the Dalton Highway. But It turned out to be the most powerful day of my life!

At sixty miles on the day, and at about 10:30 P.M. I hit the official Arctic Circle boundary line. It was a photo opportunity. Fortunately, the rain stopped, and the sun came out. That far north, the sun doesn't set in August, and its presence was a reassuring sight.

Slightly rested, I climbed back on my bike and continued south. I was just thinking that I didn't have many hills left in these legs. Then I saw it—Beaver Slide. I actually stopped in my tracks, and looked at it three times before it set in—that thing off in the distance going straight up and over a mountain was the road. Those bastards! No cute curves. No dynamite.

Straight up and over the top of the mountain—the steepest grade I had ever seen on a road, any road—and this one was gravel. I'm very stubborn and had never walked a bicycle up a hill in my life. But I really didn't think I could get my fully loaded bike over that hill. Then something strange happened. After getting mad, somehow I calmed down and concentrated on finding the quiet place in my mind. I focused on my breathing. I filtered out all else. I got into some kind of meditative state as I approached the mountain. I kept hearing, or telling myself—I'm not sure which—"You have the power within you."

Even in this state I figured I might have to ride a third of the way up, take a break, and then continue. I took a few breaths and started up the mountain. At a third of the way, after a tremendous amount of effort already, and at a very high heart rate, I somehow got into this unexplainable, very powerful rhythm. I just kept pedaling.

It wasn't long before I could only hold a speed of three miles per hour—any slower and I would literally just fall over. I kept going, and kept focusing on the word *power* and on my breathing. It was nothing short of transforming.

I was aware of the extreme pain that I was in—but at the same time able to remain in the quiet place in my mind. I would also pick a post or a patch of grass up ahead and focus on it. When I got there, I would find another one farther up the road. I kept asking myself if I could endure the pain to make it to that next landmark. The answer was always yes. Somehow I managed to keep inching onward and upward.

I was just seconds away from passing out when, with one final burst that involved some screaming, I made it to the top. I had used every physical and mental trick I knew. I could not have pedaled another inch uphill if my life had depended on it. But it was exhilarating to have made it all the way to the top without stopping. I had pushed through the pain. It was a rebuilding of my confidence, and a recharging of my spirit.

I had tapped into these same powers of the universe and of my body and mind to survive and recover from a near-fatal bike accident five years earlier. In that case I had been hit by an elderly driver and dragged thirty feet while riding my touring bike through Los Angeles. I ended up with a bunch of broken bones and in a coma and on a respirator at UCLA Medical Center—and was not expected to live through the night. Eight months later, after grueling physical therapy, spiced with plenty of mental visualizations, I managed to get back on my bike and pedal across the country.

It's amazing what you can forget in five years. I used to know that I had the power within me to do whatever I needed in my life. As I closed in on forty, I was in dire need of a reminder of my physical and mental abilities. The simple act of coordinating my powers to climb a mountain did just that. When faced with a seemingly insurmountable obstacle, just make yourself get started, and keep at it until you get where you want to go.

A calm determination came over me to use these same skills and same persistence to improve my life—to follow through on some things, though sometimes tired and burned out. After a brief rest at the top of Beaver Slide, I found myself once again cranking out miles and riding steep hills without fail—and somehow, through it all, remaining in the quiet place in my mind. Day four on the Dalton Highway was providing nothing short of a mystical experience, and it wasn't over yet.

As the evening grew later the trees cast odd-shaped shadows on the road. Many of them looked like grizzly bears. I was delirious and on a gravel road on my bike in some of the most remote wilderness in North America at two thirty in the morning. *Intense* doesn't even begin to describe it. My legs were shot, and should have been growing weaker with every passing mile, and each new hill. But somehow I was gaining strength. I was climbing stronger—more focused, more determined, even more efficiently.

On the downhills I could barely see the road. My speedometer reported my bike reaching 46.7 miles per hour while screaming down one of these hills practically blind. But I was unexplainably confident.

I could pick the one right line in the road and stick with it. I was doing it by sheer intuition.

Any mistake would have meant certain disaster. But I was completely in the flow—now one with the road and the environment that had been my enemy. I could do no wrong. Hill after hill—up successfully—screaming down to pick up momentum for the next. Almost poetic. Just plain great. I was alive, aware, exhilarated. It was nothing short of magical. A line from my journal reads, "Tom, remember being in that zone, the Michael Jordan level zone (without the millions of dollars)."

At about three o'clock in the morning, after riding against the strong wind all day, and up and down the steepest hills I had ever seen, I arrived at Yukon River Crossing. I was beyond exhausted—no legs, back shot, barely able to stand. But as I pitched my tent alongside the Yukon River I had a smile on my face. It had been a long, amazing day on the Dalton Highway, 123.7 miles to be exact. The magic of the road had been in full force.

Eventually, I made it to the pavement of the Alaska Highway. After a total of sixty-three days I would successfully arrive in Key West. But, my measurement of success by the end did not even resemble what it had been when I started out of Prudhoe Bay. There were other incredible days on the journey. In one of them, at an obscure café along the Alaska Highway, I met Martina, an amazing Swiss woman who was bicycling solo from Prudhoe Bay to the tip of South America. I would end up pedaling along with her for ten days and the entire length of British Columbia. She was young, tanned, and toned from the road. In any other setting we would not have hit it off—but the Dalton Highway gave us an instant camaraderie.

She was a magical contact on the road. Even I eventually figured that out. The conversation in my head went something like this: *Tom— hello—beautiful Swiss woman on a bike heading the same direction as you— slow down and forget the silly world record thing.* I can only hope that I was able to teach her half as much as she taught me. But my ten days of riding with Martina are the subject of another essay.

The entire journey from Prudhoe Bay to Key West was chock-full of amazing experiences, including encounters with six bears along the way, endless instances of the kindness of strangers (as always happens on any bicycle trip), and did I mention Martina? But the real lasting magic had occurred on day four of the journey.

When I reached Key West, I realized that the lessons from the Dalton Highway had really been what I needed from this entire journey. They had been made possible by my willingness to follow my intuition and get out and do what I felt like I should be doing—no matter how crazy it seemed. Somehow things always seem to work out when you do that. The Indians in Alaska have a saying, "There are spirits that protect holy fools."

I was now in Key West. I was lean and mean. More importantly, I was freshly reminded that I have the power within me to do whatever I need to do in my life. Two months later, I turned forty uneventfully. I'm a genius.

Tom Snyders (www.bikecomedy.com) is also known as "The Bicycling Comedian." His Prudhoe Bay to Key West adventure was a segment within an ongoing seventeen-year bicycle trip in which he has so far pedaled over 123,000 miles across 50 states and 11 countries. Tom pedals his bicycle to all of his stand-up comedy performances throughout North America. He has appeared in over two hundred comedy clubs. He also performs at many bike events. Tom has made nine national television appearances to date, including three on Live with Regis and Kathie Lee, *and has also been featured on* Comedy Central *and* ESPN.

The Great Bicycle Experiment

C. B. Burgess

Looking back, I remember it all very clearly. It had been my first big trip home since I graduated from law school and moved "away." I had literally written my last exam, piled all my earthly possessions into my battered old Westfalia, and headed west all the way across Canada to start a new life in British Columbia. My family in "the East" were all quite concerned. I guess it hadn't been easy for them to see the baby of the family head out all on his own. Two years later, in the fall of 1999, I had returned for my first visit. My destination had been Atlantic Canada, Nova Scotia and New Brunswick to be more precise.

I recall how disheartened I felt to see my beloved parents for the first time after a two-year absence. They simply did not look "well," especially my father. Their skin had a pale sheen to it and they had both aged a great deal since I last saw them. My father seemed heavy and sluggish, while my mother had literally withered away. I know my dad weighed at least 215 pounds (he later confessed it was closer to 225). I had mentioned my observations to my siblings, but they apparently did not share my concerns. I guess when you see someone every day you tend not to notice the cumulative effects of such gradual changes. But to me, after two years away, their aging had been strikingly obvious. Actually, my entire family had appeared to be in rather poor physical condition. Of course, having spent the last twenty-four months working and playing in Vancouver (the fittest city in Canada) may have raised my expectations about somewhat.

I like to tell people that on the plane ride back to the big city that fall,

I had made a very selfish decision. *I simply can't go to any funerals in the near future,* I remember thinking to myself. So I had vowed to get my family to make some changes in their less-than-healthy lifestyles. Most of all, I had wanted to get to my father, whom I believed needed the most improvement and would also serve as the linchpin for the remainder of the family. And thus, I had set about hatching my evil plan. A plan so deceitful and manipulative that it just had to work.

I had personally had the cycling bug for years, ever since I had bought a pair of cheap mountain bikes for me and my then-girlfriend while still an undergraduate in university. Since then my appreciation of, and investment in, bicycles has increased exponentially. I had experienced the tremendous efficiency of the ever-evolving cycling technology and the true pleasure of riding a good bike.

Now, my father is "old school," have no doubt about it. He was raised in a rigidly patriarchal family and his attitudes and beliefs reflected his upbringing. In my dad's world, men put food on the table and women cook it. It was that simple. He had retired early at age fifty-five from a career as a research scientist for Agriculture Canada. The problem was that he promptly sat down on the living room couch and watched cable TV for four years afterwards. By age fifty-nine, he was overweight, unhappy, living without purpose and depressed. This had also taken its toll on my mother, his steadfast partner of some thirty-eight years. Neither of them was very active, healthy, or happy.

Knowing my dad as I did, I knew that the key to getting him to change was to play to his old-school male ego. Though he would never admit it, even today, my father was very controlling and jealous of my mother. So I knew I had to use my mom in order to get to my dad. Thus, in October of that year, my mother received a brand-new mountain bike as a present. And this was no cheap bike by any means. I got her a good one and it was worth its weight in gold as far as I'm concerned. Although I had bought and paid for it myself, I let my sister and brother also take credit for the gift. I didn't mind sharing the spotlight with them. It didn't matter as long as the effect was the same. Of course, my ever unselfish and sacrificing mother had immediately professed that she didn't need such a good bike nor was she in any way deserving of such an expensive gift. "But I already have a bike. It's at the cottage," she had complained with tears forming in her eyes. Laughing lovingly at her continuous martyrdom, I had asked her when the last time was that she had actually ridden her existing bike. "Fifteen years ago" was her reply. "Well that's because it's not a good bike," I had told her. "That thing probably cost a hundred dollars at Kmart. The technology has really changed. This is a really good bike. Just give this one a try."

When my father found out about the present, it didn't take long for his ego to surface. "What did you give your mother a new bike for?" my father inquired in a slightly annoyed voice. "She'll never use that. She can't bike anymore. She'll break her neck." I knew by the jealous tone of his voice that I had him exactly where I wanted him.

Despite my father's dire predictions, my mom did in fact start using her new bike that fall without mishap. Sure enough, reports soon trickled west from my siblings that, yes, Mother was indeed riding her bike and had even done some weekend trips to small towns around New Brunswick with a recently widowed friend. My father, already jealous at not having gotten a bike himself, was all the more so now that my mother was out and about having fun with new friends and no longer as dependent on him.

Having successfully completed phase one of my plan, it was therefore with mischievous glee that I boxed up a shiny new hybrid for my dad that Christmas. He called me right away when it arrived to thank me. I guess it was fairly obvious what it was. He had known it was a bike even before he unwrapped it. After he had opened it, he called me again to say how nice it was. "Thanks for the present," he had said. "I'm not sure what the hell I'm going to do with it, but thank you. It's very nice."

Now, it gets damn cold and snowy in New Brunswick during the winter, so my dad's new bike was relegated to the basement for assembly and appraisal. This too was part of my devious plan. I knew it would drive him crazy to have to sit there and look at it and not be able to ride it. He had several months of cold, housebound days before spring arrived for the cycling bug to grow and fester inside him.

Eventually spring did come to the Maritimes that year and reports soon began to make their way to me from family and friends about my dad. It seems that he had actually been sighted riding a bike around Fredericton. No one could believe their eyes. Yes, my father had tried the bike out one sunny spring afternoon and ridden it exactly once around the block before walking it home exhausted. The next day he rode it twice around that same block. He had added one lap per day until his stamina returned. Soon, he was riding around the neighborhood, and eventually around the city. He began calling me to ask me questions about gearing and shifting, and to report his weekly mileage. Shunning modern cycling apparel, he wore old jeans instead of cycling shorts, taping the pant legs up with electrical tape. Much to my chagrin, he had also taken the oversized trac-tor-style seat off an old stationary exercise bike and replaced the bike's original touring saddle with it. "My ass is too big for that tiny thing," he told me. "I don't know how anyone could sit on something like that." You can imagine what a spectacle that created. But my plan had worked. He had the bug and now no trail was safe from my father's excursions. Soon he was calling me to report that he had done ten miles one morning alone. Then it was twenty and then thirty miles per day. He and my mom were now biking together, doing two outings per day. Trail maps and cycling magazines started to flood my parents' mailbox. They began using the internet to research trips and equipment. I promptly sent my dad a bike rack for his truck. That was three years ago.

Today, my father is sixty-two years old and weighs a hundredand eighty-two pounds. My mother has reaped similar benefits. They are both very happy and healthy. Dad recently told me he hadn't been in such good shape since he was twenty-five. He has a spring in his step and a quick wit that betrays his active intelligence. He rises early each morning and follows a strictly healthy diet. Three excursions per day during the height of the season are the norm. He now owns four bicycles and accumulated over six thousand kilometers this past season (May to September). My mom has two of her own as well. That first bike I gave him that started the transformation? Well, it's still his favorite, even though he now owns some at least four times as expensive. It is just about worn out. Most of its components have been replaced at least once. As for the TV remote? Well, it gathers dust on the coffee table, unless of course there is cycling on OLN.

He now spends the winter following the Tour de France and rabidly devouring each issue of the at least four cycling magazines he subscribes to. Catalogs from just about every bike manufacturer in the world cover the coffee table as he plans his next acquisition and the myriad upgrades and modifications necessary to make it just right.

Outside in his garage, my father has set up a small bicycle shop where he is constantly cleaning and tuning their stable of bikes before and after each ride. I sent him a repair stand and some tools to get him started and he has looked after the rest. The car? Well, it has been permanently relegated to the driveway year-round. The neighborhood kids now bring him their rusty, neglected charges for inspection and appraisal. He gladly accepts all their mechanical challenges free of charge, no matter how hopeless, with what can only be described as enthusiastic disgust, muttering a "Forgive them Father, for they know not what they do" under his breath for every squeaky, rust-coated chain that he unseizes. Bicycles have become sacred things to my dad. He too has realized the power of the bicycle, and has also taken to giving them as gifts. Friends and acquaintances now seek his advice on their cycling needs.

Most recently, he was elected president of the Fredericton Trails Coalition—a nonprofit association responsible for the development and stewardship of cycling trails throughout the province's capital region.

Collectively, he and my mother have pretty much conquered all of Atlantic Canada, including the remote Magdalene Islands, and have even flown all the way out to British Columbia to join me on a multiday tour of the world famous Kettle Valley Railway.

And still my evil plan continues. I have outfitted my entire family with bikes. No less than a dozen have made their way east to put smiling faces on out-of-shape relatives. Family rides of six or seven are not unusual. My fifteen-year-old nephew received a new one this past spring. Having been born with a severe learning disability and forced to attend a private school in order to get the scholastic assistance he requires, he was overweight, unable to read, picked on by his classmates and suffering from extremely low self-esteem. After a summer of nonstop riding, he has lost twenty pounds and is both happy and healthy. Cycling now consumes his days and nights, and he often rides with kids two or three years his senior. When he broke his frame in midseason, I promptly sent him another one. His interest in riding has motivated him to start using the internet and buying cycling magazines to keep up on all the different makes and models—which has helped him with his reading. He now lives for trials and big drops. The neighborhood kids come to him to fix their bikes and teach them tricks. He has a renewed confidence and maturity about him that is undeniable. On his birthday in September, he declared that he wanted to race downhill this spring. As for me, I'll be backing him all the way. May the Great Bicycle Experiment never cease.

Thirty-four-year-old Carl Burgess lives and rides in the vast cycling mecca that is Canada, where he divides his time between the coastal cities of Vancouver, British Columbia, and Halifax, Nova Scotia. An avid all-around cyclist, he enjoys touring, mountain biking, and road riding, as well as building and repairing all types of bicycles. Carl continues to use the gift of bicycles to improve the lives of family and friends, encouraging positive change just one pedal stroke at a time. He would like to dedicate this story to the memory of Moxy the Wonder Ferret.

The Life of an Inspired Cyclist

Jake Stephens

My first bicycle had lasers built into the reflectors that were controlled by my handgrips. The handgrips were red and each grip had a row of diamonds that was obviously the control panel for a variety of secret functions that none of the other kids had on their bikes. Of course, on my street, none of the other kids really rode bikes—except the ones too old to play with, who could jump an entire brick in the street—I saw it with my own eyes. I rode anyway. I rode as fast as I possibly could—back and forth between the street limits my parents had set. I sprinted. I skidded. I launched missiles at imaginary secret spy biker kids. I invented cryptological mechanisms to keep others from using my bike's superpowers. I used a smoke screen, I rode in my Batman Underoos, and most importantly I had jet boosters that sent me hurtling off to a hundred miles per hour, at my command. I was five, and I could count to a hundred, really really fast. Easy.

My half-block-long street limits had infinite possibilities. I rode everywhere—through any piece of yard that wasn't fenced in—especially if I was hiding from secret agents and trying to get a good stealthy shot with my plasma gun. In fact, some of the best terrain was in backyards, and if I hadn't been playing in those yards when those people weren't home, I never would have found my first baby raccoon, learned how to skid properly in really thick grass, or perfected my powerslide. Nor would I have lost my first Swiss Army knife one week after getting it. (The prices paid by secret agent bicyclists, especially when they are five years old.) I even learned that banana-seat bicycles did the best wheelies, and that a roofing nail through a well-pumped tire could make some amazing skid marks—and even sparks, if you got the technique right. You gotta love coaster brakes.

In many ways, my bicycle became the skin through which I touched the world. The first time I remember really, really crying was when Dad ran over my bike after I left it in the driveway. Somehow, though, I got another one, and several bicycles and many bike rides later, I knew the world I lived in in terms of my bicycle. It was defined in terms of curbs, trails, sand patches too thick to ride through, places where ramps were, neighborhoods where other kids rode bikes, hills, and the as-yet-uncharted areas, sketched in the back of the mind for future bike rides. Dad would take me riding everywhere. Over bridges with no shoulders, to the edges of the nearby marsh, to see new construction sites. We even visited friends and would stop and get a root beer on occasion. By the time I was sixteen, I had no qualms about doing a twenty-plus-mile loop on the BMX bike, and even did a forty-five-miler once with the dadster—him on his road bike, me drafting, and trying to stay off the industrial highway.

Around age thirteen the family had no car. Dad bike-commuted to work. Mom would call from the grocery store after shopping and all of us would ride up and load our handlebars with plastic bags, carefully balanced; you had to ride really smoothly to keep the bags from swinging into the spokes. Sometimes the six of us would parade home together, all loaded with groceries. It must have been quite a sight.

The bicycle defined my existence. I can't tell you how cool the movie *Rad* was to me. It was like God's spoken word of inspiration. The first time I saw it was at a slumber party, and I watched it three times before dawn. Later it was the Hans Rey trials-riding video. Most recently, it was watching my first Tour de France on TV—Mount Ventoux as that Lance guy attacked, definitively—and later, watching La Vuelta, with U.S. Postal sporting triple chainrings.

Thus inspired, I eventually perfected my 360 bunny hop. My tabletop air technique. My unchartable level of focus while descending on a mountain bike. My rear-wheel pogo. Thus inspired I have attacked on climbs, knowing I am not a climber. Thus inspired I have ridden a five-hundred-mile tour with no itinerary except Go, and slept on the beach at night. Thus inspired, I came to know the world in terms of how it could be touched by—and felt through—a bicycle. I have learned to breathe and flow in terms of the revolution of a bicycle wheel. Thus inspired I have discovered what it is that the bicycle means to me, how it has defined my life, and, in essence, what a bicycle is. If you are reading this, then this is our common bond.

The bicycle is inspiration. Religions have been founded for lesser gods—and if god is beauty, and the greatest beauties are simplicity and flow and grace—then the bicycle may be the greatest god ever devised by man.

When I ran into a steel cable in the dark at 25 mph on my mountain bike, it never even occurred to me that my bicycle might be to blame. Who will blame god for his moments of intimacy? I had bunny hopped off the college rugby field at full speed during a night ride, free-falling for forever onto the grassy slopes of a field that rolled away beneath me—invisible and rising, like the carpets of paradise. Cool wind touched my arms, the field flattened out, and then suddenly I came to a jolting stop. I saw the wire, a quarter-inch thick, when it was six inches from my chest. Mostly I just got a pair of really cool scars out of the deal—one on each arm, just below where the shoulder muscles recess onto the arm—and a thrashed cotton T-shirt.

But what stopping like that really illustrates is what the bicycle is really about: flow. The bicycle is about flow. Riding it is about flow. It is about the chess game. It is really about going 90 miles per hour. It really is about turning, and exploring, and breathing, and one's entire being dripping into one fat drop of liquid motion. The tires breathing into the dirt, the spokes churning fire-bound until electricity sets the bike and its rider ablaze.

Ablaze with motion, with peace, with fluidity. Liquid motion fueling itself on the drive of desire, freedom, and the taste of cool air. It is about moving fast enough to go places, and slow enough to see them. It is about intimacy with one's environment and painting that world in terms of contours. Contours of energy. It's the context of friction. The taste is the tangy, desirous familiarity of limits, felt and known as a blind man would come to know a new face. It is knowing where one lives. It is swerving, dodging, hopping, dancing, spinning, smiling, and it is focus. The freedom of focus; the focus of freedom.

In a race, it is barreling one's conscious into a liquid instant. In a race, it is animal aggression, it is a smiling tiger chasing its prey—slow or fast, but only what is necessary. Always relaxed. Always alive. Pouncing, playing, and breaking the game. And then suddenly, those wheels go into warp drive—stopping and starting simultaneously, the intergalactic motion of a wormhole uniting universes. There really are lasers built into your handgrips, and controls for the plasma rocket-booster warp drive, grenade launchers, and a cloaking device. In a crit, I've even realized there's an ejector seat button, but I can't always quite remember which one it is. I think it's adjacent to the diamond that says, ATTACK.

You're still not training hard enough. You're not breathing smoothly enough. You're bunny hop is still inadequate until you can clear an upside down trash can from a suburban curb. You're not fast enough—and you're not playing lightheartedly enough either.

This is the life of the inspired cyclist. Know flow. Rest harder. Ride longer. Visualize. Breathe. Act. Flow. Transform Desire into Motion. Flow more. Flow until you become liquid energy. See the world, your neighborhood. And go ride your bicycle.

Jake Stephens, 27, grew up in Jacksonville Beach, Florida, playing in the ocean, surfing, and riding BMX bikes. He spent his college years at Virginia Tech, rock-climbing religiously, mountain-biking on the side, until finally the road bike called him back. He currently rides out of Arlington, Virginia, and will race the road full time with Team Snow Valley, one of the top amateur teams in the U.S. Also a singer-songwriter, Stephens can be found singing songs about bicycles, in the DC area.

Bicycle or Boyfriend

Tammy Gomez

When I wrote my first anti-car poem, I owned a Mazda B2000 pick-up truck. Its recurring anthemic line, "death to autos in the parking lots," urged others to refute car culture, even as mine sat in a well-lit and secure parking lot. How I justified having a truck was this: It allowed me to pitch my mountain bike into the bed and drive it to the hinterlands of Colorado, New Mexico, and Texas in search of memorable off-road adventures.

> with our faces we are cheering
> —despite its four-wheel drive and power-steering—
> death to autos in the parking lots
> death to autos in the parking lots

The truck was primarily a facilitator of better mountain biking experiences. My boyfriends know this about me. They know my love. It comes easily and is expressed deeply. My boyfriends learn quickly of my deep bicycle love. They take a second seat to this love, this affliction, this affection. Witnessing my fast grip on the handlebars, and my solid stance on the foam rubber saddle, they begin to accept the mandate of our relationship. If you hang with me, you gotta ride too.

My first bicycle boyfriend rode a green ten-speed. He'd ride it to work, where he towel-dried luxury sedans and upscale station wagons at a full-service car wash—in the late 1970s. I'd feast my eyes on him as he rolled away from the schoolyard in the afternoons, his T-shirt sleeves flapping against toned and tanned biceps, his strong forearms glistening in the sunlight, and his pumping torso motion giving me an early teenage experience in lust.

One likes to imagine what a body could do if the legs were straddling you instead of that horizontal boy's bike crossbar. Sexy to watch. I got that horizontal bar between my thighs plenty of times. Except for my starter two-wheeler—a girl's-style bike with a purple frame and daisy-print banana seat—and my first ten-speed (a mustard yellow Kmart special), I've always *insisted* on owning boy's-style bikes. I read something, back in the 1980s, about better "triangulation" and "structural integrity" with boy's bike frames and detested the notion that a so-called girl's frame might have evolved as a marketing strategy to sell more bikes to chicks. A girly-fication of bike frames or bicycles, if you will. And I wasn't falling for that. So—my better-triangulated boy's crossbar bikes, though sixteen-inch frame to fit my frame, have suited me just fine over the years.

Cars always seem to figure into the equation, into the mathematics of my bicycle affinity. Funny to admit it, but I saw the now classic *Breaking Away* at a drive-in theater, sitting behind the wheel of my Datsun hatchback. I always like to root for the underdog, so it was natural for me to make the inspiring main character—bicycle racer Dave—my new movie hero. I also got a big crush on bicycling via that movie. And my boyfriend at the time, sitting in the passenger seat, well, he was more smitten by the Heineken six-pack that we were drinking than with bicycling, so I soon dropped him—off. Why would I have expected a north Texas city boy to be as enamored of bikes as I was? The Lone Star State is in a chokehold by the petroleum industry—with no signs of letting up—and only very recently has the notion of bike culture started to challenge the status car quo.

So off I went, to the mountains of Colorado, for some off-road, high country love. Boulder, Glenwood Springs, Aspen, Denver. I loved Boulder for its bike lanes—what a cool concept! (Hey, it was the

1980s.) And its proximity to the Flatirons was so alluring, and everyone there looked so fit, so healthy, so tofu-curd. I'd never seen so many luggage racks, wait, those weren't luggage racks. Those were hitch racks and upright mounts on the roofs, back ends, and beds of most cars and trucks in Boulder. Oh, the bike transport technology, oh the terminology—I had so much to learn.

In Denver, I was overjoyed to see bike racks, bike lanes, and—men on bikes. I loved seeing business execs careening in flow with downtown car traffic, their neckties whipped back over their shoulder and their office day dispositions seeming to relax in the face of the happy hour breezes. But especially, most especially, my eyes veered to the sight—my first glimpse of that most beautiful species—the bicycle messenger men. Toned calves, fast pedaling strides, quick, smooth, and confident dismounts. Style and finesse, that's what the messenger men connoted for me. They were like Mercury gods of the urban landscape, sleek-spoked, street-savvy, dashing young men with a message. Or a legal transcript. Or other business district deliverable. These men seemed as waterproof and durable as their shoulder packs, as heroic and determined as downhill slalom Olympians. The sight of such a sure-footed, steady-wheeled bicycle boy bent over his handlebars, bent on delivery, evoked in me a tremendous commingling of lust and awe. Silently cheering these messenger heroes, I have pushed my own bike and my own body to achieve such prowess on the streets.

Sidelined, I will not be sidelined
be no bystander
with life on standby
no, not me, no, not I

I have grown to enjoy that rush, the feeling of liberated velocity, that those courier men first exhibited for me back in Denver. I wanted that feeling. I wanted to be speedy diva on knobby tires, fleet on the streets, fast and ferocious, mighty and mountain-biked. So I rode and rode, pushing my pedals and my self to rougher terrain, steeper slopes, unpermitted pastures. But I also wanted boys to cheer for me. One autumn weekend, my Mazda B2000 had conked out in Basalt, Colorado. That bright Sunday morning, I perched against the front edge of the engine, under the uplifted hood of the truck, assessing the problem. I took apart the entire carburetor, and replaced the broken piece. As I refitted the engine parts, relieved and confident, a biker (black leather, long hair) motored by and did a double take. He was so impressed that a chick could fix her own truck that he stopped to meet me. Next day, he rode his cycle up the rocky mountain road to my cabin—with a fistful of red roses. My new boyfriend and cabin-mate became hot with envy when he learned of my motorcyclist-admirer. I considered the standoff these two men presented in my mind: "In this corner, wild-eyed and motorized, we have Dwayne the biker dude. And, in this corner, featherweight Marcus G—mountain biker and Taoist arts student!" The choice was easy. Ditch the biker and his hot unruly engine. Keep the soft-voiced, hard-riding bicycle boy.

Marcus and me were side-by-side cruisers, he on his white Cannondale, me on my beloved Maruishi—for the next eight months. He was fast and reckless, like his whimsical kisses. I was more prone to the paths and predictable habits of a sensible, responsible girlfriend. When we relocated to New Mexico, I deferred to Marcus's opinions and preferences, for he had lived in Santa Fe before and was familiar with its secret bicycle hideaways. We spent many hours, between work shifts at touristy restaurants, gliding through town—on and off the sidewalks and roadways—stopping only when we approached places too beautiful to pass up.

during our bike rides,
you would point and say "here"
and there would be the sweetest
softest grass to get lost in, our bicycles

tumbled on the ground, next to us

It was the most romantic of bicycle summers. If there could have been a leading lady and leading man of the fat-tire world, I would say that Marcus and me should've, could've, been it. We made Cliff's Liquor Store a regular stop, as they sold mini bottles of champagne, which we'd carry with us to the rose garden off of Old Pecos Trail. Everything seemed love story perfect: I began to notice birds following us, across St. Francis and down Don Juan streets, and older people seemed to longingly watch us, struck with memories of their own crazy, footloose love as they watched me and Marcus cruise past—pedaling free. But that blissed-out look on our faces was as much about the bicycle as it was about each other. We mutually enjoyed the vibrant energy and muscular capability that riding at high speeds had bestowed upon us. There was always something to celebrate because our bikes conveyed us to elation. Who needs antidepressants when you're crunching beautiful scenery with your bicycle?

did you feel good after noon
riding home on your bike
smiling at the folks you passed
knowing ultimately we do think alike?

Our highlight weekend was in Durango. Need I say that Durango is in Colorado? It is an outdoor adventurer's mecca and a mountain biker's nirvana, without a doubt. My man Marcus and I set up camp at Junction Creek, on the edge of the San Juan National Forest. We biked and hiked on the Colorado Trail, inhaling the mountain flower fragrances and splashing in the creek waters for several days. I racked myself as I took a spill on the singletrack path, but feeling so intoxicated by the natural environs, I barely noticed the pain. I was getting stronger and more macha and Marcus could sense that I was more easily keeping up with him. He decided to challenge me one afternoon as we were cruising the paths of Animas City Mountain. We spotted drizzles of lightning in the sky and knew we had to quickly descend and go for cover. Marcus opted for a steep angle descent route, as I shook my head in self-doubt. He took a deep breath, snarled at his fear, and screamed all the way down. His wheels knocked against gravelly rock and began a slight skid, but he made it. He triumphed with a grin and peered at me with a testy stare. Did I have the balls to follow in his path?

I will not live vicariously through the men I am involved with
I will not live vicariously through the men with whom I am involved
I will not live vicariously through the men . . .

It took several seconds, but it felt like the span of a thunderbolt explosion. I stormed down the slope full throttle with ferocity, my new mantra echoing like the pulse beats in my throbbing temples. *I will not live vicariously.* I will not stand by and be a nail-filing, doting girlfriend. I will learn to be my own hero. My newfound commitment to be a do-er and not a watcher compelled me to careen toward victory, alive and panting with adrenaline. I have not stopped since. Though the boys come and go—and Marcus did go—my chromoly Pegasus continues to faithfully deliver me to astounding heights of physical accomplishment and spiritual upliftment.

Back in a north Texas city, I now catapult through drive-time madness, managing miraculously to maintain an upright agile angle through the melee of honking taxis and impatient SUVs. Avoiding collision and ignoring derision, me and all the other wondrous two-wheeled monsters and maidens of the pavement and dirt paths are silently maneuvering as gracefully as any Mercurial deity ever could. And my bicycle boyfriends? There are many. There's Jeremy, my mutant bike-welding pal; Conrad, my bike buddy in Lincoln; my Critical Mass crusaders Cri and Mitch; Wisdom, director of a bike co-op in Chiapas; and my comrade Dave at the Yellow Bike Project. I love them all, but for now, I ride alone and free.

as demon-drivers defy my silence
they think to vanquish me in their
dusty sad exhaust
they pushing a little pedal to the floor
it's less than twelve inches
but they act like it's more
if they honk, i ask what for?
can i wink at you once more
can i wink at you once more!?

Tammy Gomez, a native Texas writer and performance poet, has not owned a car since 1992. She is currently working on an original script for the stage, SHE: bike/spoke/love, *which is a bicycle love story. Tammy is featured in the new PBS documentary* Voices from Texas, *which profiles the work of contemporary Mexican-American poets living in the Lone Star State.*

Note: The italicized lines are excerpts from her original poems: "Death to Autos," She: bike/spoke/love—*a spoken word bicycle drama, "Luminous Rose," and "Magistrate of Celebration."*

Medical Experience

Claire M. Unis

Before medical school, when I lived in California's eastern Sierra, I could lose myself in biking. Living in a town where I knew almost no one, at first I took off on trails alone. Inhaling the thin, pine-scented air, I tested my endurance on rolling fire roads that started just past the last shops in town and crisscrossed one another en route to unnamed hillsides and rocky plateaus. I passed hours without seeing anyone else. There were only the pumice crunching under my tires, an occasional squirrel or bird, and sun beating down on my shoulders and knees as I pumped along. My mountain bike had been a graduation present, so I was new to the sport. It didn't occur to me that something untoward might happen; I was young and strong and undaunted, and this was my year off after college to play. Everything within reach of the horizon was mine.

Late in the fall, after a full season of exploring most of the Mammoth Lakes trails, I took on Lower Rock Creek. Notoriously technical and precarious, it was considered one of the classic, tougher downhills in the area. I rode with two athletically fit friends—Heidi and I had hiked Mount Whitney in twelve hours only a few weeks before that, and Natalie had begun training for her snowboarding season—but Lower Rock Creek was a challenge of skill and daring, neither of which we possessed in abundance. Still, we were psyched up to ride.

As we entered the winding trail, which mercifully started out smooth and even, I remembered an article I had read in the local paper. Written by a young man on whom I had a passing crush, it was called

"Speed Is Your Friend." He had been referring to riding through pumice, sandlike volcanic rock that toppled many hapless mountain bikers who tried to brake or turn in the mush. But the author had also extrapolated the mantra to other terrain, pointing out that aggression and lack of fear could get one through a multitude of biking conditions. Including, presumably, blindly snaking singletrack.

With that in mind, I took off. Natalie and Heidi preferred to take the rocky sections of trail cautiously, walking the more awkward sections. I rode over everything I could, often stopped just in time by perilous climbs or sudden drop-offs. My eager pace seemed to be faster than theirs, so I kept moving.

Just past a creek crossing, before a turn, I negotiated a narrow passage between two boulders, and then Bam! I was chucked forward off my bicycle onto the rocks beside the trail. My right hand hit first, with my pinkie pointing off to the side, then my right shoulder, back, and hip. I dusted myself off, checked out my bike, and tried to get off the trail. I wiggled my fingers. My hand was throbbing and sore; I had the feeling that my biking glove was somehow keeping it together. I looked up the sides of the valley in which we were biking. To the north it rose in a field of boulders some two hundred feet to the road above. A rusty car that had tumbled down at some point in the distant past lay nearby, testimony to the steepness of that slope. To the south, a red volcanic outcropping rose sharply from the creek basin. Our trail was the only one running east-west, and it didn't promise to get easier any time soon.

Natalie and Heidi arrived just as I decided to try riding out, continuing on the same path.

"Oh my gosh, Clairebelle," Natalie play-scolded, "what did you do?"

"Just had a little wipeout," I admitted sheepishly.

"Are you okay?" Heidi asked.

"Yeah," I mumbled. "My hand hurts a bit, but I think I'm fine."

As we rode on, it became more and more obvious to me that I had, in fact, seriously injured my hand. Every bump sent a jolt of pain up my arm, and over the next forty-five minutes of riding it became excruciating to use my right hand to brake. What had been something of a sporting challenge turned into an exercise in focus and determination. I grimaced at the wavering aspens marking the last half mile of the trail, sparkling gold and green beside the dirt path.

Thankfully we had left our cars near the bottom, so we had only to load the bikes and climb in for the trip home. "I'm afraid I might have broken my hand," I commented to Heidi as she turned her truck onto the highway back to Mammoth.

"I doubt it," she said, mistaking my desperate pace to get back to the car for my usual downhill riding style. "You probably just bruised it badly. Put ice on it when you get home."

The next morning I couldn't fasten my bra or button my jeans, and my hand was red and swollen. Rather than go to the local ER, I drove five hours to my parents' house with my hand bandaged and tied to the sunroof of my car for elevation (using the sum total of my medical knowledge up to that point). My father, a radiologist, read the X-ray himself: A fractured bone bought me a half cast and six weeks of rest. Job-wise, the timing was fortuitous: I had been close to starting a two-week vacation from work in the coffee bar. Unfortunately, my time off had been intended for medical school interviews, which I would have to attend with a bulkily bandaged arm.

For the first interview, less than two weeks after I fractured my fifth metacarpal bone, I decided not to wear the plaster splint. Instead I taped my last two fingers daintily together, polished my nails, and smilingly discovered my error when a firm handshake almost sent me yelping from the room. Thereafter I wore the splint and had to explain to numerous interviewers that it was the result of a mountain biking mishap. Eyes lit up with surprise and conversations lingered unexpectedly on sports and mountain living. No one seemed to notice the research I had not done, or the organic chemistry grade I had failed to improve.

I've since wondered whether my broken hand helped me. Perhaps I was accepted to medical school because I stood out—the suntanned biker with firsthand knowledge of orthopedic injuries. I was carefree and energetic. I lived in the sweetest place on earth, and if they didn't admit me, I would go back there and keep on flirting with rocks and pushing myself to ride that trail without a single stop.

My first acceptance letter arrived before the bone had healed. I think it was my sense of joy they wanted. Not my knowledge base or my test scores, but the relaxed confidence that life in the mountains had given me.

My bike was the first thing I packed to bring along.

Claire Unis will finish her pediatrics residency in June 2004. She currently lives in the San Francisco Bay Area, where she rides her bike to work and enjoys weekend mountain bike rides in the surrounding hills. Other essays of hers have appeared in the Awakenings Review, Sport Literate, *and an anthology of writings about diabetes.*

Bicycle (Carriage) Built for Two

Gin Kilgore

"Are you and Michael going to bike to your wedding?" We got this question a lot, which is not surprising considering how bike-centered our lives seem to be. We met through Chicago's Critical Mass four years ago and have been collaborating on crazy bike-related projects ever since. We live car(e)free, rely mostly on two wheels for transportation, and spend much of our spare time helping others discover that biking is the perfect form of urban transportation. (Let no wind, rain, snow, job interview, or night at the opera knock you out of the saddle! For tips, visit www.bikewinter.org and www.cyclingsisters.org.)

Apparently, I can't even get through a paragraph without donning my advocate hat. However, I am not what you would call a bicycling "enthusiast." I average over a hundred miles a week, but there's not much lycra in my dresser. My bikes aren't fancy, just functional. I do not do much "recreational riding," but rather pick up pleasures along the way from here to there: the surprise summer tailwind, a lingering sunset, hitting all the greens on Armitage Avenue . . . I do not love my bicycle any more than I love the air I breathe. It is simply, marvelously, the tool that allows me to get around, have fun, save money, stay fit, and explore my community. Michael and I, like so many of our friends, do not live to bike; we bike to live.

There was going to be a strong bicycle presence at our wedding whether we planned for it or not. Many of our friends would have biked to our ceremony, even if it had been thirty miles away in some rural nook. But we wanted the event to reflect the way we live our lives and interact with our surroundings, so we chose to stay close to home, opting for a public park and a reception hall in our neighborhood. Our invitations announced that we were "biking to the chapel" and that there was going to be a bike parade between the ceremony and reception, which are about two miles apart. They also provided detailed, multimodal directions on how to get around Chicago car(e)free, because we really didn't want our "special day" to generate needless car trips.

But the question remained: Were we going to bicycle to our own wedding? Perhaps ride our own bikes to the ceremony and then ride off on a tandem? My mom/wedding outfit maker was prepared to create whatever I asked for. Short dress? Short dress with longer shell to put on at the park? Suit? Long dress with special ties to bundle it away from the wheels? I have modified many skirts along these lines. Indeed, I often wear formal clothes on a bike just to show it can be done. Ultimately, I decided I wanted to wear a full-length, slightly tulle-enhanced cotton dress, and I just didn't want to worry about keeping it out of the greasy, grimy jaws of my bike. It finally occurred to us that the bride and groom usually do not drive themselves to their own ceremony—why should it be any different with biking?

Our chauffeur was Tim Herlihy, of Urban Bikes on Broadway; our limo, his pedicab. Riding to the ceremony flanked by our two-wheeled wedding party was an affirming way to start the festivities. The familiar streets, curious smiles, and shouts of "what the?," "hey look!," and "congratulations!" reminded us that the day was both routine and special.

The bike parade from the ceremony to the reception was even better. We had expected the Critical Mass contingent to be on bikes, but a surprising number of our other friends and relatives swelled the parade to nearly a hundred people. There was Michael's childhood buddy, a recent convert to bike commuting, who rode all the way from Detroit as a surprise. There was gallant Gareth, who solo-rode a tandem to the ceremony in case a bikeless out-of-towner wanted to be in the parade. (He rescued my friend Amy from getting sucked into one of the few motor vehicles in our convoy.) Mom, my original bike-commuting role model, rode triumphantly at the front of the pack, while Dad stayed by our side sporting his best suit and father-of-the-bride grin. Everyone was in their best "polka semi-formal" outfits (another invite request), proving once again that you do not need lycra to look festive on a bicycle.

So, no, we didn't bike to our own wedding, but most of our witnesses did; promenading along the boulevards of Chicago's northwest side was the best gift we received. However, we did walk home—down Kedzie, past solid old buildings under an ancient still ripening moon, looking forward to a lifetime of routine, special days.

As a graduate student in the mid-ninties, Gin Kilgore began using a bicycle to shuttle between classes and teaching jobs throughout Chicago. Adding cycling to her "transportation toolbox" allowed her to maintain her car-free lifestyle. She now works on pedestrian advocacy through the Center for Neighborhood Technology, a nonprofit organization promoting sustainable development that creates livable urban communities for everyone.

Gin met her husband through Chicago's Critical Mass rides and is involved in a variety of grassroots efforts to promote walking and cycling and reduce dependence on private automobiles. She helped found Bike Winter, Cycling Sisters, and Break the Gridlock, and in 2003 was awarded the Pedal Power and Golden Derailleur Awards for her work to promote year-round cycling. She is particularly interested in the transportation needs of children, in part because she has so many fond memories of walking to and meandering from school with her friends. These early trips helped her develop a habit of routine physical activity, sense of adventure, and love for public spaces.

Loving a Cyclist

Jayne Relaford Brown

You and your bicycle make a singular creature together, like a griffin or centaur, a human with a wheel. I hold your slow-moving figure in my headlights as if it were in the palm of my hand, the center of my heart. In your big ring now, you crank slow and steady through the rain and headwind, up the Sangre de Cristo Mountains of eastern Arizona, the last 10 miles of the 175 you'll ride today. I've watched you struggle and persist for the last fifteen hours. *Just keep pedaling* is your life-mantra, whether you're riding the bike or writing your dissertation. I've heard you say it so many times, but I've never seen your cycling-insanity in all its beauty.

There is absolutely no no sane reason for you to keep riding. This is not a race. No one's paying you, no team depends on you. They'll give you the T-shirt. How could there be any shame in quitting after battling 40-mph headwinds and freezing rains here in middle of nowhere? But you persist. And watching the set of your back, the slow, tenacious cranking of your slight figure cutting through the night, I have never loved you as acutely as I do right now.

You stare into the window of a closed bike shop, where the silver Cannondale frame hangs from the rafters. I've learned to recognize the thick down tube at a glance, and tell you, "There's another one, and there." We've taken this walk for months, stopping to stare into the darkened shop three blocks from our house. You don't go to look at the frames or touch them when the shop is open. It is as if you fear that if you touched or rode one, you would be lost, and for a graduate student there is no money for the bike.

When we first met, you were doing centuries on a heavy Schwinn, tired of being scoffed at for having the one bike with a kickstand at the starting line. You bought a friend's bike, lighter and better, but it's not your heart-bike. Finally, the money's saved, the bike is possible. I've never seen you so happy as you test-drive the different bikes down our cul-de-sac, and I take your picture on them as you bank and coast around and around the end of our block. You try several of them, just for show, and to be certain you've made the right choice, but it's no surprise when you come grinning back again on the silver bike with the thick tube, the one you've stared at through the window for so long, and say, "I think this is the one."

Anyone who falls in love with a bicyclist should be prepared for life to change completely. I'm not a bicycle widow; I'm a sag wagon. Our first vacation together was like some magical dream, and seduced me to this life. For a week, you pedaled the coast of Oregon and I drove leisurely, stopping at every scenic pullout and ocean view, pulling into the new campsite and reading a novel or writing until you came. As I passed you on the road, I'd pull over for a little picnic and a kiss.

I could not have imagined the radical turn in my life that began with that idyllic week. Who could have predicted that a few years down the road I'd be reading *Bicycling* in the bathroom, understanding terms like *drilled frame, index shifting,* and *Shimano components*? That I'd be sitting on the grass at finish lines for hours reading student papers while hired deejays played too-loud tunes and repeated the same announcements again and again for incoming riders? That I'd find myself traveling down the California coast for six days in a 36-foot Ryder truck full of cyclists' luggage? Or driving behind my love at 5 mph in the middle of the night in eastern Arizona, accelerator foot cramping, listening through heavy static to the one faint country music station coming through? I have hung out and shopped for six-hour blocks in Tucson, New Hope, Randolph Center, and Redlands as you rode, always finding my way back to the little makeshift bicycling city of the finish line an hour before you're likely to be done, scanning the line of returning cyclists for that certain jersey.

You even got me riding for a couple of years. I loved drafting along behind you toward the ocean, matching your pace (even though I know you were holding back on speed and distance for our "Sunday-driver" rides). I got a glimpse or two into what addicts you to cycling. When I finally made it all the way up Torrey Pines, a hill well known to Southern California cyclists, without getting off and walking, I cried with happiness (and a touch of nausea) at the top. But I'm not one of the select— I bonked on the fourth leg of our Vermont trip, whining and practically stomping out each word: "I can't . . . go . . . any . . . more!" When I worked up to doing my first metric century, I was proud, but it was getting clear this cycling thing could take a big chunk of time. Just after we moved to Pennsylvania, I took one of my last rides, following you up a narrow, heavily trafficked country road, a road that narrowed even more with every little bridge. Having to ka-thunk ka-thunk over dead squirrels so guys in pickups didn't run us over did me in. Only a cycling addict could call that fun. My bike's in the shed, and my hat's off to you.

When we moved here from California, I kept asking you what you were going to do when winter came. "Ride my bike," was all you would say.

"Seriously, what will you do?"

"Ride my bike."

"Maybe you could swim at school. You used to like swimming a lot."

"Ride . . . my . . . bike." Like, *Read my lips.* Okay, I gave up. Come winter you'd have to do something else, and you could figure it out then. But you kept riding. Balaclava and wetsuit booties, frozen slush of sports drink in your water bottles, frost-pinkened skin, numb feet—as soon as the snowplows cleared the streets, you rode.

You call to say you've crashed. A dog burst suddenly from a cornfield and across the road just as you lifted your water bottle to your lips. You're fine, you say, but finally allow as how I could come and get you before the big hill by our house. You don't tell me yet that after the crash you lay in the road for several minutes, recollecting your wits and breath, hoping no car would come over the rise before you could move.

You name an intersection I'll know, about a mile from where you are. I hurry there, and watch you roll, wobbly-wheeled, up to the truck. At home, peeling off your lycra tights and shorts, your jacket and your jersey, we see the history of how you hit the road. You'll be okay, but every plane and pointy place of you along one side is scraped or bruised, and I get scared to think how close it always is, how thin the skins that cover you.

Even as we're dressing your wounds and assessing the pain in your shoulder and neck, as you're telling me how you lay there in the road, I can't imagine asking you not to ride. Bicycling is not something you do; it's who you are. If anything, I'm more scared you've been injured in a way that will keep you off your bike. You're restless if you have to miss a day, a little surly and depressed at two. When your bike's in the shop, you're a lost soul. The hundred and fifty bucks we spend to schlep your bike along on airplane trips are dollars well spent toward a vacation with the one I love. As we move through middle age together, the best wish I can have is that you ride till ninety. And that I can still come to your finish lines and see your shining face as you get off that bike, saying, "Wow, that was hilly—it was great!"

On our second California AIDS Ride, I worked security, and we slept together in a little pop-up tent surrounded by two thousand bikes. The park lights outside threw shadows of wheels and frames across the nylon walls, and when we looked out the door, we could see nothing but bicycles at eye level in every direction. "Your perfect world," I teased, but it was true.

It's a world I've married into, and though I'll always be part foreigner, I've come to feel at home in it. BIKE. EAT. SLEEP. BIKE. EAT. SLEEP, and so on, said the AIDS Ride shirts that year. You can't imagine better days than that. And traveling with you, enjoying the radiance and relaxation on your face after a good day's ride, sleeping on the ground beside the cyclist I love in a magic land made up of bicycles, neither can I.

Jayne Relaford Brown lives in Dryville, Pennsylvania, and teaches writing at Penn State Berks-Lehigh Valley college. She gardens, writes, studies yoga, and drives sag wagon for her life partner of fifteen years. My First Real Tree, *a book of her poems, is published by FootHills Publishing.*